DEBATING DIVERSITY

I cannot exaggerate the importance of this book. It addresses perhaps the most crucial issue facing the world today – racism, ethnicism, and the politics of difference – with an intelligence and integrity that are all too often missing in discussions . . . The presentation is clearly, even compellingly written.

Edwin Wilmsen, University of Texas, Austin

Debating Diversity challenges current attempts to reach understanding among racial and ethnic groups. If the ground of discussion does not itself accept diversity, efforts even by presidents must fail. Those who participate in efforts to reach understanding about diversity, or simply wish such efforts to succeed, should measure what goes on against these findings.

Dell Hymes, University of Virginia

Immigration, racism and nationalism are major political themes throughout the Western world, vigorously debated by politicians, the media and the public at large. In the process, discourses are created and new ways of speaking about ourselves and others emerge.

Debating Diversity is a highly original and controversial work which turns the debate itself into a topic, and suggests that a major 'problem' of diversity may be the way in which it is debated.

Based on empirical analysis of data taken from the context of 'migrant policies' in Belgium, *Debating Diversity* discusses the way in which 'moderate' voices in the debate construct a powerful discourse of tolerance. This 'tolerant' discourse is found in news reporting, policy statements, socio-scientific research reports and government-sponsored antiracism campaigns and training programmes. Despite the vast differences between this rhetoric of tolerance and the discourse of radical racist and nationalist groups, a remarkable consistency is revealed. The authors refer to this as 'homogeneism', a fundamental non-acceptance of diversity.

An intimate connection is shown between the Belgian debate and aspects of wider European nationalist ideologies, and parallels are drawn with conclusions of research on racism and nationalism throughout the world, particularly in France, Germany, The Netherlands, the UK and the US.

Jan Blommaert is Professor of African Linguistics at the University of Ghent, Belgium. **Jef Verschueren** founded the IPrA (International Pragmatics Association) in 1986 and currently directs its research centre at the University of Antwerp. Both authors have previously collaborated on *The Pragmatics of Intercultural and International Communication* (1991).

D1188636

DEBATING DIVERSITY

Analysing the discourse of tolerance

Jan Blommaert and Jef Verschueren

London and New York

First published 1998
by Routledge
11 New Fetter Lane, London EC4P 4EE

Simultaneously published in the USA and Canada
by Routledge
29 West 35th Street, New York, NY 10001

© 1998 Jan Blommaert and Jef Verschueren

Typeset in Goudy by Routledge
Printed and bound in Great Britain by
TJ International Ltd, Padstow, Cornwall

British Library Cataloguing in Publication Data
A catalogue record for this book is available from the British Library

Library of Congress Cataloging in Publication Data
Blommaert, Jan.
Debating diversity: analysing the discourse of tolerance
/Jan Blommaert and Jef Verschueren.
Includes bibliographical references.
1. Discourse analysis—Social aspects. 2. Language and culture. 3. Racism.
4. Pluralism (Social sciences) 5. Toleration. I. Verschueren, Jef. II. Title.
P302.84.B58   1998
401'.41–dc21   98–15143   CIP

ISBN 0–415–19137–8 (hbk)
ISBN 0–415–19138–6 (pbk)

CONTENTS

CONTENTS

ILLUSTRATIONS

ACKNOWLEDGEMENTS

This book represents collaborative research carried out over the past eight years. It would be a hopeless task to try to thank everyone who has contributed either to the approach or to the substance, directly or indirectly. It would be unforgiveable, however, not to mention Chris Bulcaen, who did much of the research that led to the content of Chapter 6, Gino Eelen, who did preparatory work for a section of Chapter 5, and Stef Slembrouck, who translated significant portions of *Het Belgische Migrantendebat* (Blommaert and Verschueren 1992a) for incorporation into this English text. Further, we are grateful to the editors and publishers of the journals *Language in Society, Journal of Intercultural Studies* and *New Community* for their permission to reproduce major portions of earlier articles (Blommaert and Verschueren 1991, 1993 and 1994b, respectively). All the research was carried out in the framework of a programme financially supported by the Belgian National Fund for Scientific Research (NFWO/FKFO) and a Belgian government grant (Federale Diensten voor Wetenschappelijke, Technische en Culturele Aangelegenheden, IUAP-II, contract number 27). Last, but not least, the manuscript might still be waiting for completion if one of the authors, J. Verschueren, could not have spent the first few days of his stay at the Bellagio Study and Conference Center (8 February to 8 March 1997), granted by the Rockefeller Foundation, working on revisions.

ABBREVIATIONS

Sources of materials discussed are abbreviated as follows:

AGALEV *Anders Gaan Leven* (green party)

BRTN *Belgische Radio en Televisie, Nederlands* (Dutch broadcasts of the public Belgian Radio and Television), recently relabeled VRT (for *Vlaamse Radio en Televisie*, 'Flemish radio and television')

CGKR *Centrum voor Gelijkheid van Kansen en Racismebestrijding* ('Centre for Equal Opportunities and the Fight against Racism'; successor of the *Koninklijk Commissariaat voor het Migrantenbeleid*)

CVP *Christelijke Volkspartij* (Christian Democratic party)

DM *De Morgen* (daily newspaper, socialist)

DNG *De Nieuwe Gazet* (daily newspaper, liberal, sister to *Het Laatste Nieuws*)

DS *De Standaard* (daily newspaper, Christian Democratic)

EU *European Union*

GvA *Gazet van Antwerpen* (daily newspaper, Christian Democratic)

HLN *Het Laatste Nieuws* (daily newspaper, liberal, sister to *De Nieuwe Gazet*)

HN *Het Nieuwsblad* (daily newspaper, Christian Democratic, popularized version of *De Standaard*)

HV *Het Volk* (daily newspaper, Christian Democratic)

KBS *Koning Boudewijnstichting* ('King Baudouin Foundation')

KCM *Koninklijk Commissariaat voor het Migrantenbeleid* ('Royal Commissariat for Migrant Policies'; precursor to the *Centrum voor Gelijkheid van Kansen en Racismebestrijding*)

PVV *Partij voor Vrijheid en Vooruitgang* (liberal party, later renamed VLD)

SP *Socialistische Partij* (socialist party)

VB *Vlaams Blok* (extreme-right Flemish nationalist party)

VCIM *Vlaams Centrum voor de Integratie van Migranten* ('Flemish Centre for the Integration of Migrants')

VLD	*Vlaamse Liberalen en Democraten* (liberal party; earlier PVV)
VU	*Volksunie* (moderate Flemish nationalist party)
VVB	*Vlaamse Volksbeweging* ('Flemish People's Movement', a nationalistic pressure group)

INTRODUCTION

Culture, ethnicity, race. Cultural pluralism, multiculturalism. Tolerance, integration, assimilation. Racism, xenophobia, Neo-Nazism. Discrimination, exclusion, repression. Equal opportunities, affirmative action, preferential treatment, reverse discrimination. Disadvantage, minorization. Political correctness. Migration, migrants, immigrants, refugees. ... These are just some of the beacons guiding a debate on diversity, which is sweeping through public life in North America and Europe, and of which echoes can be heard – usually loud and clear – in many other parts of the world.[1]

The debate seems omnipresent. Setting migration quotas, controlling illegal entry, protecting the rights of minorities, these are topics of daily political decision-making. But not only politicians participate in the debate. The media offer ample time and space to the coverage of race relations and inter-ethnic conflicts, rarely without offering a point of view. Every educated American seems to have an opinion about whether bilingualism or 'English Only' ought to be encouraged. Many bookstores now have sections on 'cultural studies', overflowing with research and opinions on race, culture, ethnicity and the multicultural society. Once you find 450-page volumes such as *Multiculturalism: A Critical Reader* (David Theo Goldberg (ed.) 1994), you can be sure to be picking up the scent of a true tradition, especially when they are matched in the children's section by a wide range of books, some of them excellent, educating for tolerance of diversity. It is not surprising, then, that the *Hungry Mind Review* (the Midwestern alternative to *The New York Review of Books*) devoted its entire Fall 1994 issue, cover to cover, to reviews of migration- and diversity-related publications, essays on the topic, reader responses to a questionnaire on race, and, to top it all off, an interview with Henry Louis Gates, Jr., chairman of the Afro–American Studies Department at Harvard. Well-known public figures and intellectuals eagerly participate in the debate. Thus Arthur Schlesinger (1992), brilliant historian and winner of two Pulitzer Prizes, felt it was necessary to warn against 'the disuniting of America'. In Germany, the controversial essayist Hans Magnus Enzensberger (1991) uses all his powers of irony to launch a lucid attack on 'foreigner policies', in the form of a little book the size and tone of which are counterbalanced by the much more voluminous and pragmatic *Heimat Babylon*, co-authored by Daniel

1

Cohn-Bendit (Cohn-Bendit and Schmid 1992), celebrated student leader in Paris, May 1968, and now responsible for multicultural affairs in the city of Frankfurt. In France, the literary scholar Tzvetan Todorov (1989) confronted the public with a captivating cultural history of French reactions to diversity, and Julia Kristeva (1988), a high-profile linguist and psychoanalyst, injected the discussion with a healthy dose of self-searching. Dozens of names could be added (Habermas, Balibar etc.), without turning to those individuals who have made a name for themselves precisely by participating in the debate.

Positions differ greatly. Not only do we find overt racism, advocating the expulsion or repression of minorities, as among white supremacists in the United States, or Neo-Nazis in a new Europe where viewpoints of the extreme right are rapidly gaining political respectability. But the issue would be a simple one if rejection were to be confronted with an equally clear acceptance of diversity. In fact, most of the debate takes place between members of the 'tolerant majority', whose shades of opinion are sometimes full of nuance, but sometimes as irreconcilable as the most extreme of extremisms. The dispute between affirmative action and preferential treatment is a subtle one, the former trying to correct historical wrongs by favouring members of minority groups in cases of equal qualification, the latter pursuing the same goal by granting more-than-equal opportunities to the disadvantaged. And so is the difference between pleas for cultural pluralism, the mere acceptance of cultural differences within a society, and multiculturalism, tending towards the celebration of difference. On the other hand, there is an abysmal divide between John Edwards's (1995) cautious support for the morality of certain preference practices, predicated on the assumption that the purity of the merit principle is not beyond doubt, and the somewhat cynical suggestion that disproportionate poverty or disadvantage result from low IQ (Richard Herrnstein and Charles Murray 1994), a lack of cultural capital (Thomas Sowell 1994), or simply a bad attitude (Dinesh D'Souza 1995), so that any form of remedial action is by definition in vain. Racist theories and practices are fuelled by statistics-laden demonstrations of genetically determined lower intelligence among blacks (the same Herrnstein and Murray 1994), while, simultaneously, a concerted socio-scientific effort is made to expose their multiple hidden manifestations and fallacious underpinnings (as in Paul Gilroy 1987, Margaret Wetherell and Jonathan Potter 1992, Robert Miles 1993, John Gabriel 1994, John Solomos and Les Back 1996, to name just a few). Significant gaps in attitude and reasoning appear between those obsessed with judging the social acceptability of every word that comes their way, those who enjoy ridiculing such obsessions, thus turning Political Correctness into a dirty word, and Deborah Cameron's admonition that the 'movement for so-called "politically correct" language does not threaten our freedom to speak as we choose' but 'threatens only our freedom to imagine that our linguistic choices are inconsequential' (1994: 33). There is a growing discrepancy between overtly positive approaches to migrants and refugees (see, e.g., Sarah Spencer (ed.) 1994) and an avalanche of new measures to curb immigration, both legal and illegal, both in Europe and in

North America. Similarly, the English Only or Official English movement and advocates of bilingualism are coming close to an all-out battle, with major advances for the former resulting in the imminent threat of a 66 per cent cut in budgets for bilingual education (for a survey of the issues involved, see Thomas Ricento 1996). Finally, Molefi Asante's radical multiculturalism of the Afrocentrist type meets Schlesinger's (1991) judgement that 'Self-Africanization after 300 years in America is playacting' and his ardent plea for the rediscovery of an American national identity: *E Pluribus Unum*.

Positions, as well as lines of argumentation, are also subject to change. Thus Israel Zangwill's 1908 (British, early twentieth-century) melting pot metaphor for an (American) assimilationist model keeps moving in and out of public consciousness, competing with alternatives, from cultural pluralism and multiculturalism to David Hollinger's (1995) postethnic perspective, allowing for an individual's multiple affiliations and 'denying the right to grandparents to determine a person's primary affiliation'.[2] In the history of affirmative action, arguments based on compensation for past harm (which used to be common currency in America but never gained popularity in Britain or elsewhere in Europe) have almost entirely yielded for those emphasizing the need for a proportionate representation of a society's actual diversity. Moreover, in the United States, affirmative action seems to have come full circle. As indicated by an ominous 'affirmative action chronology' distributed by the United States Information Service, the policy seems doomed after a thirty-year life span, from President Johnson's Executive Order 11246 in 1965 requiring employers who receive federal funds to establish minority hiring goals, to a number of Supreme Court rulings in 1995,[3] underscored by Republican calls for a re-examination of federal affirmative action policies, President Clinton's ordering of a federal review, and California Governor Pete Wilson's dismantling of some of his state's affirmative action programs. Such developments, though, are not necessarily transparent. For some, the policy changes may be a welcome return to older practices, with more freedom to exploit and less responsibility for the fate of minorities; for others, they may be the logical conclusion from observed malfunctioning and an opportunity to shift the focus towards more direct remedies for social and economic disadvantage, avoiding the easy-to-abuse detour of skin colour or family name; others still may use the arguments of the latter group to camouflage motives characteristic of the former. Whatever the case may be, the rhetoric is always interesting. Thus, when Louisiana Governor Mike Foster followed Pete Wilson's example in January 1996, Wilson's spokesman declared: 'Once again, California is leading the nation on a political idea of fundamental fairness.'

In this book we will show that the fact of the debate may be more of a problem than diversity itself. In other words, a major part of the problem consists precisely in viewing diversity as a problem. After a detailed analysis of multiple manifestations of the debate on diversity, we will conclude that this – i.e. viewing diversity as a problem – is what the 'tolerant majority' tends to share with the extreme right. We are not witnessing the end of racism, as D'Souza would have it, but rather racism without end, one of the characteristics of which is to evade fundamental issues by hiding behind definitions of racism in narrowly biological terms. A widespread consensus on the status of diversity as a problem will be shown to give rise to some of the most efficient practices of discrimination, subtly veiled from sight by a rhetoric of tolerance which radiates the best of intentions.

Many readers will at this point be reminded of Etienne Balibar's *racisme différentialiste*. In an analysis very similar to ours, he describes a racism that is no longer predicated on biological conceptions of race, but on a relativist rhetoric of cultural difference. He also describes the subtle ways in which this cultural relativism shifted from an emancipatory weapon (as a counterbalance against domineering cultural imperialism and condescending evolutionism) to an argument in defence of the supposed incompatibility of cultures, the need to allow cultural groups to develop without outside interference, and the thesis that culture contact and hybridization distort the natural order of things in such a way as to cause violent reactions. Thus, according to Balibar, 'we see how differentialist theories themselves claim to *explain racism* (and to prevent it)' while '[f]rom a theory of races or of the battle of races in human history [. . .] we have moved into a theory of "ethnic relations" (or *race relations*) in society, *which does not naturalize racial appearance but rather racist behaviour*' (Balibar 1988: 35; our translation, italics in the original). In other words, we are confronted with a set of social assumptions, an ideology, as well as with a complex of institutional and everyday social action in which human diversity is at once celebrated and qualified as dangerous, threatening, problematic. It will be our contention that the 'problem' consists to a large extent in the way in which it is put into words, or that the language in which these issues are talked about is far more than just a neutral vehicle of meanings and attitudes. The discourse on diversity is an instrument for the reproduction of social problems, forms of inequality and majority power.

Such an observation, however, raises numerous empirical, theoretical and political (or ethical) questions. In addition to addressing the classical ethnographic dimensions of the phenomenon (who gets involved in the debate, how, when and why?), one may ask what is wrong with viewing diversity as a problem if so many people seem to have problems with it. What is the exact content of this view? How is it expressed? What assumptions is it based on, and how is it arrived at? What are the ideological processes involved? How can this be investigated? What are the social and political implications? And, last but not least, are there any alternatives?

Answering these questions in the abstract would be a futile exercise. That is why we focus on the 'debate', as the empirically observable side of the processes constituting public opinion, policy-making and legitimation. An analysis, however, could not be convincing if it were simply to piece together loosely connected manifestations of the debate, imposing a pattern or imagining coherence. Therefore we have chosen to present a detailed investigation of the debate on diversity, with special emphasis on 'migrant policies', as it has been conducted in Belgium, more specifically in the Dutch-speaking Flemish north, over the last six to seven years. Even within such topical, geographical and temporal confines, the risk of imposing patterns is real, since the debate itself consists of often disconnected instances of discourse. Therefore special attention will be paid, in Part III of this book, to a demonstration of how elements of the overall debate converge in specific discourse types (the language of a training programme for police officers, Chapter 6), in a single text (a widely distributed brochure educating the public in multicultural matters, Chapter 7), and in the legitimation of some typical 'antiracist' policies (Chapter 8). We shall concentrate on mainstream rhetoric, coming from members of a societal majority which is – genuinely or strategically – convinced of its own tolerance, as represented in the major news media, in political policy documents, educational efforts and socio-scientific research reports. Part I will sketch aspects of the theme (Chapter 1) and the approach (Chapter 2). The approach is rooted in linguistic pragmatics in its widest sense as an interdisciplinary cognitive, social, and cultural perspective on language and language use. It is 'linguistic' because language is focused on as the empirical layer of the debate allowing entry into wider conceptual and societal processes; it is 'pragmatic' because only an interdisciplinary look at usage aspects of language could open the gate. All this will be explained at length in Chapter 2. Part II will then scrutinize the way in which diversity is rhetorically turned into a problem (Chapter 3), the concepts that are central to this process (Chapter 4), and the global structure of the ideology involved which we label 'homogeneism' (Chapter 5).

But why would Belgium be such an interesting case? It is certainly not the only place where the phenomena to be analysed can be found. A growing literature on similar developments in Austria, Britain, France, Germany, Italy, Spain, The Netherlands, the United States and Australia can be called upon to testify to the wide spread of debates on diversity, involving issues of racism, nationalism and ethnicity (see, to name just a few, Michael Billig 1995, Alistair Davidson 1997, John Edwards 1995, Philomena Essed 1991 and 1994, Siegfried Jäger 1991 and 1996, Luisa Martín Rojo et al. 1994, Marco Martiniello and Paul Kazim 1991, Bernd Matouschek et al. 1995, Robert Miles 1993, Tariq Modood 1992, Tzvetan Todorov 1989, Immanuel Wallerstein 1988, Pnina Werbner and Tariq Modood (eds) 1997, Cornel West 1993, Ruth Wodak et al. 1990). Diversity is hotly debated in the context of European integration, and often takes the shape of disputes over criteria for citizenship (see Martiniello (ed.) 1995 and Wicker (ed.) 1997). Significantly, the European Union (henceforth EU) declared 1997 the Year of the Fight against Racism. Thus the particularity of the case study (which has produced two books written in Dutch; see Blommaert and Verschueren 1992a, 1994a) should not distract from its more general relevance.

At the same time, Belgium may have more to offer than some other societies when it comes to dissecting the debate on diversity. A not-so-serious reason , not to be mentioned again in this book, is to be found in the results of a pan-European poll in late 1997, carried out in the context of the European Year of the Fight against Racism, which 'showed' the Belgians to be the 'most racist' Europeans, with a 55 per cent self-identification as 'more or less racist'. There is, however, a more serious case to be made. Belgium combines a position at the heart of the European integration movement with a strong language-based tendency towards regional nationalism. At one end of this equation, Belgium has been in the forefront of European integration ever since the humble beginnings of the European project in the 1950s. Every Belgian government since the 1960s has vigorously defended measures aimed at closer cooperation between EU members, and in recent years Belgian politicians have defended the idea of 'deepening' (as opposed to 'widening' by the inclusion of new member states) the institutional and organizational apparatus of the EU. Belgium is acutely aware of the transnational transfers of power, goods and people, and of the inadequacy of the national level to design policies for industrial, commercial, monetary, military and other purposes.

At the other end, however, there is a long and well-known history of gradual dissolution of the unitary Belgian state along the lines of two language-based autonomous communities, the Dutch-speaking Flemish and the Francophone Walloons, who have divided three territorial units among themselves: the Dutch-speaking northern part called Flanders, the French-speaking southern part called Wallonia, and the bilingual enclave in Flanders called Brussels. Officially there is a third autonomous linguistic community, a small (and powerless) German-speaking minority residing in the eastern parts of Wallonia. Nationalism in Belgium has been marked by a strong focus on ethnolinguistic units ('communities'), clearly aimed at creating ethnolinguistically homogeneous territories, thus mapping language and space in a rigid and legally complex way. As a result, Belgium has probably the most elaborate and intricate language legislation in the world (see, e.g., Kas Deprez 1994, Liesbet Hooghe 1991).

In other words, ethnicity has always been a forceful actor in Belgian history, deeply connected with political rights and obligations distributed in physical and social space. Especially in Flanders, ethnic awareness has long been a crucial political fact, translated metonymically into the popular collocation 'language and culture'. People speaking a particular language also have a particular culture and belong to a particular ethnic group (where the three parameters – language, culture, and ethnicity – are treated as coextensive), which, according to this well-established view, automatically entails political rights or obligations (remember Balibar's *racisme différentialiste*). If an individual moves within the space allotted to his or her ethnic group, he or she enjoys full rights and freedoms; if, on the other hand, someone leaves his or her 'ethnic' space, he or she may lose certain rights and freedoms. A Fleming who leaves Flanders and crosses the border into Wallonia cannot expect to be addressed in Dutch. All transactions in the public sphere will be in French. Similarly, a Francophone residing in a Flemish town will be treated administratively as a Dutch-speaking citizen.

Intrusion and blending are highly problematic within this system. Among the most enduring and critical political problems in Belgium is the presence of pockets of Francophones on Flemish territory (most of them in the Brussels suburban areas), and the bilingual status of Brussels. In addition, Flemish nationalists revolt more and more explicitly against the presence of a growing and affluent community of EU and NATO officials in Flanders, most of whom speak neither Dutch nor French and are thus seen to 'pollute' the ethnolinguistic landscape of the region in which they have chosen to reside. Similarly, and fully in line with the foregoing, the lasting presence of ethnolinguistic minorities of Turks or Moroccans is something that runs counter to the whole logic of the political history of Belgium. Thus, in Belgium issues of immigration are deeply connected to issues of nationalism and local political history, and the specific shape of nationalist tendencies in Belgium (in particular, the connection between ethnicity and territory) creates a fertile ground for heated arguments on diversity in terms of 'natural' rights, obligations and freedoms.

We have explored the connections between discourses on immigration and nationalist discourses (Blommaert and Verschueren 1992b, 1996, Verschueren n.d.), and the close relationship between racism, ethnicity and nationalism has also been emphasized by others (see, e.g., Balibar and Wallerstein 1988 and Peter Ratcliffe (ed.) 1994). It may be precisely in this domain that Belgium offers a rich and interesting field of study. The ideology we will reveal has at its core a fundamental non-acceptance of diversity. Since the case we are studying is not at all isolated, the rigorously scientific dissection we present may further our understanding of social and political processes ranging from the newly reinforced inter-ethnic tensions and conflicts in the United States, to the war and the subsequent fragile peace in ex-Yugoslavia, and the new nationalisms emerging elsewhere. The attempted clarity of the analysis may reveal less-than-obvious interconnections, causes, reasons, motives, as well as more accidental properties which may nevertheless have far-reaching consequences. And, as always, understanding is needed before remedies can be imagined. For instance, 'ethnic cleansing' practices will be shown to have roots in an ideology which the warring parties in ex-Yugoslavia shared with Western European societies, and the suggestion will be made that an inability to operate in a different frame of mind is ultimately responsible for Europe's failure to prevent the carnage.

As authors of this book and members of the society from which the empirical data are derived, we are necessarily involved in the debate we are describing. Most of the readers may be able to take a more distant, fully observational, attitude – looking from the outside at properties of an exotic small country. At times, the story we are telling may sound as if it comes from outer space. That is exactly the feeling we often have when talking about this in front of a non-Belgian, international audience abroad. Such is perhaps the predicament of whoever makes an effort to question what is usually taken for granted. Unfortunately, the story is a true one, or has enough truth to it to be disturbing. We hope it is being told well enough to shake at least some readers out of their contentment, even if, in the words of John Kenneth Galbraith, 'it is the nature of contentment that it resists that which invades it with vigor' (1992: 12).

Part I

DIVERSITY
The issue

1

THE MANAGEMENT OF
DIVERSITY

The management paradigm

In January 1994, UNESCO launched a social science research and policy-making programme bearing the acronym MOST, short for 'Management of Social Transformations'. As explained by Federico Mayor, UNESCO Director-General, today's world is seen as complex and troubled, badly in need of well-informed policy choices to address '*social* problems that have so far resisted national efforts to deal with them'. These include 'growing inequalities within and between nations, ethnic tensions and conflicts of all kinds, unemployment, migratory movements, urban insecurity and squalor, and loss of cultural identity'.[1] Some of the identified problems have economic, ecological and demographic overtones, such as the social transformations resulting from new patterns of accelerated urbanization, or the uneasy linkage between global interests and local life. But the list is headed by the twin worries of (*cultural or ethnic*) *diversity* and *migration*. Thus the *management of diversity* is made into a prime policy concern on an international level. Recent events are believed to disprove the theory 'that increased transnational communication and integrated political and economic structures would erase people's feelings of ethnic identity'. And it is assumed that '[d]espite technological progress, ethnic and cultural identities remain an inherent part of an individual's constitution'.[2]

Diversity is high up on the social agenda in many countries. But it is hard to find a society with widely shared attitudes that are as simple as UNESCO's valiant and (seemingly) unambiguous plea for cultural pluralism or multiculturalism. As a result, *debating diversity* has developed into a fully-fledged genre of public discourse. Whatever the positions that are taken, the debates usually share with UNESCO the idea that diversity needs to be 'managed'. In Western democratic countries, where tolerance is highly valued as a self-ascribed property, the radical elimination of diversity in the form of segregation, undisguised discrimination or the expulsion of foreigners, is not available as a public option – though it is openly advocated by a growing number of people at the extreme right of the political spectrum. In the rhetoric of the 'tolerant majority', i.e. the layer of society which professes the virtues of openness and tolerance,[3] the management of diversity takes two forms, which often occur in combination.

A first management option, appearing under different guises, consists essentially in a policy of *containment*. After the self-congratulatory rhetoric about the defeat of Communism has died down, the Western world has found a new threat to mobilize against. Vivid images of lethal migration waves are implanted into public consciousness. The formulation of migration policies has become a major concern.[4] By far the most practicable method of containment is to close borders, at least for categories of unwanted individuals, however curious this may be in the face of increased internationalization at the most visible and most widely advertised levels of economic, social and political life. In the United States strategies and new legislation are being drafted to limit both legal and illegal immigration. Legal immigration, according to one proposed bill, should be reduced by one-third (to about half a million per year, down from 800,000), not only by giving preference to the immediate family members of US citizens and residents, but also by preventing immigration by unskilled workers – while keeping up the image, in the words of the chairman of the House Judiciary Subcommittee on Immigration, that 'America is the most generous country in the world'. To reduce illegal entry by 75 per cent in the next five years, the bill would authorize 5,000 new border patrol agents; it calls for more physical barriers (say, a fence) along the US–Mexico border; it advocates the use of abandoned military bases to detain illegal aliens; and it would institute an enhanced Social Security verification system to determine an individual's eligibility for employment (see Hugh Mehan 1997). In Europe, meanwhile, the Schengen agreement allows for free traffic of persons and goods between its signatories: Belgium, France, Germany, Greece, Italy, Luxembourg, Portugal, Spain and The Netherlands. But this 'wind of freedom' which, as the propaganda has it, blows over Europe is nicely counterbalanced by much stricter controls at the outside borders (symbolized, e.g., by the 'shackle points' to detain suspicious characters on the Eurostar trains crossing beneath the English Channel) and by the Schengen Information System, also known as the Schengen computer but more aptly labelled Big SIS, designed to keep track of people moving around inside the borders. Moreover, individual states of the EU have been busy adapting their policies. Germany, for instance, used to have some of the most liberal asylum laws in the world, but managed to change them overnight to some of the potentially most restrictive. Under the new laws, asylum is no longer granted to citizens of countries that are officially defined as 'safe' by the German authorities; in those cases, no investigation of any kind is necessary. In addition, refugees entering Germany via neighbouring 'safe' countries (in practice, all countries that have a common border with Germany!) may be turned back automatically. Smaller European countries are following suit. The Netherlands recently sent over fifty Zaïrian refugees back to Kinshasa on a chartered plane; what has happened to them in Mobutu's Zaïre, shining example of democracy, is not exactly on record. Neither do we know the fate of the Somalis whom Belgium sent back to Mogadishu by military transport plane while the civil war was at its hottest. Belgium built 'closed reception centres' for asylum seekers, and proved to be highly inventive in attempts to limit the number of unwanted foreigners, including: measures such as fines for airlines (and at a later stage even bus drivers) carrying passengers without proper documents (or even without enough funds) into the country; a proposal to expel foreign students who happen to run out of money or who flunk their exams 'without good reason'; the denaturalization of immigrant Belgian citizens who are suspected of certain crimes; the refusal even to consider some visa applications;[5] and, last but not least, a system of incentives for legal experts in the service of the government to hike up the rejection rate for asylum applications.

Containment of diversity is also achieved by discouragement and a narrow interpretation of legality. An obvious discouragement measure was California's Proposition 187, endorsed by voters at the end of 1994, which would deny public services, including schools and non-emergency health care, to illegal immigrants. A common Belgian discouragement practice is to stretch the visa application process as long as possible. Disfavoured applicants are often provided with the necessary information in instalments, obliging them to make several trips to the embassy, even if they live at a considerable distance. Those Eastern European citizens who still need a visa may have to wait for many months, even if their visit is an official one, as in the case of a scholar invited to a Belgian university on a grant given by a Belgian ministry. Though applicants are, obviously, never informed of such policy guidelines, inhabitants of China or a number of African countries may not have a chance of getting in unless they travel on business or in a group, or if they intend to get married and the Belgian partner has made all the required commitments and arrangements. To top it all, visa applicants from certain countries (e.g. Brazil) are now routinely subjected to AIDS tests *and* are being asked to sign a document declaring that they will not engage in any form of political activity while in Belgium.[6]

Discouragement also takes the form of extra demands which foreigners, once they are legal residents, have to live up to. In Belgium, foreign professionals or businessmen who want to start a practice or a business of their own are legally required to acquire a so-called 'profession card', a requirement which does not hold for Belgian citizens and which often involves a lengthy administrative procedure the outcome of which is so uncertain that it not infrequently lends itself to bribery; only recently some politicians are beginning to question this obvious form of discrimination.

As to a narrow interpretation of the law, take the example of political refugees. In most cases they will not be able to obtain a visa, either because of the barriers erected by the prospective host country, or because it is simply too dangerous to apply in the country they want to escape from. Given the increasing likelihood of being denied access at the borders of Western countries, they will almost necessarily have to enter illegally. But this fact makes them illegal aliens. They are looked upon as having already broken the law before they can apply for political asylum. And under a narrow interpretation of the legality, their avoidance of standard procedures leads to grounds for 'suspicion' and ultimately rejection. To make things worse, the increasing likelihood of being denied permission to stay induces many not to apply at all; needless to say that for them there is no redemption when caught, even after fifteen years of full integration into local everyday life.

Still there is migration, producing a particular kind of diversity. For diversity one has failed to prevent, a policy of containment also takes the form of eliminating differences as much as possible. It is at this point that we enter one of the central tenets of the debate on the management of diversity, related to notions such as assimilation, integration, multiculturalism, cultural pluralism, and the like. Since the debate itself is what this book is all about, we must wait for the results of our analysis before we can say more about the substance of this angle on containment.

The second option for managing diversity rarely occurs in isolation. It usually presupposes containment. In fact, it is not so much management of diversity as such, but rather a way of managing the negative side effects of undiverted and unaccepted diversity: the *fight against racism and discrimination*. The fight is so popular that racists are forced either to define racism as a universal attitude or to declare themselves not to be racist. Participants range from small local action committees, massive grassroots movements and government agencies of various kinds, all the way up to the UN Human Rights Commission which has just developed a programme of action for the Third Decade to Combat Racism and Racial Discrimination. The battle itself, its goals and its methods, are hot topics of debate.

A misguided debate

In Richard Lewontin's words, 'The most striking feature of global human history is the incessant and widespread migration and fusion of groups from different regions. Wholesale migration is not a recent phenomenon brought about by the development of airplanes and ships; it has been an economic necessity at all times' (1982:113). Yet, at the end of the twentieth century, top-level politicians, social scientists, journalists and social activists alike, seem to feel the need to provide an ecological wrapping for the basic biological fact of diversity. The suggestion is made, explicitly or implicitly, that migration somehow disturbs a natural connection between human organisms and their environment. Surely, many of the circumstances which induce people to move are deplorable; and so are many of the conditions they end up in. But looking at the history of humanity, we cannot avoid the observation that people have roots only at the most metaphorical level and that the need to move around is part of the *condition humaine*. Thus, moving is, in and of itself, not a problem; nor is the resulting diversity. Moreover, whatever changes take place in the world, migrations will not stop; nor will the sharing of geographic space by people with different ethnic, cultural, religious, linguistic or regional backgrounds. Diversity is as inevitable and as restrictive as gravity. It is not to be deplored, nor to be exalted. It is simply there, to be used as a resource.

The management paradigm which dominates the debate on diversity, ignores its status as a simple fact of life. In other words, as will be shown in detail, the debate itself turns diversity into a problem to be managed. That is why even UNESCO's uncompromising acceptance of diversity is not without ambivalence: the acceptance in question goes hand in hand with a definition of diversity as a problem, which is why a programme is launched to research the potential of 'management'. As will be seen in the case of the Flemish version of the debate, explicit acceptance is easily combined with implicit 'doubts', if not rejection, among members of the tolerant majority. When analysing the debate, we will witness the ideological construction of a problem.

The eternal 'other'

Conventional wisdom tells us that *debates* are open discussions of opposing points of view. In that capacity, they are associated with democracy, and they are seen as the absolute opposite of authoritatively imposed *dogmas*. This dichotomy hides the fact that public discourse in democratic societies is not as free and open as it might seem at first sight. In other words, debates are themselves objects (as well as instruments) of control. They are not controlled by just a few individuals. Control, to the extent that it is exerted consciously, requires more cunning than in the case of dogma. A lower degree of predictability is involved. But they are controlled none the less.[7] Wide societal debates tend to be dominated by the economically and politically powerful segments of society, availing themselves of influential means of communication. The smaller the society, the stronger the control because of the more limited variability of communicative resources – an observation which clashes with that other conventional wisdom that democratic institutions lend more power to individual citizens in smaller societies. This is why the processes involved have a better chance of being analysed with a high degree of clarity in a small country such as Belgium, especially after a further shrinking of the spheres of influence as a result of federalization: in Flanders, a community of less than six million, all major decision-making processes pass through the same set of narrow channels dug by and protecting vested interests, both political and economic. The free flow of ideas and arguments is a cherished but dangerous illusion.

The debate on diversity is a case in point. As we will demonstrate at length, it is clearly dominated by the (powerful) majority, to such an extent that minority members are not even allowed to participate. 'Management' is always in the hands of the powerful, and the management of diversity is not an exception. Debating diversity serves the function of defining the terms of management. Despite an overtly professed democratic attitude, the 'managed' have little say in all this. Therefore the debate is really about the 'other', viewed from the perspective of the majority. There is nothing new about the 'other' as an object of discourse. Nor is there anything new about the linkage between the discourse and unequal power relationships or between the (recounting of) observations and the observer's partiality. For that reason, we should dwell for a little while on the connections between that much wider and older issue and the geographically and temporally more restricted object of investigation, thus further enhancing the relevance of the latter. This little excursion will also explain why the debate on diversity, though misguided, is conducted with such vigour.

The main point is simply this: the way in which 'others' are depicted is never to be dissociated from collective or individual perspectives, influenced or determined by an habitual frame of reference, power relationships, personal stakes and motivations. Even a well-developed field of scholarship such as anthropology seems to have the greatest possible trouble trying to free itself from such constraints. So-called 'ethnographic objectivity' is often a hidden form of ideological reinforcement of existing views and relationships, as has been convincingly argued by anthropologists such as James Boon (1982) and Johannes Fabian (1983, 1986). Other authors, including Edward Said (1978, 1981, 1993), have extended the argument to different forms of expertise, including media coverage.[8] All these authors come to the same conclusion: anthropological theories – whether professional or not – and the descriptions of other peoples based on them or underlying them are unmistakably liable to ideological bias related to a temporally situated world view, reigning norms of social organization, and actual power relationships between the observer's group and the observed (cf. Michel Foucault's *autre pouvoir, autre savoir*, 'different power, different knowledge'). Whatever counts for discourse constrained by professional norms of objectivity is all the more prevalent in popular ways of looking at and dealing with 'others'.

A constant element in these processes is the facile recourse to the notion of 'culture', that 'clumpish term, which by gathering up so many activities and attributes into one common bundle may actually confuse or disguise discriminations that should be made between them' (E.P. Thompson 1993: 13). In particular, 'culture' is used to explain or justify images of or opinions on the 'other' which are generated by factors outside the other's culture, however clumpish that term may be.

Thus Henry Kissinger (1982) felt free to compare Pham Van Dong with Zhou Enlai in terms of the former's representing a people (the Vietnamese) characterized by untameable obstinacy and deriving his strength from the obsessive ambitions of a single nation, and the latter's leadership over a country (China) that had left its mark on history due to its cultural greatness and his conviction that his country's attitude could serve as a moral example for the rest of the world. Boorish stubbornness and cultural refinement are set in contrast, not as individual properties of Pham Van Dong and Zhou Enlai, but as characteristics of Vietnamese *versus* Chinese culture. The value of this description can hardly be assessed without taking into account the historical circumstances in which Kissinger met both leaders in 1975. The People's Republic of China was on its way to full rehabilitation in the eyes of Americans, after having symbolized the Communist threat for a couple of decades. This promising ally, newly accessible after its defying Moscow's leadership in the Communist world, required positive image building. On the other hand, Kissinger's view of Pham Van Dong was no doubt coloured by America's humiliating Vietnamese adventure as well as by the fact that, at the negotiating table, the Vietnamese were hard to handle. It is useful to depict an enemy negatively and a friend positively. Under such circumstances, cultural and historical explanations for differences in observed behaviour are most welcome, especially since reactions to individuals can then be translated into legitimized political attitudes towards the nations they represent.

Kissinger did not invent this technique. Long before him, Julius Caesar claimed in *De Bello Gallico* (About the Gallic War) that the Belgians were the bravest among the Gauls – a claim which tells us less about the ancient Belgians than about Caesar's need to explain a near-defeat. The other side of the coin is that similar processes of a political and ideological nature influence the image one creates of one's own culture or community. Therefore Caesar's flattering comment used to appear in all Belgian history schoolbooks – a fact that simply reflects the nineteenth-century attempt to define a Belgian nation and to provide, *a posteriori*, a historical legitimation for its creation.[9] Little did it matter that Caesar's Belgium and the present Belgian state lack comparability, whether in terms of population or in terms of geographical space.

Such strategies of self-representation are matched in everyday life by the standard stories told about one's own country when abroad. Such stories are almost ritual, with a stable form and content. They do not normally relate day-to-day experiences and concerns. Rather, they represent a primitive form of ethnography, ideologically detaching personal experience from the generalized and stereotypical depictions offered in response to (expected) patterns of expectation.

Full awareness of these seemingly trivial processes is crucial for an understanding of our thinking about ourselves as well as 'others'. In the case of discourse about 'others' there are additional complications on top of the tendency to be led by stereotypes, implicit norms and patterns of expectation. If we consciously try to avoid generalizations and to orient ourselves towards direct observation and personal experience, we are still stuck with the question of how not to corrupt our 'knowledge of the other' with our own projections. Moreover, even in cases where there is direct personal contact, we may only know the 'other' as he or she is manifest in relation to us. It is surprising to what extent the 'culture' displayed in intercultural contact may differ from the 'culture' emerging in everyday life within a given community. Intercultural contact always involves a degree of cultural adaptation: some properties (usually the more profound ones) are suppressed, while others are emphasized.[10] This is no more than a micro-level manifestation of a more general historical process which follows Toynbee's rule that the power of a cultural phenomenon to spread is inversely proportional to its depth. Culture, therefore, is not a stable or a self-contained but an interactional phenomenon, characterized by a high degree of variability (within 'cultures' as much as between them), constant negotiability, and multidirectional adaptability.

Yet the most common presentation of (a) 'culture' is one that denies or underestimates precisely this flexibility and dynamics. People are supposed to have,

once and for all, identifiable cultural 'roots'. As one popular intercultural communication training programme would like us to believe, when moving into a
different cultural environment, people go through 'transplant shock'. Or, as a
Flemish anthropologist would have it, cultures are tough creatures: they die
slowly, if at all.[11] About 'foreigners' or 'others' in general it is easy to say '*They
are . . .*', using terms expressing both generalization ('*they*') and timelessness
('*are*'). The other is *the* other, condemned to *remain* the other: *the eternal other.*
Strangely enough, the intensity of intercultural contact – as through long years of
colonization, extensive anthropological research, or simply sharing a neighbourhood – does not seem to matter. Often the 'other' tends to become more different
and more strange.

In Antiquity and the Middle Ages, scholars 'knew' a number of 'Plinian races'
– named after Pliny the Elder's account of natural history. These were most
remarkable creatures with one leg, a single eye, people with enormous ears, with
dog heads, two heads, or no head at all. Peter Mason (1990) notes that these
Plinian races were always located in hardly known territory: just beyond the
explored horizon in Africa, South America or the Asian mountain ranges. They
were known from hearsay. Once, a traveller is said to have seen them in a far-away
place. From then onwards they live on in the imagination and in a tradition as
part of some 'public opinion' about potentially terrifying and dangerous strangers.
We are still familiar with a couple of Plinian races: the abominable snowman
inhabiting the snows of the high Himalayas; and extraterrestrials. There are
remarkably stable descriptions of such creatures, which have become familiar
appearances in movies, books and cartoons. Yet no one has ever encountered
either a yeti or a Martian. They both live beyond the common horizon, in territories that could be explored only with the greatest of efforts. But the Plinian races
are humanoid. In our description of extraterrestrials we are guided by a human
profile to which we add slightly 'abnormal' properties. Thus Star Trek's Mr Spock,
from the planet Vulcanus, looks like us except for his large, pointy ears. Others
have deviant skin colours (green, blue, or even transparent), an oversize head, no
hair, or an electronically distorted voice. Usually they are extremely intelligent,
they speak English fluently (or as fluently as is expected of a well-educated non-
native speaker), and they have characters, emotions and intentions translatable
into ours: they hate, love, are wise or aggressive, are homesick, or want to rule the
universe. Moreover, they use advanced technology and sophisticated aircraft.
They are *human beings* onto whom we project a number of physical and/or
psychical abnormalities. They are what we are not, but what we somehow could
or would like to be.

With the shifting of horizons as a result of voyages of discovery and colonization, the Plinian races were gradually replaced by better-known, but no less
barbaric and frightful, 'pagans' and 'savages'. As a result, the definition of the
'abnormal' shifted from physical properties which proved not to exist, to deviant
values and behaviour. Such was the fate of the American Indians – some of whom
'on a more distant island', according to Columbus, had tails. Mason (1987)

18

describes how, when the Indian was no longer a Plinian race but had turned into a pagan, an image developed in Europe which had no doubt more to do with European fears and wishes than with properties of the Indians themselves. The Indian was depicted as a cannibal, an idolater, and someone with highly deviant sexual behaviour. These were exactly the same qualifications as those ascribed to European witches in the period preceding the great voyages of discovery. Witches were said to eat the ashes of burnt children, to worship Satan, and to organize wild feasts marked by adultery, bestiality and homosexuality. Such qualifications were seen to reflect the ultimate evil and inferiority of the Indian or the witch. They thereby served to legitimate the drastic measures taken by the conquerors, just as they had rationalized the stake. Because of their evilness, the Indians had to be mercilessly converted. If they resisted Christianization, their stubbornness and their refusal to change for the better could be legitimately punished by death, as in the case of the witch. Thus the Indian was, following present-day critical anthropology, a projection of an intra-European enemy consisting of a complex of features founded upon superstition and stereotypes of immoral and antisocial conduct. In other words, the Indian was categorized in terms of the pre-existent functional frame of reference of the non-believer, the degenerate adversary of the established order (or the order to be established), against whom tested measures could be taken. The Indian was an exotic transformation of the European miscreant – just as the villainous and expansionistic extraterrestrial was to become a translation of the Russian threat. Shifts in the general philosophical and ideological climate later produced a diametrically opposed picture. The philosophers of the Enlightenment saw in the Indian, with equal amounts of projection, the uncorrupted primitive – just as Spielberg transformed the terror-inspiring extraterrestrial into the loveliest children's friend in movie history, E.T.

It is not hard to draw parallels between the fate of the American Indians and that of people elsewhere throughout history, until today. The Western view of the African in his prototypical sensuality and rhythm is the negative mirror image of Weberian capitalist-Protestant ethics (see Jan Nederveen Pieterse 1990). The perceived Arab tendency towards verbosity and antagonistic dispute is the opposite of self-ascribed European norms of negotiation, consensus and rational dialogue. The more and more frequently emphasized Islamic inclination towards fundamentalism is supposed to contrast sharply with Christian tolerance and democratic pluralism. In all these cases we pay less attention to true characteristics than to what the 'other' might represent in our socio-psychological and moral frame of reference. We reconstruct the other in terms of our own categories, expectations, habits and norms. Not everything in our own reality fits those categories and expectations, and not all of our behaviour corresponds to these habits and norms. But the deviation, the 'abnormality', is attributed to the 'other' as an essential property. The foreigner, or the 'other' in general, is thereby getting *abnormalized*. When we brand Africans as lazy, we use as our measure the assumption that we normally embody diligence, tenacity and dynamism. When we portray Moslems as fanatics with an incorrigible craving to conquer and to convert, we start from the belief that we are tolerance personified. All of this is a matter of self-presentation, potentially detached from who, what and how we really are.

Abnormalization and the immigrant

In the debate on diversity, the tendency to abnormalize the 'other' combines with the assumption underlying the 'management' paradigm that diversity itself is somehow abnormal and problematic. The full burden of this double problematization befalls the immigrant, the 'other' who happens to come to us rather than to be a long-time neighbour or the object of our own exploration. Again, there is nothing new about this. Even in a typical immigrant society such as the United States, there is a long history of constructing the immigrant as a physical threat to the community, importing epidemic diseases of various kinds, and as a scapegoat for most of the community's social ills. Alan Kraut (1994), for instance, chronicles epidemic encounters and shows how xenophobic reactions to them – all the way to AIDS – focused exclusively on biological factors, thus turning immigrants into real enemies, while ignoring social and economic conditions conducive to the spread of disease, such as the extremely poor living and working environment in which most new immigrants used to find themselves.

As if foreboding later developments in Europe, at least one early twentieth-century Flemish observer managed to cast the American 'negro problem' in an interpretative mould that abnormalizes immigrants and immigration:

> Imagine that between 1926 and 1928, half a million Riffians and Arabs would move to Northern and Western Europe and that they would settle in a couple of big cities such as London, Paris, as well as in Northern France and Belgium. Just estimate the housing shortage, the adaptation problems in economic production, the influence on wages and the trade unions, the tensions between inhabitants and immigrants, the stories about the customs and habits of the immigrants who would wander around in the North, the consequences for industry and agriculture in the South, and you will come close to understanding why there is a black problem in the United States.
>
> (Marnix Gijsen 1928: 74)

The historical details of Gijsen's (unintentional) premonition are not completely accurate. Nor is the comparison he tries to make with the African-American population in the US. But the air of normality with which this Flemish author surrounds the problematic nature of diversity, especially when linked to migration, explains fully why there is a debate, however misguided it may be.

As explained before, irrespective of the intensity of intercultural contact, we tend to create a complex of ideas about the 'culture', the 'mentality' or the 'character' of the 'other' in relation to ourselves. The Belgian migrant debate, as it

unfolds in the mass media, in socio-scientific research and in political policy decisions, also contains such a complex of unquestioned conceptualizations. Our
analysis will reveal that the Belgian migrant debate is essentially based on a
distancing and confrontational view of 'us' *versus* the 'other', captured in (often
implicit) terms of 'normality' *versus* 'abnormality'. Migrants are our Indians, no
longer a Plinian race, but at least 'pagans' (of the expansionistic and fanatical
Islamic type) and 'savages' (barbarians who chop off hands, imprison their
circumcised wives, and allow polygamy). In contrast to the Indians of old, they do
not only *symbolize* the intra-European enemy. They *are* the enemy. They seem to
have penetrated in our midst, abusing our openness. They seem to form a threat to
our society which risks destruction as a result of its own tolerance if we remain
unopposed to their abnormalities. Hence the necessity of adaptation and 'integration' – a term which assumes a very specific meaning in the Belgian debate, to be
explained in full later. Hence also the necessity to construct the migrant problem
in such a way as to preserve the existing power relationships – or at least to avoid
questioning them.[12]

The limits of awareness

Whatever aspects of critical theory, cultural criticism, theories of discourse and
power, and postcolonial analysis may have forced themselves into the preceding
paragraphs, by now they have acquired the status of common lore in a segment of
the humanities and social sciences. Why then did we have to repeat them?
Certainly not to convince the non-believer – which would require a wider theoretical and empirical effort. Though our immediate purpose is more modest, at the
same time the implications go further. Not a single member of what we designate
as the 'tolerant majority' will recognize him- or herself in the Western or 'colonial'
ideas and attitudes sketched (almost by way of caricature) and criticised above.
But that is exactly why this book had to be written. Our analysis reveals that
professed awareness of a Foucauldian perspective on social life – i.e., the common
philosophical and socio-scientific lore referred to – does not stand in the way of
rhetorical operations which, at various levels of implicit meaning, clash with
overtly accepted 'critical' beliefs and attitudes. In particular, there is a level of
ideological work which is shared by mainstream pro-migrant rhetoric, i.e. the
rhetoric of tolerance, and anti-migrant rhetoric alike.

It will be our task to demonstrate all of this. But first we have to make another
excursion, describing the link between cognition and group relations, and
explaining how language will be used as a window onto the ideological processes
at issue.

2

GROUP RELATIONS, COGNITION AND LANGUAGE

Framing group relations

The empirical data for this study were collected from publicly accessible types of discourse on 'migrants' (a fuzzy category the functioning of which will be described at length) produced by the mass media, government sources, political parties, and social scientists whose work was widely broadcast in the media. To the extent that these different sources are interrelated, the 'migrant debate' is predominantly oriented at formulating policies, i.e. the management of diversity. Irrespective of the content of the adopted positions and of the formulated proposals, it is clear that they affect *group relations*: existing or desired relations between a majority of 'Belgians' and a minority of 'immigrants'. In the foregoing chapter we already hinted at the dependence of group relations on their conceptual framing. Before venturing into an analysis of actual data, the general validity of this point about the cognitive anchoring of intergroup perception and interaction has to be shown.

Not only are perceptions of the 'other' highly influenced by the socio-psychological positioning of the self. At the most elementary level the conceptual framing of group relations depends on *definitions of group identities*, as much for the self as for the other. And this is where a major problem emerges from the start. As Dov Ronen (1979: 9) says,

> Until future research proves otherwise, we ought to take for granted only two basic human entities: individuals and all humanity. All entities between these two, save a mother and a new-born child, are arbitrary formations created by our perception of ourselves vis-à-vis others.

In a further explanation he argues:

> One's religion, mother tongue, culture, also one's education, class, sex, skin color, even one's height, age, and family situation are all potentially unifying factors. Each factor can also be ignored as irrelevant in the formation of an 'us.' Various unifying factors, such as language, religion,

22

and color of skin, seem 'natural.' I propose that none is. Language, culture, a real or assumed historical origin, and religion, form identities for an 'us' in our minds, and only so long as they exist in our minds as unifying factors do the entities of 'us' persist.

It is not difficult to come up with examples to complete this picture. Indeed, there are numerous ways in which groups can be distinguished, but it is hard to come up with objective criteria which could be used to identify 'natural groups'. The role which each individual parameter plays in determining group identity depends fully on group-internal and group-external perceptions and conceptualizations which are historically and socio-culturally shaped.

Let us take the factor *race* as a society-structuring element. Race, whatever the exact content of this notion may be, used to be of primordial importance in the South African context, but much less so in a country like Brazil, and it may in the long run lose most of its power to structure social life in postapartheid South Africa.

Religion, to use another example, has steadily been losing its relevance in the interaction between 'religious' and 'non-religious' groups in Western Europe, even though, until very recently, it played a crucial distinguishing role. In Belgium, for instance, being Catholic used to mean joining a Catholic trade union, sending one's children to a Catholic school, and voting for the Christian Democrats – and certainly not for the Socialist party. Today, the traces of this pattern, the so-called 'pillarization' of Belgian society, are still clearly visible, while they have lost most of their significance in religious terms. But, during the last decade, religion has been revitalized as an identity-constituting parameter. This time it differentiates between a Moslem minority and a Christian majority, where the two religiously defined camps consist of both practising followers of the faith and non-religious heirs to a pervasively Islamic or Christian culture and morality.

Descent is a crucially important factor to determine membership in a Jewish community, whereas it is only of secondary importance in a definition of Catalan identity, which may simply be acquired after moving into Catalonia from any other part of Spain.

Language, finally, is perceived as a uniting factor in the relations between Flemish and Dutch (and some wish to extend this 'unity' so as to include speakers of Afrikaans), while it reinforces divisions between Serbians and Croats. Yet the level and nature of the linguistic differences, which clearly exist and which are used as distinguishing traits also in the Flemish–Dutch case (e.g. in jokes, or when expressing antagonism), is virtually the same in both cases. Moreover, in both contexts the differences find a rough parallel in a religious divide (Catholic *versus* Protestant in the case of Flanders and The Netherlands, Catholic *versus* Orthodox for Croats and Serbians)[1] and can be related to an imposed separation in the past (as a result of the Spanish occupation of Flanders and the Turkish occupation of Serbia). Thus, in an 'objective' comparative paradigm, it is quite possible to conclude that 'except for language there is little which unites Serbians and Croats' (*DS* 24 July 1991: 4). But starting from the dominant Serbian and Croat definitions of their group identities, language separates more than it unites. While some Flemish nationalists are committed to a 'Great Netherlands' because of the common language, and most other Flemish people recognize a level of cultural unity for the same reason, however different the linguistic varieties may be, Croats send their linguists to conferences abroad with the message that the Serbian and Croat varieties of Serbo-Croatian are really two different languages.

Cognition and ideology

As shown above, there are no objective (i.e. 'constant' or 'natural') criteria that can be used to identify groups. Though group formation is a natural and universally occurring process, its product is never a 'natural group'. A parameter may be dominant in one context while being ignored completely in another. Still, groups and group relations are usually objects of a wide consensus within the groups thus created: they are *felt* to be natural. In other words, *group relations and group identities are cognitively framed phenomena to be found at the inter-subjective level of the community*. Group relations and identities exist predominantly in the mind, but they are shared by many, even if they do not take exactly the same shape in every individual mind within a given 'community' produced by the cognitive framing in question. The point is that this cognitive framing is an active process, in which identifiable social actors organize the structure and distribution of knowledge and ideas about, as well as perceptions and impressions of social phenomena, and simultaneously furnish ways of speaking about these phenomena. The process, therefore, need not be 'collective' in the strictest sense of the term. The 'commonsense theorizing that occurs in the process of organizing and applying some description of the world' (Blum 1971: 117) is in itself a layered and structured phenomenon which allows for a range of interindividual and intersubgroup variability.

Group identities do not only determine our opinions and discourses about others, but also other forms of behaviour towards them. The opinions come in as tools to legitimate the behaviour. But it is rarely clear whether the opinions were arrived at independently or simply in function of legitimization. We should bear in mind, in this context, that the identification of a group has a strategic potential for forming alliances or bringing about exclusions. Therefore *power* always plays a role, both, as noted above, in the intragroup process of ideologization, and in the intergroup application of ideologies. From our analysis it will appear that power is the factor which consolidates negative perceptions and distancing attitudes in the migrant debate. It is symptomatic, for instance, that the migrant debate is conducted almost exclusively between members of the majority. Rarely is there a direct dialogue between majority and minority (with the exception of a number of relatively isolated situations of contact with little direct impact on the public debate). Moreover, it is the majority which clearly determines the shape of group relations; it defines the 'code' of interaction. In so far as members of the minority are tolerated as active participants in the debate, they are also expected to pay lip service to, and echo, the majority views. In this way, these views can also be presented as being reflected in segments of the minority community, and even as reflecting those segments' needs and desires.

These two factors, the societal and socially structured dimension of the cognitive framing of group relations and the processes of power that are involved, lead directly into a discussion of *ideology*. In the light of what has been said so far, our claim is that social and political problems related to intergroup relations cannot be understood without analysing the ideological undercurrents of the society exhibiting the problems in question.

Bearing in mind that 'ideology' may be 'the most elusive concept in the whole of social science' (McLellan 1986: 1), we shall avoid a lengthy discussion at this point and simply define an ideology as any constellation of fundamental or commonsensical, and often normative, ideas and attitudes related to some aspect(s) of social 'reality'. Usually, ideologies have a degree of persistence over time: similar ideologies are recoverable, to quote Maurice Bloch (1989: 133), 'from one power-holder to another'. Our discussion of the images of an Eternal Other has shown that there is usually a 'stock' of topoi, motives and stories which can be used for constructing user-friendly 'new' ideologies. The commonsense nature of the beliefs, ideas and attitudes (i.e. commonsensical for those who hold the beliefs and attitudes) is manifested in the fact that they are rarely questioned, in a given society or community, in discourse related to the social 'reality' in question, sometimes even across various discourse genres.[2] In the case of the Belgian migrant debate it will be shown that these beliefs, ideas and attitudes are also features of opposition, dissident or resistance rhetoric. Theoretically this may be just a matter of coincidence: the Belgian migrant debate could simply be an extreme case of successful hegemony. Yet, it presents us with a series of analytical questions which deserve further scrutiny because simple associations between hegemonic discourse and mainstream discourse on the one hand, and between counter-hegemonic discourse and opposition, dissident or resistance discourse on the other, do not hold. There is resistance discourse galore in the Belgian migrant debate, but it is hard to find any that is genuinely counter-hegemonic in the sense that it would deny or question the fundamental assumptions, ideas and beliefs that characterize the hegemonic version.

Their not being questioned means that the ideas and attitudes in question are often (though not always and not exclusively) carried along implicitly rather than to be formulated explicitly. Rhetorically constructed or supported ideological webs, which are manifestations of Vygotsky's (1978) 'mind in society', 'social cognition' (T.A. van Dijk 1995), or 'interpretive frames' (Tulviste and Wertsch 1990), serve the purpose of framing, validating or legitimating opinions and actions in the domain to which they are applicable. To quote Tulviste and Wertsch (1990: 3), such ideological webs 'determine which arguments will appeal to a group' and will hence 'provide the groundwork of our thinking and identity'.

Ideology and discourse

The most tangible manifestation of ideology is discourse (in a non-metaphorical, down-to-earth sense of discourse as an observable instance of communicative behaviour, whether verbal or not). Remembering Vološinov's view that not only ideology but even self-awareness or consciousness 'is always verbal, always a matter of finding some specifically suitable verbal complex' (1976: 86), but keeping in mind that 'verbal' may have to be replaced with the more general 'communicative', one could even go as far as to claim an ontological connection between ideology and discourse. After all, ideas can only begin to permeate social life and action when they find forms of expression. Therefore, empirical ideology research is almost necessarily discourse-centred, or should at least contain a significant discourse-analytical component. The main question is: trying not to confuse 'empirical research' with a positivist belief in 'objectivity', what should a discourse-centred approach to ideology research look like?

Providing a full set of methodological guidelines is beyond the scope of this book; some further elaborations, still highly succinct in formulation, are to be found in Verschueren (1995a, b), and the basic principles are illustrated in their application to the topic of 'ethnicity' in D'hondt et al. (1995). Let it suffice to outline briefly a few elements that are eminently relevant to the specific problems at hand. As suggested, a complete account of the ideological processes manifested in discourse requires a balanced presentation of explicit and implicit aspects as well as the way in which these interact. It was also suggested that the level of implicit meaning is of particular importance because of the commonsense nature of ideology: a world of ideas and attitudes which is basically taken for granted as a yardstick by which opinions, actions and events are measured. In the present investigation the importance of the implicit is still seriously enhanced by an intricate interaction between the sources of the data, the topic and the adopted research angle.

Even so, ideological analysis cannot bypass a phase of pre-analysis of its data. Not all social discourse data are of equal importance, and, in view of the socially structured character of ideology, data should be identified and situated with regard to the role and position they have in the process of ideologization. Are the data 'powerful', i.e. produced, controlled or monopolized by demonstrably powerful groups in society? Or are they grassroots data, reflecting the way in which reigning ideologies have penetrated the commonsense theorizing of those lower on the social ladder? Distinctions such as these are of major importance for assessing the potential social effects of particular forms of discourse. Not all discourses have equal weight, and the reasons for this do not usually lie *inside* the discourse, but *outside*, in the identity of its producer, in the socio-political and spatio-temporal context of its production. (See, e.g., Kathryn Woolard 1985, Paul Friedrich 1989, Monica Heller 1995.)

It may be wise, in view of this, to adopt a materialist perspective on the discourse data. By this we mean a perspective which views discourse more or less in terms of an economic model, including producers, means of production, processes of distribution etc. (cf. Bourdieu 1982). Discourse thus becomes a (symbolic) commodity, a source of and instrument for acquiring and elaborating power and status – a view which differs substantially from widespread 'idealist' and often transcendental linguistic views of discourse. This materialist perspective also invites an *ethnographic* and an *historical* approach to the data, complementing the discourse-analytical approach which focuses on the structure of the data itself. The ethnographic approach compels us to analyse the data in the context of a synchronic pattern of social relations and practices. It allows us to understand that certain groups in society have the powerful status of 'ideology brokers', and why. The historical approach allows us to detect large 'waves' of discourses: discourse traditions, genres, styles and transformations or fissures in these waves. It also allows us to see how and why certain discourse traditions become instruments of ideological production and reproduction (i.e., why they become 'recoverable', to use Bloch's term), and thus to view discourse practices as elements in a *process* of power elaboration.

The ethnographic situation of the data

The data sources were briefly mentioned at the beginning of this chapter: publicly accessible types of discourse produced by the mass media, government sources, political parties and prominent social scientists. The reason for this selection lies in the status and authority of these discourse producers. With regard to most crucial political debates in Belgium, the major players are politicians and policy makers, the media, and academic (or other 'learned') experts. With regard to the debate on 'migrants' in particular, it is these groups that furnish the lexicon for talking about the issue, the major patterns of argumentation, the appropriate styles. Their discourses are often echoes of or responses to those of their fellow ideology brokers: politicians refer to scientific reports; scientific questions are asked in response to political issues and investigated with funds provided by politicians for that purpose; the media refer to politicians; politicians react to media reports; and so on. At the same time, their collective discourse is reproduced through an infinite series of echoes and references in secondary sources: everyday talk, but also the rhetoric and jargon of social workers and institutional or semi-institutional centres for 'migrant work'. The various actors in the field – producers (politicians and policy-makers, journalists, experts) and reproducers (secondary actors such as 'migrant workers'[3] and individual community members) – constantly feed back to each other. A particular idea may be elaborated and 'discoursed' first by a conglomerate of politicians and scientists; next it is handed over to the media, which distribute it and provide it with subtexts, comments, interpretations; then it is picked up – sometimes only through the media and sometimes through direct communication from the responsible authorities as well – by people in the field of practical migrant affairs, integrated into their practices, and sent back to the sources of production which may then use this to legitimate their ideas, tested and positively sanctioned by 'the people in the field'. Simultaneously, the 'public' adopts bits and pieces of the rhetoric in its own discourse on migrants, and thus also becomes a source of legitimization for the producers.

The instruments used by the implicit alliance of 'ideology brokers' are genres and styles. Power is shaped and elaborated by means of a particular lexicon, a particular logic in the arguments, recognizably 'political' or 'academic' ways of speaking. Mediatization is crucial to the whole process, if for no other reason than because of the access these groups have to the media, a feature which sets them apart from most other groups in society. Not only are they the object of media reporting (with a higher likelihood than other individuals), but they can represent themselves through the media.

This is, of course, a highly schematized description of what is in effect a process of tremendous complexity, part of which we hope to elucidate in the remainder of this book. But the point is that there is a clear hierarchical producer–reproducer relationship in the Belgian migrant debate, involving on the side of the producers an identifiable set of authoritative social actors – the ideology brokers – and a less neatly structured collection of reproducers, including both laypersons and various (semi-)institutional and (semi-)organized groups. The particular constellation in which they find themselves in the migrant debate may be debate-specific. The major role of social scientists, for instance, may be less outspoken in other debates such as those, say, about unemployment. Yet the particular alliance between politicians, media and experts may be a feature of social structure in societies such as Belgium in general. (For more details about this general picture, to be substantiated by our analysis, see e.g. Norman Fairclough 1989.)

The historical situation of the data

Where does the discourse on migrants come from? What sources can be detected in contemporary realizations of discourse? The questions are important, for one of the key ingredients of the debate is a strictly local and synchronic perspective. The issue of migrants (as well as its derivatives such as the topic of racism) is presented as a feature of the *hic et nunc*, as a new and unique problem that can be treated and discussed autonomously. Ample evidence for this claim will emerge from the data later. The historical perspective allows us to detect 'deep' relations between the contemporary issue and other socio-political matters.

One clear historical source – the link with which will also emerge clearly from the data – is *nationalism*, or, to be more precise, the particular history of nationalism in Belgium. Recapitulating what was already said about this in the Introduction, the issue of diversity (as made visible by the presence of migrants) is framed in terms of culture differences and their ensuing social and political ramifications. While this culturalist orientation is shared to various degrees by other European societies (see, e.g., for a discussion of The Netherlands, Jan Rath 1991), the logic behind it is particularly appealing in Belgium, due to the political history of the country in which language and cultural identity have been (and are) central. Much of the discourse on migrants, we will show, is anchored in older and more established discourses on cultural identity and the necessity of cultural homegeneity, mostly produced by the Flemish nationalist movement. This partic- ular historical source also accounts for some small differences in policy development between Flanders and Wallonia, the culturalist orientation being more outspoken in Flanders (see Marco Martiniello 1994).

A second, more specific, source is *cultural anthropology*. Given the culturalist orientation and the impact of academic experts on the debate, the discourse on migrants draws extensively on vulgarized anthropology. The most widespread definitions of 'culture' stress the deep-rooted values, customs and traditions of the people, and advocate cultural relativism or particularism as solutions to practical problems in education, counselling, administration, health care, and so on. As argued in Chapter 1, this anthropological discourse is in turn anchored in an older tradition of speaking about the 'other'.

The *sociological* discourses underneath the debate are hybrid. There is a remarkable (but, as shown by Jan Rath 1991 and Robert Miles 1993, not excep- tional) absence of Marxist discourses emphasizing social class differences and power struggles. The predominant sociological discourse is that of the Christian labour movement, emphasizing the individual and psychological dimensions of poverty or social disenfranchisement, adopting a paternalistic stance in formu- lating remedies (better individual education, ethics, small-group solidarity), and preferring local solutions over large-scale reform. The presence of this particular sociological undercurrent can be explained by the fact that migrant policies, since their latest inception in 1989, but including earlier preparatory work, have been the province of Christian Democratic politicians and experts. Thus the discourse on migrants was appropriated by one particular ideological current (partly by default), and, by the time the issue became a nationwide political topic of debate, an elaborated terminological and rhetorical framework was already in place.

It is also important to note, in this context, two other influences: that of the political right wing, and that of Europe. The *political right wing*, which is strongest in Flanders and epitomized by the Vlaams Blok party, is an offspring of the radical Flemish nationalist movement. Discredited because of overt collaboration with the Nazis during World War Two, the nationalists reorganized in the 1950s and became an important political force in the 1960s and 1970s. The movement radi- calized in the 1980s (after the founding of the Vlaams Blok in 1978), and from that point onwards Flemish independence and anti-foreigner policies became ingredients of the political debate in Belgium. Migrant policies in Belgium were created partly as a direct response to a major electoral breakthrough of the Vlaams Blok in 1988. As a consequence, part of the formulations of the 'migrant problem' was inspired by that party, which has consistently been applying strong pressure on the government, attempting to influence new policies in the domain of migrants.

The influence of *Europe* is to be situated at two levels. On the one hand, some of the Belgian policy decisions (e.g. in the field of asylum politics; see Chapter 8) were made in consultation with other EU member states. There certainly is a degree of practical, but also rhetorical, uniformization inspired by the process of European integration. Belgian policy-makers, journalists and experts often refer to the situation in other EU member states in order to motivate their own preferences, or to emphasize either the positive or the negative of the Belgian situation – depending on which strategy is most suitable for the purpose at hand.

In addition to highlighting these sources for the new discourses, a few remarks have to be made about the precise historical period in which our data are to be situated. There was discourse on immigration in Belgium, very similar to the type we shall investigate, produced long before today's typical immigrants entered the scene. Belgium has known various waves of immigration (and emigration, the often forgotten other side of the coin), and each wave was welcomed with discourses of otherness, rejection and defamation (Morelli (ed.) 1992 provides an overview). But our data come from a particularly 'hot' historical period, in which the rise of right-wing nationalism and neo-fascism coincided with a period of economic recession, in turn triggering socio-geographic, demographic, and socio-economic phenomena such as the impoverishment of the inner cities, the emergence of intergenerational unemployment, the decline of labour-intensive heavy industries (the prime employers of migrant workers) and so on. This period witnessed an unprecedented political initiative: the creation in 1989 of a special government office in charge of migrant affairs, the 'Koninklijk Commissariaat voor het Migrantenbeleid' ('Royal Commissariat for Migrant Policies', henceforth KCM). The creation of the KCM indicated the government's acceptance of the presence of migrants as a *problem*, a *political* problem of considerable importance. Hence, along the longitudinal dimension against which data such as ours have to be measured, the particular stretch of time which they represent happens to be a critical period in the formation of migrant issues as a political matter in Belgium. Balibar claims that '[m]inorities only exist in actuality from the moment when they are codified and controlled by the state' (1991: 15). As will be shown in the chapters that follow, our analysis bears on the period in which the Belgian state assumed full control over immigrants and developed an elaborate frame of reference codifying and controlling their presence, role and status in society.

Further notes on the data base

Within the range of our data sources, a further selection was necessary. It would have been possible, for instance, to concentrate on extremist sources such as the discourse of the extreme right. We decided not to do this, for two reasons. First, analyses of extremist discourse are abundantly available. Second, though these are of interest in their own right, they do not present much of a research challenge. In relation to the topic of diversity, the political right does not make any effort to hide its discriminatory attitudes, even though a need is felt to rationalize them. What we wanted to investigate was something less easily scooped up from the discourse. The basic question was: What fundamental ideological framework is conscious thinking about, e.g., 'migrants' anchored into? From that point of view, it is not so interesting to read in an unmistakably nationalistic Flemish magazine: 'These Bosnians are not Moslems as we know them here – they sided with the Germans in the Second World War'. The negative feelings towards our own Moslem minorities as well as sympathies for the Third Reich are too obvious, and too expected, to be of much interest. It is much more intriguing, and relevant, to hear a high-placed political figure, in charge of migrant policies, declare that it had been a mistake officially to recognize Islam 'in such an ill-considered manner, without first evaluating the consequences for this small country'.

We concentrated, therefore, on 'mainstream' sources, touching upon extremist materials only to the extent that they entered the mainstream (as objects of discussion or – as happens quite regularly – as contributions to the opinion pages of quality papers or as voices on radio and television programmes). Since tolerance and openness are self-ascribed attributes of most mainstream Western societies, acceptance of diversity is a predictable feature of the explicit message in most of the investigated instances of discourse. That is why we refer to our object of investigation as the *rhetoric of tolerance*, and why the producers and reproducers of the investigated forms of discourse will regularly be labelled the *tolerant majority*. In the face of this explicit message of tolerance, i.e. the professed attitude visibly colouring our specific sources in relation to the topic of diversity, an angle on fundamental ideological frameworks in relation to the same topic can only be obtained through close scrutiny of implicit layers of meaning.

In practical terms our sources include, first of all, a variety of newspapers: *De Standaard, Het Nieuwsblad, Gazet van Antwerpen, Het Volk* (all four with a Christian Democratic tendency, *De Standaard* being the most authoritative one, and *Het Nieuwsblad* being a more popularized version of *De Standaard*); *De Morgen* (socialist); *De Nieuwe Gazet* and *Het Laatste Nieuws* (two sister versions of the same liberal paper); given their importance in the political landscape, the majority of illustrative examples will be from *De Standaard* and *De Morgen*. Data were also derived from magazines such as *Knack, Humo* and *Trends*, all three of them weeklies. The audio-visual media were scrutinized less systematically, but references will be made to BRTN, the Dutch-speaking versions of Belgian radio and television. Coverage of these mass media started in the late 1980s, peaked in 1992–93, and has continued until today.

In addition to mass media sources, documents issued by various political parties or their top-level representatives (the Christian Democratic CVP, the socialist SP, the liberal PVV [later VLD], and the 'green' AGALEV) are investigated. And so are communications from government agencies, in particular the KCM and its successor, the *Centrum voor Gelijkheid van Kansen en Racismebestrijding* (CGKR, 'centre for equal opportunities and the fight against racism'). Further, a KCM-sponsored training programme for police officers, preparing them for interaction with migrants, is studied in detail, as well as some highly mediatized socio-scientific research reports (the type of discourse that will be the least prominent in this book; a sizeable chapter was devoted to it in Blommaert and Verschueren 1992a).

The attentive reader will have noticed that virtually all of these sources (except for the national government agencies) are specifically Flemish, rather than 'Belgian' in general. This restriction was imposed on the data because, as mentioned earlier, there are very significant differences in the ways in which the debate develops in the Flemish and in the Walloon parts of the country. It should be kept in mind, therefore, that the use of the terms 'Belgium' and 'Belgian' in this book are not meant fully to generalize research results emerging from predominantly Flemish data. Our continued use of the terms may be dictated less by descriptive needs (though sometimes they do play a role) than by a form of resistance against the dogmas of separability which recently allowed the Flemish media minister to forbid BRTN-programmers to talk about the 'Belgian coast' and to oblige them to use 'Flemish coast' instead – thus entirely defying the logic of part–whole relationships.

Language and the pragmatics of ideology research

In this book we use language, the central medium of discourse, as a way into ideology. Such an enterprise is necessarily interpretative. This interpretative effort bears on a genuinely communicative phenomenon: the debate about diversity or about immigrants and immigration is quite literally a debate. An eminently suitable theoretical background for such an undertaking is provided by linguistic *pragmatics*, to be defined as a general functional perspective on (any aspect of) language, i.e. as an approach to language which takes into account the full complexity of its cognitive, social and cultural (i.e. 'meaningful') functioning in the lives of human beings.[4] Pragmatics provides us with the tools for tracing the construction of meaning in discourse. And ideological processes, to the extent that discourse or language is their medium, are fundamentally processes of meaning construction.

Linguistic pragmatics assumes that cognitive images and conceptual habits are reflected in the behaviour of language users, their forms of communication and their rhetorical habits. All forms of communication are accompanied by more or less hidden meaning systems which determine the interpretation of what is said. One of the basic premises of a pragmatic approach is that every utterance relies on a world of implicit background assumptions, supposedly shared or presented as shared, which combines with what is explicitly said in the construction of meaning. In other words, it is impossible to find utterances which express their full meaning fully explicitly.[5] Let us briefly summarize some of the methodological requirements for a scientifically tenable scrutiny of such double-track meaning processes.

Given the nature of the enterprise (i.e. the reconstruction of an ideology which, as suggested, and contrary to common practice in mainstream sociology, cannot simply be carried out on the basis of what is said literally), the major concern is to separate clearly interpretation from speculation.[6] After all, just as it is impossible to say explicitly everything one means, it is impossible to 'mean' (not to be confused with 'intend') everything that is possibly implied by what one says. The task is less impossible than it might seem, thanks to a significant degree of conventionality involved in the use of 'carriers' of implicit meaning, and thanks to the observability of how pieces of potential meaning actually get used or fail to get used.

Every pragmatics textbook contains numerous types of examples of conventional presupposition- and implication-carrying constructions such as 'I regret that . . . ' or 'I'm sorry that . . . ', typically presupposing that what follows is both factual and known to the interlocutors. Thus 'I am sorry that I didn't come to your party yesterday' presupposes minimally that the speaker was not at the party and that she/he assumes that the hearer noticed her/his absence. This presupposition can be elaborated strategically by adding other ingredients. 'I am sorry that I couldn't come to your party' adds an excuse to the fact which is presupposed, viz. the speaker's inability to come. Because this excuse is not brought up as a separate assertion but is simply embedded in the factive structure, it also presents itself as factually valid and becomes less susceptible to questioning or criticism. For someone with a trained eye, such intricacies of implicit meaning are quite clear.

As to the scientific study of how meaning potential is actualized in discourse, the latest pragmatic literature draws special attention to empirically observable traces of the dynamic negotiation of meaning, not only at the explicit but also at the implicit level. Thus Charles Goodwin (1994) shows, for instance, how lawyers succeed in defining Rodney King, lying face down and surrounded by four police officers, as being 'in control of the situation' while being beaten, just by framing the event in terms of categories that are normally descriptive of responsible police behaviour. Detailed analyses such as Goodwin's make the actual meaningful *functioning* of linguistic choices visible. This is possible because words and linguistic structures are observable beacons referring to wider contexts and at the same time creating contexts as largely implicit meaning complexes which serve as frames of reference for interpretation. The beacons are there, open to the eye, and we are learning more and more about the ways in which they signal the less visible but equally functional aspects of meaning.

In practical terms, a few of the more relevant phenomena that we looked at systematically are the following:

1   *Wording patterns and strategies* Words and structures are not meaningful in their own right. Meaning derives from the grammatical and lexical choices which language users make from the range of possible choices, in relation to subject matter and context. For instance, if farmer demonstrations in Brussels, no matter how much damage they do to the city, are systematically referred to as 'farmer *demonstrations*', while 'migrant *riots*' is used consistently when describing a group of migrant youngsters protesting police brutality in

the streets of Brussels and breaking a window here and there, this pattern of word choice is meaningful. Though the two types of events have many common characteristics (the dissatisfaction of a social group, the public voicing of protest, the lack of respect for public and private property), the first one is clearly placed – and kept – in a frame of legitimate social action, while the second is condemned by the very act of labelling it.

2   'Local' carriers of implicit information, i.e. the types of implication- and presup-position-carrying constructions already referred to. For instance, when a group of well-intentioned social scientists organizes a symposium under the title 'Towards a liveable multicultural municipality', this seemingly innocent form of expression carries interesting implications. The combination of the process marker 'towards' with an explicit description of the end product of the process, 'liveable', implies a denial of the liveability of multicultural municipalities as they are now, or as they would remain without special measures.

3   Global meaning constructs The way in which (explicit and implicit) meanings are combined, for instance into patterns of argumentation, is just as impor-tant as the meaning of individual utterances or their sum. Coherence and recursivity create meaning networks, in which social patterns of signification are embedded. Many examples will emerge from the data. One of the quite general or global patterns we detect, for instance, is what we will refer to as a process of systematic problematization, as in certain types of documents which invariably begin with phrases such as 'No one can deny that the pres-ence of foreigners in our country causes problems'. Note the presupposed status of the fact that 'foreigners cause problems'. Another example is the abnormalization to which foreigners are subject – remember our first hints at this phenomenon in Chapter 1. Yet another one is the recurrent reference to 'poor socio-economic circumstances' as a staple argument to explain racist incidents. All of these will be fully documented and their functioning will be discussed at length.

4   Interaction patterns The debate on diversity is a real 'debate' in the sense that it involves many types of direct and indirect interaction between different points of view. Consider, for instance, a televised debate between a member of the extreme right Vlaams Blok and a member of what we have called the 'tolerant majority': the member of the extreme right says: 'It must be possible to revise naturalization procedures that have been completed since 1974', to which the member of the tolerant majority responds: 'Also for those who have adapted themselves?' What is interesting about the example is that the response seems to accept the premise that under certain circumstances de-naturalization should be possible; the only contribution is that a condition is formulated under which this should not be possible.

These are just a few of the levels of analysis at which the search for implicit meaning proves to be particularly fruitful. The totality of presuppositions and implied meanings constitutes the general world view which a language user assumes to be or handles as if shared with others in the same community. Methods of pragmatic analysis, when efforts are concentrated in areas such as the ones listed above, allow one systematically to uncover ideologies in terms of common frames of reference.

A common frame of reference includes what is felt to be 'normal' within the group, i.e. a set of assumptions about acceptable or appropriate social behaviour which is unproblematic, natural, etc. This explains why frames of reference are hardly visible to members of the group and are not normally questioned. Forms of communication grounded in assumptions which deviate from the common frame of reference tend to be experienced as 'marked', 'shocking' or as simply incomprehensible; alternatively, they are 'explained' as expressions of maladjustment; at any rate, they are noticed. For a newspaper such a lack of fit with the expected patterns of ideas and attitudes can lead to a drop in sales figures; for a political party, a loss in votes may result. When scientific research is aimed at uncovering unconsciously adopted frames of reference, it inevitably becomes a critique and usually it meets with a wave of criticism and denials. It is always a painful experience to uncover what is taken for granted, because it forces one to question and sometimes revise one's own opinions.

To uncover the ideas of a group about their own identities, those of others and their reciprocal relations, one must indeed analyse 'normal' (i.e. unquestionable) forms of expressions. 'Automatic' expressions of ideas contain the highest degree of information, not so much about the communicated thoughts, but certainly about ways of thinking (see, e.g., Jacob Mey 1985, Donal Carbaugh 1989). It is precisely in apparently non-strategic uses that implicit, normal strategies are brought in. Concepts, when experienced as 'normal', do not require an explicit definition. Paradoxically, this makes them all the more susceptible to conscious forms of manipulation, but even in the absence of any manipulatory intent, they can still give rise to forms of communication which are misleading. The avoidance of definitions (cf. Obermeier 1986 and Blommaert 1989 on notions like 'peace' and 'human rights') entails an enormous strategic potential, because almost any referent can be assigned to a term in an *ad hoc* fashion. One result of this 'flexibility' is that terms may acquire a contextual meaning which deviates considerably from the meaning which language users would take for granted, without the deviation being noticed. The abundant use of undefined and underdefined concepts is characteristic for the discourse which we have examined.

In the foregoing, we have already repeatedly talked about patterns of recurrence, or about consistency. Together with the issue of 'normalcy', this leads us to the topic of *coherence*. While distinguishing between interpretation and speculation was no doubt the most elementary recommendation to keep in mind, establishing coherence is an important methodological goal – where 'coherence' is used both in the sense of conceptual connectedness and patterns of recurrence or of absence. This is not meant to suggest that the ideological world of meaning under investigation would itself have to be coherent in a strict sense. Ideologies may be, and usually are, full of internal contradictions. But in order for empirical claims to be possible, even such contradictions have to emerge coherently from the investigated data.[7]

Establishing coherence or 'normality' can only be done reliably if there is enough variability in the types of data, if a representative amount of data is studied, and if the data are selected on the basis of criteria warranted by the specific research goal. This is why four quite distinct discourse types were investigated. This is also why the materials we used consist literally of hundreds of documents, with a time depth of roughly seven years. Robert Hodge and Gunther Kress (1993: 210) may be right when they say that large data samples are not always necessary to *demonstrate* the mere *existence* of widely shared background meanings. However, when it comes to *assessing* the *distribution* of ideological patterns, the fact of their being widespread, a significant body of data is a requirement.

Finally, since interference with one's own ideology is to be expected, the research requires a phase of counterscreening during which meaning constructions incompatible with the tentative research conclusions are systematically searched for, in spite of the fact that it would be a mistake to think that all bias can (or should) be eliminated.

Wider perspectives

This study is only one building block for a pragmatic programme of research into problems of intercultural communication. It shares, in its own particular way, a number of crucial problems with other types of investigations in the same general area.

First, there is the role of the investigator in the communicative process under investigation. In the field of intercultural communication there is no real theoretical difference between talking with the other and talking about the other. Linguistic analysis, as a way of talking about the other, is an instance of intercultural communication itself, subject to all the influences, conditions and rules that govern intercultural interactions in general. Therefore the linguist can never be a detached bystander. He or she exerts direct control over the interaction, and 'constructs' it as an object on the basis of available assumptions. This activity is never culture-free; neither is it free from social influences (see James Boon 1982 and Johannes Fabian 1983 for stimulating discussions; other parallels can be found in Foucault 1969). The emphasis we placed on a counterscreening phase of the research process should not be misread as a denial of such basic constraints. The main question is whether pragmatics can offer a scientifically justifiable framework while being in line with its own implicit ideological assumptions based on the inescapable involvement of the researcher. Our answer to this question is affirmative, though clearly dependent on strict adherence to the principles of our methodological starting point (see pp. 32–3). The answer is also related to two other major problems in the study of intercultural communication.

Second, coming to terms with the integration of micro- and macro-influences on communication in an intercultural context proves to be particularly tricky. Most of the analyses are situated on a micro-level (the level of what is directly inferable from textual properties), while most of the conclusions are supposed to have a wider societal and cultural bearing. The problem is not, as the traditional social scientist might be tempted to suggest, one of representative sampling. It is not a quantitative, but a qualitative one: the interdependence of individual cognition and socially constructed meaning is what we have to come to grips with. Again, approaching the issue from a practical research point of view, the related problem of unwarranted inferences from idiosyncratic data can only be avoided by following a methodology which pays due attention to the coherence of the emerging picture. Further, it should be kept in mind that the wider societal and cultural implications of our work on the level of group relations (the macro-object of investigation) are not even approached in terms of micro-processes constitutive of those relations as such, but micro-processes of textual communication between majority members (minority members being at best indirectly addressed) about majority–minority relations.

Third, the problem of utilizing the full potential of the interdisciplinarity which necessarily characterizes pragmatics is also extremely acute. As will be clear from the foregoing discussion of the complexities of the research topic, for a study such as this one it is imperative to take into account data of a historical, ethnographic, socio-scientific and socio-psychological nature, going far beyond linguistic communication proper. But at the same time the purpose is to show that a clear focus on communication, from the point of view of linguistic pragmatics, contributes something to the discussion which the other disciplines cannot substitute. Every social conflict is always a communicative conflict, on which linguistic analysis can shed some new light.

In other words, although our approach is linguistic, it is clear that some of our concerns are shared with anthropology, social psychology, historiography and sociology. Some of our positions have been borrowed from critical theory. This kind of interdisciplinary set-up is simply characteristic for any valid linguistic pragmatic approach to real-life data. In this specific case, the migrant debate is not a unified object of research: there are linguistic dimensions to it, but at the same time it is clearly caught up in historical and contemporary social structures and processes, interwoven with power relationships and attitudes. As we pointed out at the beginning of this chapter, the migrant debate is largely a subjective phenomenon, in which group relations occupy a central position. These group relations constitute the non-objective – but often objectified – part of the debate. As is usually the case with group identities, 'the Belgians' and 'the migrants' are products of the mind, classic examples of what Anderson (1983) calls 'imagined communities' which are subject to all the problems that surround ethnic boundaries (cf. Barth (ed.) 1982). It is the subjective construction of so-called objectively given, 'natural' groups, and of the relations which hold between these, which will be one of the main preoccupations of this study. This field of subjectivity is virtually absent in Belgian scientific research about the migrant problem

– except for some research about image formation. As a result of this, a lot of research (including work in training and education) is based on very vague notions about the identities of those involved. What is more – as will become clear from our research – as a result of this lack of attention to the subjective constructions which inform verbal and non-verbal actions, a lot of the pro-migrant rhetoric is not really very different from that directed against the migrants. Underneath both kinds of rhetoric are the same basic notions about group identities, the problems they pose and the solutions which are possible, and also the same key analytical concepts like 'culture', 'integration', etc. We hope, therefore, to contribute to the development of a more precise understanding of what, at the moment, is seen as one of the most urgent social and political problems, not only in Belgium, but on a wide international scale. Elsewhere, the actors may be very different, as are the facts of history and social structure, but many of the underlying ideological processes are similar.

An ulterior motive for the writing of this book is to show the importance of linguistic pragmatics for dealing with current social problems. Minority politics, and the socio-scientific study of the issues involved, is usually approached in terms of quantifiable aspects of employment, housing, education, etc. The role of face-to-face communication in the implementation of any policy decision is usually ignored.[8] Even less attention is paid to the conceptual underpinnings of the related political debate. The qualitative basis of any type of discourse on or with the others in our society seems to be a phenomenon which is largely taken for granted (again, 'normal') and unquestioned (or even unquestionable). Yet it is precisely at the qualitative level that socio-scientific research seems to suffer from the three problem areas which have just been outlined. The pragmatic analysis which we will put forward is aimed at integrating the methodological insights derived from a critical consideration of these research problems into a strongly developed descriptive and interpretative framework, a reliable research apparatus for capturing otherwise intangible phenomena. Thus a pragmatic analysis should help us to disclose, and thereby to question, what is usually taken for granted.

A preview

The analytical bulk of this book resides in the two parts which follow, each containing three chapters. The chapters of Part II sketch the ingredients of an underlying ideology in terms of which the Belgian 'tolerant majority' approaches a so-called 'migrant problem'. Chapter 3 presents a general picture of what that problem looks like, judging from the discourse which makes up the debate. The central concepts used in the framing of the problem will be studied in more detail in Chapter 4. The resulting ideological picture will be summed up, in Chapter 5, under the label 'homogeneism'. The dominance of this ideological framework will be briefly shown in the same chapter. Further demonstrations of how homogeneism 'works' will be given in Part III, with chapters on a training programme for police officers (Chapter 6), a document used in a campaign to educate the public (Chapter 7), and various ingredients of a massive antiracist movement (Chapter 8). The Epilogue, finally, will offer what we consider necessary conclusions and implications.

Part II

THE INGREDIENTS OF AN IDEOLOGY

3

THE 'MIGRANT PROBLEM'

The demographic background

Though quantification is of little importance to this study, it is no doubt useful to have a statistical point of reference to situate the 'problem' which inspires or emerges from the Belgian 'migrant debate', and in particular its Flemish version. According to the official figures for 1991, released by the National Institute for Statistics, the number of foreigners in Belgium (defined as people without Belgian nationality) amounted to 9 per cent of the population (904,528 individuals in a total of 9,986,975). In Flanders, however, the figure is only 4.5 per cent, as opposed to 11.4 in Wallonia and 28.6 in Brussels. The majority of the foreigners are citizens of other EU countries: 5.5. per cent for the country as a whole, 2.4 per cent for Flanders, 8.9 for Wallonia, and 13.2 for Brussels. Non-European foreigners (including refugees and nationless people) constitute 3.3 per cent of the population; in Flanders the figure is 2 per cent, compared to 2.3 in Wallonia and 14.6 in Brussels.

As to countries of origin, the largest group of foreigners are Italians (26.7 per cent), followed by Moroccans (15.7), French (10.4), Turks (9.4), Dutch (7.2), Spaniards (5.8), Germans (3.1), British (2.6), Greeks (2.3), Portuguese (1.8), Zaïrians (1.3), Americans (1.3), Algerians (1.2), Tunisians (0.7), Yugoslavs (still counted as one category in 1991 – 0.7), Poles (0.5), citizens of Luxembourg (0.5), and a mixed residual category (8.8).

These groups are not spread out evenly over the different parts of the country. Only 11.2 per cent of the Italians reside in Flanders, as opposed to 75.5 per cent in Wallonia and 13.3 per cent in Brussels. Of the Moroccans, 29.2 per cent reside in Flanders, 15.5 in Wallonia, 55.3 in Brussels. French: 15.6 per cent in Flanders, 55.5 in Wallonia, and 28.9 in Brussels. Turks: 49.8 per cent in Flanders, 25.2 in Wallonia, and 25 in Brussels. Of the Dutch, 83.7 per cent live in Flanders, 9.2 in Wallonia and 7.1 in Brussels. Etcetera. In absolute figures, the largest number of foreigners live in Wallonia (41.1 per cent), as opposed to 28.5 per cent in Flanders and 30.4 in Brussels. Inside the various regions, it should be noted that immigrants are strongly concentrated in urban areas, and more specifically in the older industrial centres of the country. Brussels counts the highest percentage. In

Flanders, Antwerp has the most important concentration. In Wallonia, this role is shared between Liège and Charleroi.[1]

Against this background, the first point of interest is that the 'migrant debate' was more vivid in Flanders, with the lowest number of foreigners, than in the two other regions during the period of investigation. This was partly due to the way in which the theme was exploited by the political right wing. But the way in which this challenge was responded to was equally responsible for the resulting picture, as our analysis will show. Though the response was at first sight a national rather than a regional one, e.g. with the establishment of a 'royal commissariat for migrant policies' (KCM), the tone was set by a Flemish political and intellectual reflex.

In this chapter, we will survey some basic components of the debate. Given the fact that, as pointed out before, the debate is conducted by and among members of the tolerant (and powerful) majority even though the subject matter concerns majority–minority relationships, our first topic will be the way in which the majority perceives the 'other'. Second, by contrast, aspects of self-perception will pass the review. Further, the formulation of the 'problem' will be investigated. Finally, solutions to the problem will be scrutinized.

Perceptions of the 'other'

One day's harvest

The 'other' is a highly visible player in the political and social drama of every day. Intensive discursive practices have granted the 'other' a secure place in the consciousness of average members of the autochthonous Belgian majority. As a random sample, one could take the respectable Flemish dailies and weeklies available in a regular supermarket on any given day. When we did so for purposes of presentation on 6 June 1992, when we started the writing of Het Belgische Migrantendebat, no special crises or hot issues were in the air. A few weeks earlier, the coordinator for migrant affairs within the Flemish government had made the controversial statement that the discussion about migrants' voting rights at the local level should finally be reopened. Her own party, the Christian-Democratic CVP, had voiced public disapproval, and it was not until a few days after 6 June that the incident would enter the news again as a result of a parliamentary inter-pellation by the liberal PVV, applauded by VB delegates, calling for her resignation. Thus this political firecracker had barely any news value on 6 June. Neither were there any riots, other irregularities, or exotic festivities to be reported. There had not been any demonstrations, neither for nor against the multicultural society, and the ritual slaughtering of sheep – an annually recurrent theme – would not enter the picture until a few days later. All was quiet on the migrant front, or so it would seem. Yet, leaving aside the numerous letters to the editor, the harvest of articles about migrants or foreigners in general, collectively or as individuals, consisted of no less than 37 articles (six in De Standaard, six in

Gazet van Antwerpen, five in *Het Nieuwsblad*, five in *De Nieuwe Gazet*, two in *Het Volk*, one in *De Morgen*, one in *Het Laatste Nieuws*; nine in *Knack*, and two in *Trends*).

The types of newspaper articles vary. Some deal explicitly with (groups of) 'migrants', as in texts entitled 'Allochthonous police officers give parking fines' (DS; note that the terms 'allochthonous' and 'autochthonous' are in common use in Dutch today, resulting from rhetorical changes to be described later in the chapter), or 'Brussels school supervisor indignant about violence of youth gangs' (GvA). Others report on individual members of that category, as in 'Suspect in murder case arrested' (GvA), or 'After forty years, T.S. still living in "Little Italy"' (DS). Other categories of 'foreigners' are the focus of articles such as 'German asylum procedure drastically shortened' (DS). Individuals from that wider social formation also receive due attention, as in 'J.E. [a Nigerian soccer player] convicted of rape' (DM). Further articles deal with attitudes towards or relations with 'migrants' or other 'foreigners', as in 'Older migrants do not cause trouble' (DNG) or 'Germany – afraid of foreigners' (*Knack*).

The same spectrum can be found almost any day during the last few years, though shifts in emphasis can be observed. Let us briefly review the categories and opinions in terms of which the 'other' is habitually perceived.

Categorization

The categorization of the 'other' in Belgian (and more specifically Flemish) public discourse, generically referred to as *vreemdelingen* ('aliens', 'foreigners')[2] or sometimes *buitenlanders* (literally, 'people from outside of the country'), is characterized by two basic dichotomies, each embedding a further bifurcation, supplemented with a few additional types of properties. The first dichotomy, which we already used for purposes of presentation in the foregoing paragraphs, opposes *migranten* ('migrants') to other *vreemdelingen*; within the second category a further distinction is made between *vluchtelingen* ('refugees') or *asielzoekers* ('asylum seekers') and a nondescript mass of others who do not fit that category. The second basic dichotomy, to be found not only in day-to-day discourse but also in most official demographic statistics, is of a clearly political nature and distinguishes between *EU-vreemdelingen* ('EU-foreigners', i.e. citizens of other European Union countries) and *niet-EU-vreemdelingen* ('non-EU-foreigners'), a group which is further split up into *Europeans* and *non-Europeans* (see Figure 3.1).

These basic dichotomies intersect in various ways, in interaction with different types of additional properties which structure speaking and thinking about the 'other' in Belgian society. Those additional properties include:

1 *Geographical origin* (Turks, Moroccans, Africans, East Europeans) This is related, but cannot be reduced, to the second basic dichotomy. What counts is not only broad categories of nationality, but also the specifics of a

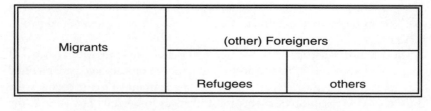

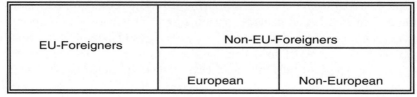

Figure 3.1 Basic dichotomies

place of origin. Thus third-generation immigrants of Moroccan descent remain 'Moroccan', in spite of their Belgian citizenship.

2   *Legal status* A distinction is made between those foreigners residing legally in the country, and the *illegalen* ('illegal aliens'), often including refugees seeking political asylum.

3   The *motivation* for having moved to Belgium. This is the basis for a distinction between political and economic refugees.

The resulting categories are far from being transparent. However, the language usage follows relatively clear patterns which impose a conceptual frame on the foreigner issue, in which only some of the analytical possibilities are actually realized.

In the Flemish discourse under investigation, the prototypical 'foreigner' is the 'migrant'. This is why the problem of group relations which forms the topic of debate is usually referred to as the *migrantenproblematiek* (the 'migrant problem'). The term *migrant*, though by no means a difficult formation, is a late addition to the Dutch vocabulary. It was not to be found in the authoritative Dutch dictionaries of the 1970s, but it became a household word as soon as it appeared after 1980. The term classifies people as 'being in the process of migration'. In contrast to *immigrant*, a term which was readily available in Dutch as well as in most related languages, *migrant* really focuses on migration as an activity and a process rather than on the end product, the reaching of a destination. While an 'immigrant' has completed an act of migrating, for the 'migrant' the option of departure remains open. New terms rarely become fashionable by accident. In this case, the sudden popularity of 'migrant' goes back to the need for a euphemism for *gastarbeider* ('guest worker'), which had been in common use ever since postwar Belgium started to attract large groups of foreign workers, first Italians, then Spaniards, and later Moroccans and Turks. The economic crises of the 1970s and the ensuing unemployment problem reduced the need for 'guest workers', who were increasingly being perceived as a troublesome burden to society, to such an extent that the term *gastarbeider* itself became loaded with negative connotations. Consciously or unconsciously, the new euphemism was well-chosen: a barely used term, free of unwanted associations, which left the return option open without making it rhetorically impossible to lend explicit support to the tolerant idea that the guest worker population was here to stay.

There is hardly any doubt that *migrant* was a mere substitute for *gastarbeider*. For one thing, it is possible to talk of 'EU-foreigners' and even 'EU-immigrants', but the term 'EU-migrants' is never found. EU-foreigners, however, can some-times be called 'migrants' if they entered the country as 'guest workers' before the signing of the European treaties which regulate the free movement of people within the European Union. Thus a category of 'older Italian migrants' can easily be referred to.

Second, the term 'migrant' is usually reserved for groups of non-EU-foreigners who originally moved into Belgium as 'guest workers', in particular Turks and Moroccans. Since the majority of those are Moroccans, the terms *migrant*, *Marokkaan* ('Moroccan') and *Maghrebijn* ('inhabitant of the Maghreb' or 'someone coming from the Maghreb') alternate freely. Thus, in a series of arti-cles on the work of deputy police officers of 'migrant' descent, we find the following descriptions of the same category: *Maghreb-agent* ('Maghreb police officer'), *migrant-agent* ('migrant police officer'), *Belgisch–Marokkaans hulpagent* ('Belgian–Moroccan deputy'), *Belgen van Maghrebijnse oorsprong* ('Belgians of Maghreb descent'), *Arabisch sprekende kandidaat-hulpagenten van Belgische nation-aliteit* ('Arabic-speaking candidate deputies with Belgian nationality'), *jonge Marokkaanse Belg* ('young Moroccan Belgian'), *wijkagenten van Marokkaanse origine* ('neighbourhood police officers of Moroccan origin'), and also *hulpagenten van Arabische origine* ('deputies of Arab origin') and the even wider *allochtone agenten* ('allochthonous police officers'). According to the same articles, those deputy police officers are supposed to ensure better communication with a popu-lation group referred to as *migranten* ('migrants'), *Maghrebijnen* ('people from the Maghreb'), or *allochtone Brusselaars* ('allochthonous inhabitants of Brussels').

The typical migrant, then, is called Mohammed or Fatima. Hence the title of an article inquiring into the possible discrimination of migrants in processes of personnel selection: *Liever Jan dan Mohammed?* ('Jan rather than Mohammed?'; *Trends* 6 June 1992). For the same reason, two articles about the murder of a young woman, in which the term 'migrant' is not used at all, but in which the murderer is called Mohammed 22 and 19 times respectively, will predictably be remembered as a brutal crime committed by a 'migrant'.

The fact that the term *migrant* is reserved for non-EU-foreigners who have come to Belgium as guest workers, also appears from reporting on other *vreemdelingen* ('foreigners'). No one calls a Nigerian soccer player a 'migrant'. The sportsman in question is described as *de 22-jarige Nigeriaanse profvoetballer* ('the 22-year old Nigerian soccer pro'), *de Nigeriaan* ('the Nigerian'), *profvoetballer*

J.E. (soccer 'pro J.E.'), *de bonkige Nigeriaan* ('the bulky Nigerian'), *de Nigeriaanse aanvaller van Lierse* ('the Nigerian striker of [soccer club] Lierse'), *ex-Lierse voetballer* ('ex-Lierse soccer player'), *de Afrikaanse voetballer* ('the African soccer player'), and even *de zwarte parel* ('the black pearl'). Similarly, articles about black prostitutes do not mention migrants but rather *de zwarte meisjes* ('the black girls') and *Ghanese vrouwen* ('Ghanaian women').

Not only is the applicability of the term 'migrant' restricted in this way, its general acceptability for the limited and poorly defined category in question is already in decline. Euphemisms are generally short-lived, as they tend to absorb the negative connotations adhering to the terms they served to replace. Today, if one wants to avoid stirring up any negative emotions, the term *allochtoon* ('allochthon') is used in opposition to *autochtoon* ('autochthon'), distinguishing population groups which can somehow be shown to have a foreign origin from those that are supposed to 'belong' to the territory historically. This new dichotomy does not manage to supersede the earlier ones. The term *allochtoon* should normally refer to every 'foreigner', irrespective of geographical and ethnic origin or of their reasons for being in the country. But since it was introduced in the context of 'migrant research' and 'migrant policies', where it *is* often (though not always) used in its general and proper sense, the term developed quickly into a new euphemism for the prototypical foreigner, the 'migrant'. Hence the possibility of using the general label 'allochthonous police officers' while designating a restricted category of deputy police officers mostly of North African descent.

As is clear from the examples, the free variation between 'migrant', 'Moroccan' and 'Maghrebi' is purely associative, based on a network of concepts and entities which do not emerge from an analysis but rather from a stream of consciousness. The categorization is barely related to reality. It deviates profoundly from the elementary semantics of 'migrant' (and even of the term 'allochthon' in its non-professional use) by imposing a referential narrowing of the concept. Moreover, generally available anthropological knowledge is ignored. A large proportion of the Maghrebines living in Belgium are Berbers, and hence not 'of Arab origin', as is suggested in the articles on 'migrant' deputy police officers in Brussels (unless only non-Berber Moroccans were accepted as deputy police officers, which would considerably lower their representativeness for the 'migrant' community). Those Berbers may be 'Arabic-speaking', but in that case with Arabic as a second/foreign language. Here we are not revealing new facts. Everyone writing about the 'migrant problem' knows them. And yet we encounter, over and over again, not only the *semantic narrowing* which we have already explained, but also an *associative widening* from 'migrant' to *Arabier* ('Arab') and, as will appear repeatedly from what follows, to *islamiet* ('Moslem'). The result is a hopelessly underdefined concept, hardly an adequate representation of the social formation concerned.

The apparent ease with which the term 'migrant' is intuitively handled contrasts sharply with the vague characterization of the referential object which emerges upon closer scrutiny. Hence the free fluctuation of narrowing and widening. Most socio-scientific and political texts open with an historiography of migration, thus revealing a deeply felt need to provide an historical explanation for the presence of the minorities in question in Europe or, more specifically, in Belgium or Flanders. The result is extra emphasis on the 'otherness' of those others. They are virtually defined as 'tribes', groups of people with their own separate history without any 'natural' links with our territory – in spite of the fact that in many cases their history has been a *Belgian* history for decades. And though there is explicit recognition of the fact that the target group is not homogeneous but quite diverse in terms of religion, culture, social position, nationality, geographical origin and ethnicity, the content of this diversity is rarely explored explicitly, analysed, or used sensibly in the formulation of points of view or in news reports.

Returning to properties related to legal status which intersect with classifications of foreigners, we see that 'migrants' do not get conceptual access to the category of *asielzoekers* ('asylum seekers', 'refugees'). 'Asylum seekers' are *politieke vluchtelingen* ('political refugees', where usually black Africans, Asians, or Latin Americans are thought of) or *economische vluchtelingen* ('economic refugees', now mostly East Europeans) posing as political refugees. Though the motivation for their migration was comparable to what drives East Europeans towards the West, 'migrants' are never conceptualized as 'economic refugees'. And though the King of Morocco can hardly be seen as an example of democracy, yet he is approached for advice on our 'migrant policies' so that 'migrants' of Moroccan descent can hardly be considered 'political refugees', even in cases where there might be very good reasons for doing so. Still, 'migrants' are mentioned in the same breath as 'asylum seekers'. The link that is brought into view is *illegality*: both 'asylum seekers' and 'migrants' can be *illegale vreemdelingen* ('illegal aliens'). This shows immediately that the terminological shift from *gastarbeider* ('guest worker') to *migrant* implies a form of social degradation in at least one respect. While 'guest worker' represented an officially recognized status, 'migrant' is only descriptive of a species: one cannot be a 'guest worker' without being received as a guest (even if treatment is not always perfect), but it is easy to belong to the 'migrant' species even if one does not have any permission to stay in the country.

An article entitled 'Recognized political refugees or illegal aliens: They remain foreigners'[3] unwittingly clarifies these complex relationships:

GHENT – Whether a foreigner in our country is recognized as a political refugee, which gives him the same rights and duties as a Belgian, does not make any difference for the average citizen. Guest workers, illegal aliens, political refugees ... They are all lumped together: they are foreigners. And irrespective of their status, they are up against the same problems.[4]

This report raises a few problems. First, the term 'guest workers' surfaces here, years after it had virtually disappeared from official and semi-official texts. Here it is used because it seems to be the only unambiguous way to single out the category in question vis-à-vis other categories of non-natives. 'Migrants' was not suitable because that label may also cover 'illegal aliens'. In this text, 'guest workers' (read: 'migrants' residing in the country legally) are presented as a category somewhere in between 'recognized political refugees' and 'illegal aliens'. Second, there is a clear implication that the different categories could and should be treated differently (as well as a further implicit complaint that not all people realize this). While this would be acceptable if the categorization had only focused on the distinction between legal and illegal immigrants, it is hard to see the relevance of the three-fold distinction with respect to the degree of hospitality the members of the labelled categories should enjoy. Third, the three-fold distinction involves a hierarchy, in which political refugees are clearly entitled to preferential treatment. This final implication is directly related to the concepts of democracy and political freedom which are constitutive of the European's self-perception (as will be demonstrated later).

Attempts to define categories of non-natives are rare. Usually they lack clarity as a result of blatantly absent ethnographic foundations, or else the introduced clarity disappears in later usage. Thus *De Standaard* made an effort – later honoured with a media award – to represent the diversity of groups of foreigners in the Brussels area. The concluding article in this series (published under the less-than-clarifying title 'The strange mutation of Brussels'[5]), however, starts as follows:

> BRUSSELS – During the foregoing days we have presented *different groups of 'unknown and richer' foreigners* in the Brussels area: Dutchmen, Frenchmen, Germans, Japanese, Scandinavians, British people and Americans, and also Poles and Zaïrians. All these groups appeared to be very different. And then we did not yet touch the four largest (and best known?) groups of *migrants* in Brussels: Italians and Spaniards, and especially Turks and Moroccans. Foreigners in Brussels, therefore, cannot be put under one label, except in population statistics. Only to make the distinction between Belgians and foreigners is clearly insufficient.[6] (italics ours)

Indeed it is ethnographically insufficient just to distinguish Belgians from foreigners. But it is equally unwarranted to maintain the misleading contrast between 'migrants' and 'other foreigners' (further qualified in this text as 'unknown and richer', where 'and' can probably be interpreted as 'or'). Though the formulation might seem to eliminate this contrast, since 'And then we did not yet touch the four largest [. . .] groups of migrants' by no means excludes the 'other foreigners' from the scope of 'migrants', still the contrast is maintained by the patterns of complementary distribution in which the terms 'foreigner' and 'migrant' are used. Later, in a report on the media prize awarded to the series, the articles are described as being 'about "other migrants"' (DS 17 June 1992: 1).

Again 'other foreigners' seem to fall inside the scope of the category of 'migrants', while in the same phrasing they are excluded from it by means of the special interpretative status signalled by the quotation marks.

Moreover, the distinction marks two *sliding fields*. As usual, the explicit use of the term 'migrant', in the quotation as well as throughout the entire series, is reserved for the traditional groups of original guest workers. The wording of the distinction implies that the differences between the described groups of '"unknown and richer" foreigners', though 'very' significant, may be less overwhelming than they would have been if 'the four largest groups of migrants' were also to have been included in the survey. The fact that this judgement does not primarily bear on the Italians and Spaniards appears from '[. . .] and *especially* Turks and Moroccans'. Here we find a first conceptual shift. The Italians and Spaniards, put into the 'migrant' category with the Turks and Moroccans for historical reasons, are incorporated into the category of 'other foreigners' on the basis of a judgement related to the measurement of difference – a judgement which is itself no doubt related to the political construct called Europe. The shift takes on a definite shape further on in the same article: in the conclusions the only formations that are left are 'Moroccan and Turkish migrants' *versus* 'other groups of foreigners'.

Meandering through the series we can also observe three sporadic shifts in the other direction: for the Japanese, the Scandinavians and the Poles. About the Japanese it is said that they can be described 'as a model of a recently arrived migrant group'; the Scandinavians are presented as a 'growing group of migrants'; and for the contribution about the Poles we get the title 'Polish migrants as yet uncharted due to a lack of data'.[7] The shift towards precisely these three groups is not accidental in the light of the conceptual associations attached to the term 'migrant'. Migrants (read: Turks and Moroccans) exist in the majority's perception as a problem group, the main problem being – as will be clarified later – a *lack of integration*. The article about the Scandinavians, 'Swedish colony wishes to maintain cultural identity in unifying Europe',[8] deals exclusively with the observation that the Swedes in Brussels do *not* regard themselves as *im*migrants, but as Swedes who stay in Belgium temporarily for professional reasons and who do not feel any need to integrate. The article about the Japanese bears the title 'Japanese not really in search of integration'.[9] It emphasizes the temporary character of the presence of most of them, as well as the development of their own facilities such as a Japanese school. Further:

> The Japanese like living close together, and show *therefore* all characteristics of new *migrants*: they look for each other's company.[10] (italics ours)

The Poles, on the other hand, become 'migrants' because of that other aspect of the associative complex, *illegality*:

> The Poles can be regarded as a very distinct group of migrants. The majority of Poles are black market labourers, who have entered the

country illegally, work here illegally, and apparently find work very easily.[11]

The higher degree of problematization of this group, which is no doubt related to their not belonging to the category of 'richer' foreigners, unlike the Swedes and the Japanese, has engendered institutional attention directed at them in the framework of 'migrant policies':

> At the Royal Commissariat for Migrant Policies the development of the group of Polish migrants is watched closely, to the extent that information about them is available.[12]

As a result, the Poles were most clearly incorporated into the category of 'migrants'. For the Scandinavians and the Japanese, the term is used only sporadically. But in the articles on the Dutch, the Germans, the Zaïrians, the French, the British and the Americans, the word does not occur.

In the terminological developments outside of this specific series of articles, similar processes can be observed. But the overall picture is one that keeps restricting 'migrants' to people of Turkish or Moroccan descent, a restriction which is being inherited by the supposedly wider term 'allochthon'. The incorporation of other groups of foreigners into the category remains rare and only occurs for very specific rhetorical and argumentative purposes. Thus in October 1996 there were elections for the *Antwerpse Migrantenraad* ('Antwerp Migrant Council') in which, for the first time, Dutch and Chinese people could participate in addition to the traditional groups of Moroccans and Turks; but this move went hand in hand with the demand to change the council's name.

The fate of the Poles is such that they have come to occupy a virtually completely separate position: they are referred to specifically as Poles, sometimes East Europeans, but almost never 'migrants'. This may be due to the visibility they acquired in urban and rural areas alike, or simply to their specific and well-organized pattern of moving in and out of the country which resulted partly from the abolishment of visa requirements (which makes their entering legal, though not necessarily their stay, nor the activities they engage in while in Belgium). So many people make use of their services, moreover, that they are rarely thought about as a problem category – a major aspect of the public perception of the more narrowly conceived 'migrant' population.

Opinions and attitudes

In spite of the underdefined nature of the target group and the vagueness and imprecision characterizing its description, there is no lack of opinions about 'migrants' and 'other foreigners'. Some opinions are positive, others are negative; some are voiced explicitly, others remain implicit. Let us briefly look at manifestations of the four forms of expression which these distinctions give rise to: explicit positive, implicit positive, explicit negative, and implicit negative.

Explicit positive statements are mostly to be found in official sources, where they function in the legitimization of policies. Thus we find the following introductory phrase from the European Union's 'Declaration against Racism and Xenophobia':

[...] aware of the positive contribution which workers from other Member-States and third countries have made and can make in the future to the development of the Member-State in which they legally reside, and of the benefits which the Community as a whole derives from this [...]
(Declaration against Racism and Xenophobia, 11 June 1986)

Note that the (potential) positive contribution of the people who might be the victims of racism and xenophobia is formulated completely in terms of their labour and the resulting economic benefits. This angle is also to be found in a KCM report on 'Financial–economic aspects of migrant policies in Belgium',[13] which emphasizes that today's 'migrant' youngsters are worth an investment in terms of education and professional training because later they will have to help pay for our pensions.

Also outside the economic domain, explicit expressions of a positive attitude can be found in official sources. Thus there is constant reference to an abstract form of *enrichment* for our culture resulting from the presence of 'others'. Witness the KCM report on 'Cultural diversity as mutual enrichment':[14]

The Royal Commissariat for Migrant Policies is aware of the potential riches for our own social life in this country presented by the other cultures in our midst.[15]

Political texts are notoriously polyphonic, as they reflect and incorporate the voices of all the parties involved in the decision-making process. Contorted syntax, as in the Dutch original (not wholly mirrored in the translation above), usually indicates that sentences such as this one are the product of battles between proponents of different positions. The outcome is a vague and hedged sentence which passes a mitigated positive judgement on diversity. It is not surprising, then, that rather than exploring the fact of wide-ranging diversity itself as a source of riches, the report is devoted to the formulation of 'proposals' which can count as 'an enriching offer for cultural life'.[16] The proposals themselves reveal that the 'cultural life' in question is largely to be situated at the surface level of the so-called *cultuuruitingen* ('expressions of culture'): as the subtitle of the report says, the issue is public support for social activities organized by and for 'migrants', culminating in an 'intercultural training and arts centre'.[17] Such a centre, with activities ranging from the inventorization of 'migrant' organizations to exhibits and 'intercultural festivities', was established soon after publication of the report. (Note that, as will have to be emphasized repeatedly, the state's support for 'migrants' is mostly restricted to the state's own initiatives which the majority can present as being to their benefit.)

A somewhat deeper view of what cultural enrichment due to the presence of 'migrants' could look like is tentatively offered, for instance, in the Flemish Green Party's 'migrant policies' statement:

> The intensive contact via migrants with a Turkish or Moroccan culture is enriching. We already find such enrichment in our culinary culture, in present-day music . . . but it can also help us, Westerners, in solving our problems. The function and esteem of older members of the migrant family contrast sharply with the way in which we ban older people from our society. In the light of an aged population, living together with migrants can lead to new insights.[18]

But the discourse does not take us beyond this kind of sporadic and usually vague example. A striking characteristic of the explicitly positive rhetoric is that straightforward positive contributions of the 'others' are either situated in the past or, if situated in the present or future, are accompanied by a modal auxiliary such as 'can' to stress their potentiality rather than their factuality.

Implicit positive judgements are even harder to come by, except in concessive constructions such as 'Though they also enrich our society, they . . . '. If pragmaticians are right to regard implicit information as a powerful indicator of underlying views and opinions, then the virtual absence of an implicitly communicated positive perspective on the minorities in question is a particularly ominous sign.

Explicit negative statements about 'migrants' as a group hardly ever occur. Note, however, that we restricted our sources, for reasons explained before, to what can be assumed to be acceptable for a mainstream inhabitant of the country, i.e. for the target audience of the most widespread media, the largest political formations, etc. For this mainstream majority explicit condescension does not seem to be acceptable, which is why we could introduce the label *tolerant majority*. Of course, explicitly negative characterizations can easily be found in texts representing the extreme right. But since its electoral success on 24 November 1991, even the Vlaams Blok, in search of still wider respectability, has begun to temper or even deny its hostility towards foreigners. As we shall see later, this phenomenon is directly related to the majority's (Flemish, Belgian or even European) self-perception, rather than being indicative of a basically positive attitude vis-à-vis the 'other'.

There is, however, an abundance of *implicitly voiced negative opinions*. A classic example is one of the articles from the one-day corpus referred to above, which is at first sight a perfect expression of a positive attitude, as would be suggested by the title 'Older migrants don't cause trouble'.[19] The text clarifies, however, that this opinion about older migrants is voiced only by way of contrast for the real message. A woman barkeeper in Borgerhout[20] talks about the presence of vigilantes in her neighbourhood, groups which were suspected of racist attacks on young migrants:

> But I repeat: this [bar] is certainly not an operations centre for those patrols. Mind you, I sometimes wish that such vigilantes with dogs would exist. Things would soon be different around here. Because, sir, what is the problem? Those older Moroccans do not cause any trouble, they are polite, they even step off the sidewalk when I pass. But that gang here on the square, when are they going to leave us in peace?[21]

We do not classify this as an explicit negative judgement, because the reporter builds in the distance of the literal quotation. Except for an introductory paragraph, the entire article consists of statements by the same woman barkeeper. Still, we can maintain that the reporting itself implicitly expresses negative opinions because no attempt is made to provide the quotations with an interpretative framework that would show a degree of relativization. Moreover, the indirect message of the article is further supported by a factual comment accompanying two photographs of a seemingly peaceful square: 'The Koxplein is poisoned by gangs: thus even a pregnant woman was harassed in a phone booth'.[22] The reader is thus gently guided towards the barkeeper's conclusion:

> They say this is a Vlaams Blok café. OK, they come here for meetings once or twice a year, and moreover, 99 per cent of the people in Borgerhout vote for them. They know why. As far as I am concerned they can send 100,000 additional migrants, as long as they adapt a little and leave us in peace. But the City [Council] does not listen.[23]

An understanding of this position becomes virtually automatic, since the final sentences link up directly with generally accepted 'tolerant' rhetoric about the 'migrant problem', as will be clarified later.

Often we find implicit expressions of negative attitudes *in what is not said*. An example is to be found in the articles about Mohammed D.'s murder of his ex-girlfriend Marianne. As pointed out above, the murderer is extensively identified as a Moroccan migrant. By contrast, the man who managed to convince him that he should voluntarily return from Paris to turn himself in to the Antwerp police is simply described as *zijn schoonbroer* or *zijn zwager* (both of which translate as 'his brother-in-law'), *die man* ('that man') and *de man* ('the man'). Had the brother-in-law been a native Belgian, the reports would probably have mentioned 'his Belgian brother-in-law'. Now the ethnic identification remains ambiguous, so that the readers have to rely on what would, in their vision of an ethnically structured society, count as the least marked case: the case in which the brother-in-law is also Moroccan. By not eliminating the ambiguity, however, and by not being explicit about identity, a chance is missed to draw the attention to a serious form of cooperation between a 'migrant' and the Belgian police. Thus the 'migrant' population is characterized by criminality, not by a sense of civil responsibility. This would not suffice as an individual example, but the case is symptomatic for the common association between 'migrants' and crime (see, e.g., Meeuwis 1990) which would lead to so-called 'safety contracts' between the (socialist) Minister of the Interior Louis Tobback and municipalities with relatively high numbers of foreigners. Such 'safety contracts' themselves, offering money for a more visible policing of the streets in exchange for lower crime rates, constitute an implicit acceptance of the 'criminogenic' nature of 'migrants', one of the most powerful negative stereotypes about them in Belgium.

In order to show that this type of phenomenon is not restricted to the media, where competition sometimes leads to a certain level of sensationalism, we shall again have a brief look at a political document beyond suspicion, a 'migrant policies' document produced by the Flemish Socialist Party, a party with an image of progressiveness and tolerance.[24] We read:

> In certain neighbourhoods we find mainly older Flemish people and young migrant families with small and growing children, so that for those older people there is comparatively a lot of commotion and noise. In such situations tensions are 'normal'.[25]

As an attempt to analyse some causes of tension between the native and the non-native population, this statement is either irrelevant or it implies that 'migrant' children make more noise and cause more commotion than autochthonous children would. Without this implication, the quotation would have to be interpreted as a general statement about the 'normality' of tensions between old people and young families living in close proximity, because of some 'natural' noise and commotion factor. Since the general validity of such a statement is far from obvious, and since as a generally valid statement it would not make an obvious contribution to the analysis of specific native/non-native tensions, ordinary principles of relevance dictate our conclusion regarding an implicit negative judgement. The document's authors would no doubt deny the implication (in keeping with the observed tendency not to make any explicit negative statements), while most of the readership can be expected to fail to isolate it conceptually as an issue in its own right, thus accepting it as a premiss on which the explicit line of argumentation is based. This is exactly the way in which presuppositions usually function.

Let us look at a second passage from the same text:

> But also the particular position of mainly Turkish and Moroccan women limits their possibilities of contact and their freedom of movement, so that they place themselves automatically in an isolated position.[26]

This implies the unqualified validity of a negative stereotype about Turkish and Moroccan women, which shifts much of the burden of guilt for their real or presumed social isolation on the shoulders of the minority groups. Questions remain, such as: Do these women really lead such an isolated life? By whose standards? How do they feel about their own position? Do they want any changes? If not, what gives us the right to make judgements? But if they do, what social or cultural forces make change difficult? To what extent is their position, whatever it may be exactly, responsible for the lack of communication with the autochthonous population? Or to what extent are autochthonous attitudes and styles responsible for non-communication? Such questions are prevented by the unshakeable acceptance of a stereotype. The stereotype is so strong that even facts that could be adduced to undermine it are turned around for their support. For instance, in Belgium twice as many 'migrant' girls get into higher education than do 'migrant' boys. But when this fact (well-known for a long time) was recently reported, this was explained with reference to the girls' lower status (which makes it possible for them not to have to start working immediately) and the perseverance which they develop as a result of not being allowed any freedom (while they derive some freedom and independence by going to school).[27]

The same policy document continues:

> [The young people's] desire to adopt 'our' life style, with the prosperity they expect of it, they are often unable to satisfy because of too low a level of schooling and difficulties in finding work.[28]

This third quote, then, takes for granted the wish of minority youth to adopt our ('Western', 'modern') lifestyle. Though undoubtedly some minority youth cherish wishes describable in such terms, the phrasing (in which, again, presuppositions figure prominently) does not leave much room for doubt. The straightforward reality of their wish is not questioned, nor is there any discussion of its exact content. The majority's perspective, in other words, is projected on to the minority. This reveals a latent sense of superiority, further underscored by singling out a low level of education – and the causally related problems of finding work – as the main cause of non-fulfilment of the aspirations of 'migrant' youngsters.

The sense of superiority which comes along with an unquestioning confidence in 'Western' lifestyle and values is to be found even in the most magnanimous and benevolent attempts to show tolerance and to educate people for life in a multicultural society. One such attempt is the distribution of educational films (by a non-profit organization called *Bevrijdingsfilms*, 'Liberation films') intended to engender better intercultural understanding. To give just one example, the film *Julia's geheim* ('Juliet's secret') introduces Arzu, the teenage daughter of a Turkish family in The Netherlands. Arzu faces what is perceived as a 'typical' problem: the family has promised her in marriage to a young man back in Turkey, but she does not feel like marrying him at all. The plot revolves around the parallelism between her situation and that of the characters in a school performance of Shakespeare's *Romeo and Juliet*, in which she is asked to play Juliet (initially, of course, in secret, unbeknown to her parents). However innocent the idea may be, the parallelism happens to be one between a present-day situation in a Turkish family and a situation which Europeans can imagine as possible in some remote past but as completely 'transcended' in Europe today. This clearly unintentional (but therefore all the more noteworthy) expression of a sense of social and cultural superiority is further aggravated by the film's conclusion. The Turkish father decides that his daughter's happiness is more important than his own (culture-related notion of) loss of face, and he gives in. In other words, all problems are solved if minority members are willing to adapt to the norms of our time in our society. Note that the adaptation process presented as a solution to cultural incompatibilities is completely unidirectional. More about this will have to be said later.

Meanwhile we are still stuck with the question: Who is 'the migrant'? In any case, the 'migrant' discourse developed in the media and by policy-makers does not provide an unambiguous answer. This should pose a grave problem for the entire debate. How can one solve social problems, or even reflect on them, when the social formations concerned are so ill-defined? They are, however, not *perceived* as ill-defined. They contrast sharply in the public mind with elements of self-perception (to be discussed next), so that a problem formulation and a set of solutions seem to follow naturally.

Self-perception

Cultural superiority

Today, unlike in previous centuries and a good part of the earlier twentieth century, Europeans tend to stay away from explicit claims of cultural superiority. The forms of expression have become subtler, as appeared in the foregoing examples from the self-evident manner with which a 'Western' cultural model assumes a normative status. Typical of the way of thinking is the emergence of a mixture of 'development' (technological, scientific, military, economic) with 'civilization' (values, 'culture'). It is assumed that there are countries with low development but high civilization (e.g. China) as well as countries with high development and low civilization (of which the US often turns up as an example). Countries which combine a high degree of civilization with a high degree of development include Japan and Western European nations, while unfortunately our 'migrants' are perceived as coming from countries with a low development level and a low civilization, thus being backward in both technology and cultural values.

The sense of superiority rooted in such categorizations of the world is often expressed in the observed contrast between the absence of praise for the cultural heritage of our 'migrants' and the frequency with which Europe's cultural riches are heralded. An apparent exception is an article occasioned by the publication of *Vreemde grootmoeders* ('Foreign grandmothers'), written by Mim El Messaoudi-Van Keer, a Flemish woman with a Moroccan husband. This booklet deals with the author's confrontation with the family and place of birth of her husband.

The article bears the promising title, in quotation marks, 'My book is ode to Moroccan father of my children'.[29] A more positive picture seems hard to imagine, but the subtitle immediately leads us into another direction: '"Foreign grandmothers" looks at Morocco openly and critically'.[30] We do not have to wait long for an explanation. The introductory paragraph says:

> Published as a book for young people, in fact more suitable for adults, not exactly a masterpiece, but still interesting because of *the open and warm but also critical look of the author at a still very traditional piece of Morocco and its inhabitants.*[31] (our italics)

In other words, in spite of her being married to a Moroccan man, Mim preserves a critical distance. That is why the book is presented as 'interesting'. Putting this 'still very traditional piece of Morocco' in an unambiguously positive light, without approaching it critically, might have been unacceptable for the Belgian public. It is no doubt seen as a virtue to display an 'open and warm' attitude, i.e. a serious sympathy for the other culture, as long as its remains within acceptable boundaries. The reported interview goes on to develop a picture of a perfectly normal marriage, until, all of a sudden, by means of italics in the text, the article draws the attention to two remarks by the interviewer:

> *Less attractive in the story, however, is the clearly overbearing dominance of the man over the woman.*

> *Another disturbing thing is the fanatical importance which especially fathers attach to the virginity of their daughters, while they look the other way when their sons are concerned.*[32]

As a result, the social backwardness of the described community, and, by extension, of our own 'migrant' population, is again confirmed in its most stereotypical form. What remains of the ode to the Moroccan husband is the suggestion that he is different from other members of his ethnic group: after all, he is the only Moroccan in his village in Belgium, and he studied computer science in Brussels. The turn taken by this potentially extremely positive article demonstrates the tendency to abnormalize the foreigner.

Superiority does not only emerge indirectly from the fact that really positive image formation does not get a chance, but also directly from recurrent forms of positive self-evaluation. A first aspect of positive self-appreciation is based on the perception of *cultural riches*. The rhetoric on this topic circles around terms such as *identiteit* and *eigenheid* (both terms mean 'identity'; *eigenheid* is literally 'own-ness', and connotes 'uniqueness'), defined grandiloquently and vaguely with reference to a rich cultural past as well as economic dynamics past and present, and supported by a reification of 'the language'. At a European level, where the importance attached to small-scale identity is translated into a quest for the

'Europe of the regions', the idea of cultural riches is given substance in terms of *cultural diversity*. In this context, diversity does not stand for mixture (which, as seen in Chapter 1, is viewed as a problem-to-be-managed) but rather for the juxtaposition of different entities. Such diversity is, in and of itself, regarded as a positive value, an exceptional heritage to be protected because it could be endangered by large-scale European levelling in which 'small nations' and 'small peoples' could lose their identities. In justifications for this defensive reflex, invariably the unique nature of rich European cultural diversity is called upon as an argument. This self-appreciation contains a clear element of superiority. The average European, to the extent that she or he considers the issue at all, seems to be convinced that cultural diversity, and hence riches, is far more impressive in Europe than elsewhere in the world. Intellectuals and politicians alike contribute to the maintenance of this idea. According to an oft-repeated claim by the French sociologist Edgar Morin, diversity is 'Europe's originality *par excellence*'. Alan Sked (of the London School of Economics) says, in a quite similar vein and applying the idea specifically to Belgium:

> The Belgian linguistic struggle is one of the many signs indicating that it is exactly *divisiveness* which is the most distinctive feature of European civilization – that which distinguishes European from any other civilization.[33]

And Gaston Geens (at that time chairman of the Flemish Government) voiced similar ideas during a get-together of European regional governments in Brussels (April 1990):

> He [Gaston Geens] strongly emphasized that cultural diversity is one of the most striking characteristics of the European continent and that 'we have to take full advantage of these riches'.[34]

This rhetoric of cultural diversity often complements a rhetoric of nationalism (which we already hinted at and about which more will be said in Chapter 5) or of regional identity politics. The diversity mentioned by the various discourse producers quoted here refers to differences *between* what is perceived as regional 'units', whether or not they are enshrined in political–administrative autonomy. Diversity does not, however, refer to potential differences *within* the units which form the building blocks of a 'Europe of the regions'. No wonder, then, that the discourse of Europe as the apex of cultural diversity is cherished by the leaders of smaller European member states and especially of sub-state regional governments such as in Flanders or Catalonia.

The idea of exceptional cultural diversity and richness in Europe is as naive as it is persistent. To take just one parameter of cultural diversity, the degree of linguistic differentiation (language being the most-used marker of identity in both the Belgian and the European debate on diversity), we see that Europe is the least diversified of all continents (with only 3 per cent of the world's languages, as compared, for instance, with 31 per cent of the world's languages in Africa).[35] Adding other cultural parameters does not change this picture very much – at least not in favour of the view we are criticising.

In seeming contradiction of the perception of unrivalled diversity, we discern a second element underscoring the latent sense of superiority: a perception of *European cultural unity*. This unity rests on two pillars: *Christianity* and *democratic thought*. Thus, under the title 'Monotheism explains the European mystery for Mark Eyskens',[36] an article appears in which Mark Eyskens (then Belgium's Minister of Foreign Affairs) says that:

> Monotheism has for centuries been the lever of irresistible creativity and innovation.[37]

This statement is certainly not modest, and the causal relation between (the Christian brand of) monotheism and cultural achievements is not hidden. In its next issue, the same periodical goes even further in the presentation of the same basic idea. An article is published by Frans Alting von Geusau (a law professor at the Universities of Tilburg and Leiden) which is intended to show that:

> [. . .] the revolution [which we were witnessing at that time in Eastern and Central Europe] was fed by the common Christian roots of European civilization.[38]

The 70-year-old Communist regime, in other words, was not a real product of *the* European civilization. The Christian ethics of personal responsibility, of living in truth and therefore ignoring the danger of speaking freely under a repressive regime, is held responsible for the political changes. This argument equates some aspects of a *Christian ethics* with *democratic values and thought*. While the explicitly Christian argument will only be adduced by Christians (certainly in Flanders, where they form a clearly distinct 'pillar' in society), it is democratic thought which is regarded by Christians and non-Christians alike as the common basis of a pan-European culture. Western Europe, with its transatlantic allies, is seen as the embodiment of this way of thinking, which allowed Western Europeans to think about events in Eastern Europe not so much in terms of internal changes (in which some political leaders have played a crucial role, both individually and collectively) as in terms of 'The Way the West Has Won'.[39]

Before exploring further the role of democratic values in the European self-image, we return briefly to its perceived link with the Christian tradition. Paul Belien, a well-known right-wing political commentator, says:

> Liberalism, or *freedom*, has emerged from *the Christian foundations* of Western society.[40] (our italics)

In addition to freedom, openness or any other high values may be referred to. Thus, under the title 'Church opts for multicultural society',[41] a high-ranking Catholic priest advocates the 'necessary mutual respect for each other's culture and religion, intercultural exchange and interreligious dialogue'.[42] He continues:

> *Evidently* we indicated in this matter explicitly the believer's motivation for our commitment. *As Christians* we are called upon to display *hospitality for foreigners* – especially for the poor and weak amongst them.[43] (our italics)

The link is presented as self-evident, though for some (e.g. Belien) it leads to the justification of conservative intolerance on the assumption that 'others' would threaten our values, while for others (most representatives of the Church itself) it underlies explicit advocacy of tolerance. Yet for all of them the self-image is underscored with notions such as openness and tolerance. For some, these qualities are not just typical of Christianity, but nearly unique. The step towards a sense of cultural superiority, therefore, is a small one. This tendency is by no means restricted to Flanders or Belgium, but is widely shared in Europe. One example to illustrate this refers to the Dutch liberal party leader Frits Bolkestein:

> Bolkestein's thesis comes down to the idea that Christianity, rationalism and humanism have provided the Western world with values such as the division between church and state, freedom of expression, non-discrimination and tolerance, and that the Islamic world is much less advanced in that respect.[44]

A straightforward relation emerges between Western culture, Christian values, our present socio-political system, and superiority. In its most extreme form, the phrasing of superiority takes the shape of an explicit denial of the equality between Christianity and Islam. Thus the Flemish orientalist Koen Elst published a series of articles (e.g. 'The Islamic bomb', 'Stop subservience [towards Islam]', 'The new pillar: Islamic fifth column'[45]) devoted to the description of Islam as an inherently intolerant, murderous, and therefore inferior religion; crusades, inquisition, genocides (as against the American Indians), and the like are conveniently glossed over as untypically Christian *faits divers*. More moderate expressions of such moral absolutism are legion. In those cases, as is predictable in a tolerant style, the affirmation of one's own cultural-religious superiority is usually left completely implicit – which allows for rhetorical denial. A strong manifestation of implicit cultural superiority will be seen later in the discussion of solutions to the 'migrant' problem: imposing their adaptation to (superior) mainstream values is elevated to a humane duty, in much the same way as it was the colonizers' humane duty to civilize primitive peoples. But because of the implicitness, indeed, denial is always possible at the explicit level which, in turn, yields strong expressions of tolerance and openness – precisely the values which support the claim to cultural superiority.

The noble European

Democratic values, respect for freedom of expression and other basic human rights, governments elected by popular vote, are seen as ingredients of a cultural heritage which make Europeans inherently or naturally open-minded and tolerant for 'otherness'. We should point out immediately that the jump from a *cultural heritage* to beliefs about the *nature* of a population is at least dubious. Worse yet, the descriptions adduced for that cultural heritage are rather dubious as well, even in the most official of sources. Thus the European Union's 1986 'Declaration against Racism and Xenophobia' takes it for granted

> [. . .] that the respect for the dignity of the human person and the banning of expressions of racial discrimination are part of the common cultural and juridical heritage of all Member-States.

Similarly, a note accompanying the results of an opinion poll on 'Racism, xenophobia and intolerance' starts with the following sentence:

> It is important to observe that the respect for human rights and the fundamental freedoms are part of the common heritage of political ideals and traditions of the Europeans.
>
> (*Eurobarometer*, November 1989)

In both cases, *ideals* are formulated in terms of *observed historical fact*. Clearly, attention to history must be extremely selective, blocking many schools of thought and events leading up to and during World War Two, antisemitism in general, the persistence of (often bloody) ethnic strife, attitudes underlying Europe's relations with its colonies even after decolonization, etc. In other words, these historically formulated statements about European culture and a European tradition of openness and tolerance constitute an example of a largely unnoticed rewriting of history, and whatever deviates from the perceived standard in European history is seen as a *fait divers*, an untypical and accidental episode.

Because of the supposedly evident truth of the historical observation of European openness, it can only reluctantly be admitted that a lack of tolerance can be found in Europe today:

> Yet, we find expressions of a certain degree of intolerance vis-à-vis persons and groups because of differences in race, religion, culture, social class or nationality.
>
> (*Ibid.*)

The euphemistic phrasing of this finding ('expressions of a certain degree of intolerance') contrasts sharply with the explicit themes of the research which the report is supposed to comment on: 'racism', 'xenophobia', 'intolerance'. The overall result is that these negative feelings towards the 'other' are presented as *un-European*. The European is *by nature* noble and humane, and racism and xenophobia are – as we shall see later – the outcome of malevolent agitation. This explains why, as pointed out before, explicit negative statements about the immigrant population are not to be found in official and semi-official texts: they would violate the Europeans' view of themselves as noble, magnanimous, open-minded and tolerant. The authors are clearly struggling to maintain this aspect of European self-perception, even if this requires verbal acrobatics:

> Almost one in two Europeans regards the presence of immigrants in his country rather as something positive for the future. A strong minority holds the opposite opinion.
>
> (*Ibid.*)

The logical conclusion from the content of this quote would have to be that anti-immigrant feelings are quite strong. Yet the authors' wording is an awkward attempt to lead to the opposite conclusion. Note that the 'almost one in two Europeans' with positive feelings towards the presence of immigrants would also be properly described as 'a strong minority', a term reserved for the less open-minded (and hence for the less typical) Europeans. Note also that the positive feelings of almost one in two Europeans are directed not so much at immigrants as people who would be perceived as individually and collectively capable of positively contributing to our social and cultural environment, but rather at 'the presence of immigrants', a reality at a much more abstract level (the level of the ideals which are so easily confused with historical fact). One could wonder, therefore, whether these tolerant Europeans would still give the same response if the questioning had been situated at a more concrete level or if they were to be confronted with immigrants on a day-to-day basis. In the following quote, the authors make breathtaking manoeuvres to demonstrate that even the less tolerant respondents would not be in favour of undemocratic measures against immigrants.

> The sense of uneasiness in some European countries with respect to immigration does not mean that the citizens of these countries want measures which clash with democratic values and principles. On the contrary, three out of four Europeans believe that the situation of the immigrants should become better or at least not worse: in this context they count on the European institutions.
>
> (*Ibid.*)

If three out of four Europeans do not want the immigrants' situation to become worse, does this mean that one out of four *does* want this? Can we speak, then, of 25 per cent foreigner hatred? If so, the proportion still seems quite high. And which proportion of the three out of four want an amelioration of the immigrants' situation rather than simply no deterioration?

The Fleming, paragon of openness

What we observe at a European level is to be found in undiluted form in Flanders. The final paragraph of the award-winning series 'The foreign mutation of Brussels' (see p. 50) opens with the reassuring words that 'Flemings are by nature a hospitable people, interested in other cultures, new points of view'.[46] An anthology of like-minded claims, often to be found in a moderate Flemish-nationalist corner of society, is no doubt superfluous. The need for self-affirmation seems quite strong. Again we see the strange jump from a *socio-culturally* defined group, the 'Flemings', to the attribution of properties, here 'hospitality', which would characterize the *nature* of the group. Belief in a *volksaard* or 'national character' is deep-seated. As we shall see below, this belief has significant consequences for the definition or conceptualization of the 'migrant problem'. Indeed, since we are by nature hospitable, the 'migrant problem' can never really be blamed on us. Something must be wrong with the 'migrants' themselves.

A definition of the problem

The 'migrant' time bomb

Since it has become clear through a chain of electoral successes for the extreme right Vlaams Blok that the 'migrant problem' is a theme with enough popular appeal to bring in votes, Flemish politicians (of the tolerant majority) have exhausted themselves in collective admissions of guilt because they have allowed 'the problem' to 'rot'. The reality of a genuine problem is thereby openly accepted. The problem itself is consistently described in the vaguest possible terms as a *situatie* ('situation') or *toestand* ('condition'), but this does not prevent the use of (equally vague) superlatives for its further characterization as *explosief* ('explosive'), *dramatisch* ('dramatic'), *dringend* ('urgent') and *onleefbaar* ('untenable', 'unliveable'). There is even constant reference to a *migrantentijdbom* ('migrant time bomb'). In a televised debate during which, for instance, the Belgian 'situation' is compared with those of France and Italy (where, shortly before, foreigners had been murdered), the CVP representative Marc Van Peel (who became CVP chairman in June 1996) says: 'The situation in Antwerp is becoming much more explosive'.[47] Guy Verhofstadt, then PVV chairman, joins the chorus as follows:

> And yet the situation in the field is continuously becoming worse and worse. Tension between the population groups in our country in the

different neighbourhoods of the cities and municipalities is constantly growing.[48]

One of the most dramatic formulations is to be found in a metaphor-rich article by one of Belgium's best-known political columnists, Manu Ruys:

> The migrant question also has to be placed in its geopolitical context. The European is in danger of becoming an extinct race. [. . .]
>
> The percolation started shortly after World War Two. The drops have long since become jets of water. Can the dam-burst still be avoided? [. . .]
>
> In the absence of a pan-European approach, the generation which is now growing up is in for some dramatic shocks in the 21st century.[49]

A glut of further examples, corroborating the same point, could be added. In the presence of so much testimony, no one could doubt that there is a 'problem'. But what exactly does it look like?

Public order, safety and prosperity

Usually only members of the political right claim openly that the presence of large groups of 'migrants' in Belgium threatens *prosperity* and 'endangers the future of our children'. In the street, however, this is one of the most widespread arguments to legitimize an anti-migrant attitude. 'Migrants', the story goes, would make disproportionate use of the social security system and occupy positions which 'our' unemployed would be entitled to.

The Vlaams Blok slogan *Eigen volk eerst* ('Our own people first') voices such sentiments clearly, and has in recent years been made more and more explicit, as in the words *Eigen volk eerst, altijd en overal* ('Our own people first, always and everywhere') which close their information programmes broadcast on public television, and in *Werk voor eigen volk eerst* ('Jobs for our own people first') which was the main VB slogan during the May Day celebrations in 1996. In Chapter 8 we will come back to the fact that no legal action is taken against such slogans, though they clearly violate existing laws against discrimination and racism.

The prosperity-based anti-migrant attitude, of course, does not square with the magnanimous self-image which Flemings share with other Europeans. Therefore, it can only show up in the most implicit ways in our non-extremist sources. At the explicit level, the tolerant media and politicians do their best to undermine the prosperity argument. They do so by talking and writing about the population growth which we now have foreigners to thank for, about the many crucial and hard-to-replace positions which 'migrants' now occupy in the labour market, and about the contributions they make to the treasury which must be higher than the costs calculated for their presence. In the words of Louis Tobback, then Minister of the Interior, 'Migrants constitute an enormous reserve'.[50] This sustained effort at taking the edge off the argument implies full acceptance of its premises and places the 'migrant' at the centre of a cost–benefit analysis. One of the premisses is that the presence of foreigners as such should not simply be accepted without special reasons: they are welcome to the extent of their usefulness and as long as they do not burden the state financially; in the absence of economic return, they would not deserve the right to stay.

The conceptual complex surrounding our notion of the 'migrant', as analysed above, showed a resilient association of the 'migrant problem' with *illegality*. Unlike for the prosperity issue, no attempt is made to hide this. The association even surfaces in newspaper headlines. Just two examples:

[Title:] *Migrant problem* also in The Netherlands time bomb
[Subtitle:] Government intends to crack down on *illegal aliens*[51]
(our italics)

and

[Title:] Government appoints ambassador for *migrant affairs*
[Subtitle:] Stronger crackdown on *illegal* labour[52] (our italics)

From this point, the jump to issues of *crime* and the problem of *safety* is made with amazing agility. Witness another headline:

[Title:] Government tackles *safety* and *migrants*
[Subtitle:] Dehaene: measures soon[53] (our italics)

The same explicit link, which is beginning to look like an idiomatic collocation, appears in the body of numerous reports. Just consider the following random anthology:

During the meetings of party councils frantic efforts were made to understand the why [of the electoral success of the VB]. A number of reasons are readily available: *migrants, crime and unsafety*, massive disinterest among younger people for anything smelling of politics.[54] (our italics)

Because if we want to do something *about the migrant problem or the lack of safety*, that is going to cost money.[55] (quote from Hugo Schiltz, important VU politician; our italics)

How big the distance had become between politics and the people could best be measured against the lack of understanding on the part of ministers in relation to the *growing unsafety and the problems with migrants*.[56] (our italics)

> As a result of the fact that the previous outgoing government has done little to deal with *problems with 'foreigners'*, especially young ones who were usually born in our country, *a growing feeling of unsafety* has emerged which does not only oblige older people to stay inside in the evening (certainly in large cities) behind the closed doors of their houses [. . .][57] (our italics)

Or, returning briefly to the one-day corpus of 6 June 1992: of the 37 relevant articles, no less than 22 dealt with explicit themes belonging to the areas of illegality, crime and safety. Also from earlier research of media reporting on 'small crimes' (Meeuwis 1990, and, outside Belgium, T.A. van Dijk 1983) a strong conceptual link emerges which ties 'migrants' to criminal tendencies. In spite of sporadic conscious efforts to avoid this, the global picture has changed only slightly in recent years and excessive ethnic markings of criminals are not exceptions. In this respect, black Africans and East Europeans score as well as the prototypical 'migrant'.

Except in individual cases in which specific facts are at issue, criminality and lack of safety are usually lifted up to a general and abstract level where it becomes possible, again, to display a magnanimous disposition. 'Neutral' explanations are proffered for the 'observed' criminal tendencies and behaviour:

> Youngsters who become naturalized Belgians get alienated from their origin. [. . .] They suffer the classical handicaps of the newcomer: learning problems, family tensions, a narrowed entry into the job market. The social difficulties lead to excesses, drug use, street crime, friction with the autochthonous population and with the police.[58]

The 'understanding' which is displayed here becomes a double-edged sword. With the best of intentions, the problem is removed from individual guilt and responsibility and placed in a much wider social framework. The effect, however, is that a complete segment of society is problematized – in spite of the fact that only a minute minority within this segment ever mugs old ladies or goes around shoplifting. The rationalization, in other words, emphasizes that the 'migrant' population as such *is* a problem and is responsible for crime and lack of safety in our cities.

It would be a mistake to think that the association between 'migrants' and crime lives only in the minds of the naive masses, or that it surfaces only in their unintentional (and therefore forgivable) juxtaposition in hastily written news reports. It is to be found at the highest level of those appointed by the Belgian state to conduct the official fight against racism. Thus when a symposium on *violence prevention* was held in Antwerp on 27 April 1996, CGKR Director Johan Leman criticized the *'migrant' policies* of the city of Antwerp, adding that so little was done to prevent problems that here even he might become a VB voter.

In addition to prosperity and safety, the entire domain of *public order* seems to be threatened by 'migrants'. In the migrant debate, May 1991 is almost as important a notion as 24 November 1991. In the political jargon, the traditional parties were punished by the voters during the elections of 24 November 1991 for, amongst other things, having allowed the 'migrant problem' to 'rot'. May 1991 symbolizes the 'rotting' process: a number of municipalities in the Brussels area were turned into a low-grade war zone for a few days by 'migrant' youngsters. Or, to use the words of PVV analysts:

> Broken up streets, smashed shop windows, demolished cars. Brussels was in the grip of violence for four nights. With sticks and Molotov cocktails a trail of destruction was drawn through the capital.[59]

This description is reminiscent of a few memorable manifestations in the 1970s and 1980s by farmers and steel workers which, in spite of the much greater damage they caused, have never lost their respectability by being labelled 'riots': they are still referred to as 'demonstrations', placing them in the context of legitimate social action. Such verbal legitimization has never been tried for what we now remember as *migrantenrellen* ('migrant riots'). This notion is now indelibly imprinted in public consciousness. It led to commemorative articles one year later (e.g. 'Vorst, one year after the riots'[60]), and whenever there is a gathering that threatens to disturb the public order, 'migrant riots' or even 'race riots' are referred to. Even when the facts themselves warrant only a report on *migrantenopstootjes* ('migrant disturbances'), extensive comments may later turn them into 'Brussels riots' which are 'more than isolated incidents', and 'hooligans' are said to 'disrupt the integration process':[61]

> It looks like Brussels got the migrant riots that had been brewing for some time, just like The Netherlands was confronted with Moluccan violence before, and like Great Britain saw parts of Brighton [sic] go up in flames as a result of coloured violence. The Brussels riots can no longer be regarded as isolated incidents. Nor are they due to the nervousness that usually goes hand in hand with Ramadan. There are common lines, dangerous lines. The authorities will have to take measures fast.[62]

The author tries to convince the reader that we have reached a second phase in 'the arrival of others in a certain society', the phase of the Dutch Moluccan violence and the British *kleurlingengeweld* (literally 'violence committed by coloured people'), the stage which precedes 'a third, ideal phase' in which autochthons and allochthons form 'a society enriched by the new group' – a stage which The Netherlands and Great Britain 'seem to be approaching'. The 'dangerous lines' in question, the analysis goes, derive from the fact that a small group of agitators can carry the confrontation to extremes so that further integration is impeded:

This small group exercises a dictatorship of the street, the victims of which are both the Belgians and the majority of non-Belgians in Brussels. This small group aims at an *intifada*, with at stake the gaining of control over a territory: a part of the public space. In this way they also prevent every attempt at integration on the part of the non-Belgians, and they cause considerable damage to society. Therefore, severe measures have to be taken against the leaders of this intifada.[63]

This analysis, presented here by Guido Fonteyn, leading journalist and first laureate of a KCM prize for tolerance-inducing reporting, corresponds clearly to the official version. Soon after, a study by the Brussels police is said to show that 'the most recent migrant riots were provoked by criminals who dragged along other youngsters'.[64] And KCM Commissioner Paula D'Hondt, later followed in this practice by CGKR Director Johan Leman, never failed to declare immediately after disturbances of the public order that fast and severe action was needed against the few hooligans who spoil the atmosphere. In this way, the majority of 'migrants' is again discharged in the official rhetoric, and cultural alienation and economic poverty are called upon to explain why a sizeable group of 'migrant' youngsters is susceptible to agitation. Thus, while guilt for the riots is put on the shoulders of a small minority (of 'migrants'!), the ultimate explanation is still sought within the 'migrant' population as a whole. Again the effect of 'understanding' is a further, albeit vague, problematization of the 'migrant' community.

Before analysing this problematization in greater detail, we have to shift the focus briefly to the other side of the 'migrant problem', the autochthonous attitudes towards allochthons. Let it be sufficient, meanwhile, to emphasize that the associative conceptualization of 'migrants' as tied to problems of prosperity, illegality, crime and disturbances of the public order has given rise to a range of policy measures related to foreigners as well as a blatant exploitation of the issues in political campaigns. The policy measures include a complete crackdown on immigration, implemented by the two most recent SP Ministers of the Interior, Louis Tobback (now SP chairman) and Johan Van de Lanotte. Some of these were already briefly mentioned in Chapter 1; others relate specifically to asylum policies, leading to the construction of new closed detention centres (functionally equivalent to prisons) and a brand-new and much more restrictive asylum legislation (which, amongst other things, will allow the state to detain asylum seekers almost indefinitely). In addition, the same ministers have been responsible for an increased policing of areas with 'migrants'. Louis Tobback invented the 'safety contracts' which give municipalities extra money for police services in exchange for a lower crime rate; as a result, the visibility of policemen in the street has gone up drastically. Arguments to the effect that measures are concerned which are not primarily directed at 'migrants' do not stand up to scrutiny. It is not surprising, then, that the safety issue, in its direct association with the 'migrant' population, surfaces unimpeded in political campaigns of the traditional parties as well as those of the extreme right. Thus during municipal elections in 1994, the VLD used a slogan saying 'The Flemish Liberals and Democrats are tolerant, but not at the expense of your safety'.[65] A clearer acceptance of foreigners' responsibility for a decline in safety is hard to imagine. Yet one year later, for the national elections in 1995, one VLD candidate went even further. In an elaborate advertising text he describes the hospitality of the people of Antwerp towards foreigners who behave like guests (naming Jews, Chinese, Indians), adding that 'Things go seriously wrong when foreigners abuse the proverbial Antwerp hospitality',[66] and then listing forms of social decay (the destruction of social networks by driving natives out of certain neighbourhoods, the decline of schools, the loss of value of property in some areas, youth gangs, theft and petty crime) commonly blamed on the traditional categories of 'migrants'. Those categories of 'migrants', i.e. mostly Moroccans and Turks, are never named in the text, but their ominous presence looms large over the entire electoral campaign.

Racism and xenophobia versus demagogy and poverty

Extensive media attention has been devoted over the past few years to the phenomenon of the 'extreme right' in Europe and the associated notions of racism and xenophobia: Le Pen and the *Front National* in France, the *Republikaner* in Germany, the Vlaams Blok in Belgium, all the way to various movements in The Netherlands, Italy, Spain and the Scandinavian countries. Acts of violence against foreigners, ranging from brutal identity checks to the burning of houses for asylum seekers and death threats, are unambiguously condemned. The electoral successes of parties on the extreme right (as when the VB doubled its votes on 24 November 1991) are presented as most disturbing developments, while downward fluctuations (as for the Republikaner) are received with a sigh of relief. There are explicit warnings against the treacherous nature of the democratic image which those parties increasingly tend to cherish as they get more powerful.

With implicit and explicit reference to specific persons or groups, therefore, the existence of racism and xenophobia is by no means denied. Thus the European Union's 'Declaration against Racism and Xenophobia' (11 June 1986) is predicated, *inter alia*, on the following premiss:

> Observing that attitudes, movements and violent actions of foreigner hatred which are often directed at immigrants, increasingly occur [. . .]

Similarly, the research note concerning the European opinion poll on racism (Eurobarometer, November 1989) mentions 'rising fascism and racism in Europe', and a policy statement by the Flemish SP deplores 'the alarming growth of an extreme-right ideology'.[67]

At this specifically political level – Racism with a capital R – no one seems troubled by the recognition of racism as a fact. A completely different picture emerges, however, when anti-'migrant' attitudes are at issue *at a wider societal and a personal level.* At those levels, a *denial of racism* is the rule – a phenomenon which again is directly linked to the positive self-image of the noble European (and which was already described in T.A. van Dijk 1992). Denials at the personal level usually take a standardized form that can be summarized as 'I am not a racist, but . . . ':

> As far as I am concerned they can send 100,000 additional migrants, as long as they adapt a little and leave us in peace.[68] (said by the barkeeper quoted more extensively above)

> I am not one who is against the presence of migrants in our society. Amongst my pupils there are a number of Moroccans who do their very best and who are intent on learning a rewarding occupation. But it is those youth gangs who damage the image of the entire Moroccan community.[69] (said by a school supervisor)

At the societal level, no energy is spared to reject the generality of the racism problem. In answer to the question of how important the new racism and radicalism in Germany is, the German *éminence grise* Marion Gräfin Dönhoff, publisher of *Die Zeit*, replies simply: 'I do not believe that racism is involved'.[70] This is one of the main subjects of a long interview in the Flemish weekly, *Knack*. Another weekly, *Trends* (4 June 1992: 45), makes the effort to carry out its own 'research' to demonstrate that 'systematic discrimination of migrants' does not occur in personnel selection procedures in Belgian companies.

In discussions about this topic, a subtle distinction is often made between *racism* and *xenophobia*. Apparently the term 'racism' is so heavily loaded with negative connotations that its application immediately involves a condemnation, and even one in an area of concerns that is central to the European self-image of tolerance and openness. The pragmatics of word choice, or (as Mehan 1996 would call it) the politics of representation,[71] is put into action. It seems harder to recognize that Flemings are prone to racism than to admit that 90 per cent of them are xenophobic. One common argument is that the Flemish people living close to the northern border of Belgium also do not like the invasion of Dutch people (many of whom have indeed settled there for tax reasons). The Dutch belong to the same race, so the argument goes. Therefore Flemings with an anti-Dutch inclination are not racists, but they *are* xenophobic. Rhetorically, this seems to work: the dirty word has been avoided. But semantics and logic are clearly given a day off. In simple terms, *racism* is hostility towards other races (whatever 'races' may be). *Xenophobia*, on the other hand, is characterized by aversion to 'others' in general. Hence, xenophobia is the wider concept which includes racism. If xenophobes are then called 'non-racist' because their unfriendly feelings are restricted to other 'races', the argument contains a semantic blunder: their aversion is much more general, is therefore *also* directed at other 'races', and is therefore fundamentally racist. This explaining-away of racism gets all the more dubious in the light of the uncertain status of the notion of 'race' itself.

Though a reproach of xenophobia is thus in principle worse – because more general and more inclusive – than a reproach of racism, the existing connotational context reserves the term racism for those expressions of xenophobia which go hand in hand with extreme, fascist points of view (such as a repatriation policy for 'migrants'), i.e. what we called Racism with a capital R. A typical example would be the VB's 70-point programme (Dewinter 1992) for the solution of the 'migrant problem'. Indeed, the programme in question is directed specifically at Moroccans and Turks, two groups seen as 'racially' distinct, though the term 'race' is carefully avoided and systematically replaced by 'descent' or 'origin' and 'nationality'. Note that the VB is certainly not xenophobic, since it does not seem to be bothered by European foreigners (and certainly not by Dutchmen, with whom we share 'our language and culture').

Such semantic-pragmatic processes are not as innocent as they may seem. The euphemistic use of 'xenophobia' fits into *a rhetorical strategy which links an abnormalization of the foreigner with a normalization of our own attitudes*. Fear of and aversion to 'others' is systematically presented as 'rather normal' phenomena:

> [. . .] a number of groups in the Antwerp area, and not only the Vlaams Blok, systematically reinforce and exploit the – say *normal* – feelings of suspicion which people have towards people with a different skin colour and a different language.[72] (Marc Van Peel, now CVP chairman, during a televised debate)

> Why not admit that the lasting settlement of Islamic families and groups has been a mistake and that certain reactions of the autochthonous population are well-founded and have nothing to do with racial hatred, but everything with the right to a safe and undisturbed existence?[73] (Manu Ruys, long-time editor of DS, still active as an apolitical columnist)

> A reserved attitude towards what is foreign is a constant element in human behaviour.[74] (from an interview with Daniel Cohn-Bendit, former student leader, now responsible for multicultural affairs in Frankfurt)

The theme is even widened in the context of reporting on an anti-racist campaign launched by *Artsen zonder Grenzen* (Médecins sans Frontières, or 'Doctors without Borders'):

> Moreels [then AzG chairman, now State Secretary for Development Aid] did not evade the issue that xenophobic reactions in the Third World are sometimes more vehement than here.[75]

In other words, *everyone* is xenophobic, including those against whom our xeno-phobia is directed. Honesty dictates we do not 'evade' this issue. This completes the normalization process.

Such a rationalization and normalization of anti-foreigner feelings, however they are further defined, meets only one obstacle. How should one explain that adherents of extreme anti-'migrant' positions get so much support? A heavy load dropped from the public mind, then, when a few months after the elections of 24 November 1991 it was possible to advise, on the basis of scientific research, 'Don't call VB voter "fascist"',[76] or when, half a year after the same elections, it was considered statistically proven that the majority of Flemish youngsters show 'a non-negative attitude towards foreigners' and 'a certain openness', and that they are 'tolerant, non-racist and non-fascist'.[77] The reassurance is rather fragile, though, since a diagram accompanying the report shows that youngsters' votes for VB are slightly higher than the average Flemish percentage. Thus, either reassurance should be generalized (which was probably the intention), or else the problem remains the same.

Sufficient arguments having been gathered for generalized relief, deep feelings of intolerance are exclusively ascribed to certain (political) movements and their leaders. The *voters* (without whom, after all, there would be no political move-ments in a democratic context) are presented as *misled victims whose normal feelings of suspicion are relentlessly exploited or whose xenophobia is turned into racism by malicious demagogues*. The Flemish SP's analysis adduces all the elements:

[. . .] the political exploitation of tensions and prejudice [. . .].[78]

[. . .] people's susceptibility for systematic negative propaganda such as by the Vlaams Blok.[79]

The explanation based on these ingredients is widely shared, and not only in Belgium. Witness Marion Gräfin Dönhoff:

Though it does not seem racism to me and certainly not antisemitism, still a demagogue can easily take advantage of it.[80]

Moreover, demagoguery is facilitated by circumstances which have nothing to do with racism or xenophobia, viz. *socio-economic frustrations*. This analysis is adhered to by most political parties. For instance, from policy statements by the Flemish socialists and the Flemish green party:

Today, many people find themselves in weak social situations [. . .].[81]

Especially in economically more difficult times people from the lowest classes, themselves the first victims of poverty, unemployment, rotting ... have a tendency, when confronted with large groups of foreigners, to regard them as the cause of all evil.[82]

The analysis is supported, on a massive scale, by social scientists:

Research shows that the main cause of societal conflicts and intolerance towards migrants is at a first level not so much to be found in cultural differences and related racist sentiments, but in the poor material living conditions to which both autochthons and allochthons are exposed.[83]

The formulation remains sufficiently vague. What 'research' is this about? What is the scope of *in eerste instantie* ('at a first level') and *niet zozeer* ('not so much'). What is the meaning of *culturele verschillen* ('cultural differences') and *daarmee gepaard gaande racistische gevoelens* ('concomitant racist sentiments'; literally 'racist sentiments which go hand in hand with that [i.e. with cultural differences]')? How do racist sentiments go hand in hand with cultural differences? Is this meant to suggest that cultural differences, whatever they may be, are necessarily linked to racist sentiments? What does it mean to be *blootgesteld* ('exposed') to *slechte materiële bestaansvoorwaarden* ('poor material living conditions')? How can *onverdraagzaamheid tegen migranten* ('intolerance towards migrants') result from the poor material living conditions to which *allochthons* are exposed?

In spite of perfect vagueness, the above statement of the problem is accepted as a premise for further research, a premise which fits comfortably into our self-image and thus serves a soothing function. Note that its content, as such, *cannot even be proven*. If research shows that clear expressions of racism occur more in poorer population groups, then the official version has it that poverty causes racism. But this could also mean that a latent form of racism, which generally surfaces more subtly (as described for The Netherlands and the United States by Philomena Essed 1991; for Germany see Jäger 1996), assumes a certain form of expression under certain circumstances. That we are really confronted here with *an official version* appears, e.g., from a European parliamentary report in which Enrique Barón Crespo, then President of the European Parliament, made the following unmitigated claim:

Racism and foreigner hatred are produced by fear and uncertainty about the future and are nurtured by unemployment and poverty.[84]

Daniel Cohn-Bendit is quoted at length, emphasizing the psychological aspect and relating racism even to sexual frustrations (a link which is also supposed to be based on research):

The wave of racism that we are experiencing is, in my opinion, the expression of a deep uncertainty of the people in society. That uncertainty results from the modernization of the world, which absorbs a lot of energy. The so-called achievement and competition society is experienced as something very tiring. That induces fear, because you either succeed or you do not succeed. I think that people have been disappointed by democracy because they have the impression that in a democracy everything changes only very slowly. Many people need clearly defined situations, but our society has become very complex. That, also, causes uncertainty and fear.

During the latest municipal elections in Frankfurt many young men have cast right-radical votes. Research showed that they had trouble with their role as men, that they did not know how properly to start a relationship with a woman, that in general they did not know how to handle societal developments. Migrants then form an easy target to work off stress, they become scapegoats.[85]

In the same vein, Bijttebier *et al.* (1992) mention *wanhoopsracisme* ('racism of despair') in their analysis of the election results on 24 November 1991. And even that formulation seems to be in need of further weakening:

In the case of some of Vlaams Blok's voters one can speak of a 'racism of despair' (though later it will become completely clear that the term 'racism' does not really belong here).[86]

In addition to social scientists, the opinion of successful 'migrants' is elicited in search of authoritative arguments, as in the case of a Moroccan bank manager quoted in a report on the Brussels Foyer (an 'integration' centre often considered as one of the real success stories in 'migrant'–native relations in Belgium):

He ascribes the success of Vlaams Blok and Front National to the frustrations of dissatisfied people, who – in their ignorance – burden foreigners with all the sins of Israel.[87]

And the news media have no problems siding with the analysis. Thus we find elaborate articles of the following type:

[Title:] Louise's road of suffering leads to racism
[Subtitle:] Housing problems nurture resentment against political refugees[88]

In the same vein, De Standaard picks out the theme 'Vlaams Blok is poverty party'[89] as the title of its report on a symposium dealing with the extreme right in Europe – a symposium which dealt with many more (and different) aspects of the problem. About the published proceedings of the same symposium (De

Schampheleire and Thanassekos (eds) 1991), the same newspaper later reports under the title '"Unpredictability and incomprehensibility" of extreme right in Europe investigated', and the report concentrates on explanations based on a social disruption model and offers a central place to the portrayal of the success of the extreme right as 'an anomaly' with 'dimensions that are as incomprehensible as they are unpredictable'.

The ideological construct can be schematically summarized as follows: *poverty provides the raw materials which manipulators need to bring about the unlikely metamorphosis from 'normal' feelings of uneasiness to 'un-European' racism or xenophobia.* This extremely widespread ethno-theory, reduced to its essentials, is so clearly apologetic that it cannot but miss the essence, which has to do with a deepseated aversion to diversity – as we shall see below. The need for rationalization becomes even clearer in attempts to force obvious exceptions into the same explanatory mould. At first sight, the fact that people who are not poor also cast VB votes and seem to show serious forms of xenophobia would have to break the rule. Yet,

> Another phenomenon that comes into play in Antwerp is *distancing racism*, in which rich people who are hardly confronted with migrants – except in the form of their foreign house personnel – still take a defensive stand against them. They believe that if migrants stay and get more involved, society will change and their own position in society will be in danger.[90]

In other words, those who could hardly be said to show 'racism of despair' because they are too rich, show *distanciëringsracisme* ('distancing racism') out of fear of situations that might lead them to despair as well. Both manifestations are thus reduced to the same existential uncertainty, though actual in one case and anticipatory in the other.

The threshold of tolerance

Though every conceivable effort is made to demonstrate that 'normal' reactions are maliciously exploited by a handful of extremists, a certain tension remains between the tolerant self-image and observable expressions of racism and xenophobia. The final move in explaining away racism is the *objectification* of 'the migrant problem' in the form of a *tolerantiedrempel* ('threshold of tolerance').

Not only is a certain degree of xenophobia elevated to the level of a 'normal phenomenon', but expressions of racism and foreigner hatred – about which we already know that they are caused by socio-economic uncertainty, even among the rich – are normalized in the most general way imaginable: they become 'normal' from the moment that *the number of foreigners in proportion to the autochthonous population crosses a certain threshold.* Numerous lines of argumentation and numerous policy proposals are based on this notion. It guides the discourse on *concentratiegebieden* ('concentration areas'), i.e. areas with 'too many' foreigners, which are systematically problematized and which are often called 'ghettos', as well as a package of proposals – to be discussed at length in Chapter 8 – related to *concentratiescholen* ('concentration schools') and the so-called '1 in 1000' polemic about the geographical spread of asylum seekers (referring to a principle that municipalities should not be asked to accommodate a higher number of asylum seekers than the equivalent of one for one thousand inhabitants). The threshold of tolerance is *an objectifying socio-mathematical concept that defines the conditions under which the all-European tolerance and openness may be cancelled without affecting the basic self-image*. The European does not become intolerant until this threshold is crossed. Just let him or her step back over the same threshold, i.e. just reduce the number of foreigners again, and the good old tolerance will return. In other words, even in moments of intolerance the European is still tolerant at heart, and the observed behaviour is completely due to the factual circumstances which render it impossible to exercise this essential openness. Needless to say, the threshold of tolerance is not an exclusively Belgian notion. It is commonly used in other European countries, and when François Mitterrand uttered the term it was more widely internationalized by *Time Magazine* in an article entitled 'Foreign overdose: The "threshold of tolerance" toward immigrants is crossed, provoking an eruption of racial violence'.

The quantitative nature of the notion goes hand in hand with a more 'philosophical' attempt to ground the limitations on tolerance. Consider the following:

> Freedom and tolerance, however important, must remain limited, precisely because of the mutual interaction between these two. For freedom this is clear. Unrestricted freedom for some leads to repression of others: that is true for political, cultural, social and economic relations. But also tolerance has to be restrained and cannot be allowed to degenerate into submissiveness, resignation, indifference or, worst of all, into permissiveness.[91]

Another Flemish intellectual professes the same faith:

> The tolerant human being however [i.e. in opposition to, e.g., religious fundamentalists], opts for a pluralistic society, in which all opinions get a chance with equal rights. Yet he has some reservations towards the excesses of the ideological 'free market economy'.[92]

He continues the argument with a plea for the value of 'tradition':

> In reality it is precisely the human being living from within a tradition who shows something revolutionary. For only he dares, when necessary, to swim against the current of the times. He knows that who marries the spirit of the times soon becomes a widower.[93]

Permissiveness, then, is defined as *excessive tolerance for deviations from one's tradition*. This is not tolerable, since it threatens one's own identity. However straightforward this may sound, the respectable and eloquent wording hides tangled argumentation. The stipulated path can only be followed as long as the tradition in question is confronted with disloyal members from one's own ranks (i.e. those 'who marry the spirit of the times'). But what happens in the confrontation with a different, and perhaps more vital, tradition? How can one maintain, for instance, that tolerance with respect to Islam degenerates into 'submissiveness' (or, to use the words of Koen Elst, quoted earlier, 'subservience') from the moment when we accept its practice largely the way it is, *chador* included? If we want to change the Islamic tradition seriously to adapt it to our own norms, values and lifestyle, we undermine our own argument in relation to the value of 'tradition'. In the above argument, moreover, 'tradition' is completely abstracted from the active and dynamic role which it plays in human societies. The notion is to be situated on a par with 'identity', a vague complex of properties about which it is said that they have been inherited from a distant past, inalienable, the core of our very existence. Tolerance collides with a fundamental intolerance towards others.

The 'migrant' debate also provides a solution for this conflict. The self-imposed restrictions on our tolerance, for instance in relation to Islam, are justified on the basis of a comparison of the *tolerance levels* of the Christian and Islamic traditions. The most tolerant of the two traditions – Christianity, needless to say – acquires the right to limit its tolerance: since Islam is less tolerant, it may endanger us; hence, we have the right of self-defence. Here a constructed enemy image is given reality status and finds its way easily into public opinion and into politics. One of the many recent expressions of this was produced by Guy Verhofstadt, then VLD chairman, who considers Islam to be 'in essence an intolerant and totalitarian ideology':

> The question is whether Islam can be tuned in with liberal democracy and the freedom, tolerance, diversity and argumentative debate without which an open society is impossible.[94]

The conclusion is simple enough:

> As soon, however, as Islam wants to structure the state and society in keeping with its moral principles and its opinion of what is good and bad, the *threshold of tolerance* is crossed. In liberal democracy tolerance cannot go so far as to end up ultimately in an open or even tacit repression of its own values: freedom of expression, freedom of religious practice, equality of rights for men and women, pluralism, separation of Church and state. Making the Islamic community in our country accept and live according to those values is the road to 'integration' [here the term *inburgering* is used; see comments later in this chapter and in Chapter 4] that has to be followed.[95] (our italics)

79

Practically all prominent authorities in Flanders, to the extent that they openly accept the presence of 'migrants' at all, support some version of this view. Even KCM Director Paula D'Hondt, when officially in charge of the formulation of 'migrant' policy proposals for the Belgian government, utters her despair when confronted with the mosques which 'keep shooting up like mushrooms' and which represent a type of Islam that, in her opinion, is not sufficiently 'autonomous' in relation to Islam in the Islamic countries:

> I do not know whether it was a mistake to recognize Islam. I do know, however, that it was a mistake to do it in such an ill-considered manner, without evaluating the consequences for this small country.[96]

In spite of the confidence with which tolerance and pluralism are seen as fundamental properties of our society, nothing prevents Verhofstadt (1992: 65–6) – and many with him – to include in the list of unacceptable concessions to Islam facts such as the hiring of foreigners by the police, or the permission for young Islamic girls to wear the *chador* in public schools. The latter example is supposed to have broken 'for the first time since long ago' the 'principle of ideological neutrality'. The logic in this argument is seriously warped, because the 'neutrality' in question bears on the public school system itself, not on those who receive schooling; hence the 'neutrality' is broken by banning a specific religion- or culture-related habit, as much as it would be by making it obligatory (see Dembour 1996 for a discussion). As for D'Hondt's remarks, it should be kept in mind that although Islam was officially recognized by the Belgian state in 1974, twenty years later this official recognition has still not led to any measures for implementing it. As a consequence, Islam still does not enjoy the privileges it is entitled to. An Islamic council, elected democratically, was not recognized by the government because it was judged to be insufficiently representative or insufficiently free of ties with the Islamic countries. There is no subsidy system yet. And no training for Islam teachers is available.

Though basically a quantitative notion, the 'threshold of tolerance' is thus further substantiated with an ideological or philosophical and a moral or ethical-behavioural content. But both the quantitative and the more philosophical aspects are kept utterly vague. How many foreigners may present themselves, or what aspects of belief or behaviour they should display before the 'threshold' is crossed, remains an *ad hoc* decision. As is always the case with underdefined social concepts, this indeterminacy opens the road to endless possibilities for manipulation. The bottom line is, however, that the 'threshold of tolerance' may turn the very *existence* of foreigners, as well as their *way of being*, automatically into a problem.

Diversity

Objectifying the 'migrant problem' or the 'migrant question' by means of the notion of a 'threshold of tolerance' becomes possible only on the basis of *the assumption that (a certain degree of) cultural, ethnic, linguistic or religious diversity is essentially problematic.* It does not come as a surprise, then, that the 'migrant' debate is filled to the brim with explicit statements to that effect, varying from rather general and non-committal claims such as 'Everywhere in the world peacefully living together is complex and difficult'[97] to rather extreme and concrete analyses, as in the following reader's letter on the occasion of the 1992 race riots in Los Angeles:

> Usually events in America present a preview of what will change here in ten or fifteen years. It was like that with the drug problem, juvenile delinquency, the omnipotence of television, the changed sexual ethics, Aids. All these problems first surfaced in America and only later in Europe.
>
> The race riots in Los Angeles have to be a warning to us: a multicultural or multiracial society leads to chaos, looting and violence. Do we want the same conditions in Brussels and in Antwerp ten years from now?[98]

Though letters to the editor cannot normally be assumed to be as indicative of a general mood as regular reporting, this one is interesting because it was published in two newspapers (from the same group) on two different days. The fact that the reasoning which it represents touches a recognizable sentiment is also apparent from its frequent appearance in the opinion pages where radical Flemish nationalists such as Peter De Roover write unambiguously about 'the multicultural mistake' and are given a forum for premonitions of the following kind:

> Let us say openly that we do not want and cannot let Flanders grow into a multicultural country.[99]

Somewhere between the extremes we find a quite general consensus couched implicitly beneath the words, as when a group of social scientists organizes a colloquium under the title 'Towards a liveable multicultural municipality'.[100] The process marker 'towards', in combination with a description of the end product of this process, 'liveable', imply clearly that a multi cultural community is *in itself* seen to form a *problem*, and that special *measures* have to be taken to make it *liveable*. Briefly, *an homogeneous community is regarded as the norm*, and diversity is only acceptable to the extent that it does not touch social harmony as viewed by the majority.

In the light of this normative view of society, cries of alarm are heard about a *nascent Moslem pillar* (as in 'The new pillar: Islamic fifth column' and 'From guest labour to Moslem pillar'[101]). It is presented as a problem that, during the sixth annual conference of Moslems in Europe, held in Genk around Easter 1992, 'a plan for the definitive and lasting settlement of Islam in Europe was formulated'. According to the picture we get, Europe will be overrun by Moslems before long. Another dramatic formulation goes as follows:

> But the turn which the migrant question is taking transforms the problem of discrimination into a phenomenon of Moslem awakening and radicalization.[102]

Imagine that 'all kinds of action groups systematically develop organizations and institutions aimed at the permanent settlement of the Islamic community in Western countries', and that part of the planning is 'the establishment of Koran schools, Islamic youth associations, financial and social institutions, media instruments'.[103] A Moslem 'pillar' would perpetuate diversity and is therefore unacceptable. This is not only one individual's opinion. There is an immediate outcry as soon as the idea is voiced, for instance, to set up an autonomous Islamic school network – though there is a vast Catholic schooling network (more extensive than the public network in Flanders!) and a well-developed Jewish network as well. The 'migrant' is not allowed to institutionalize his being different, simply because he is perceived as too different. In other words, 'migrants' present us with *a form of diversity that is by definition a problem*. This ideologically based problematization, which, of course, goes against the loudly professed value of pluralism, will be further analysed in Chapters 4 and 5. But the core which we have revealed so far already offers the necessary ingredients for a good understanding of the range of solutions for the 'problem' that emerges in the 'migrant' debate, as conducted by a wide cross-section of the autochthonous majority.

Solutions

During a televised political debate[104] Filip Dewinter, one of the most popular VB leaders, defended the retroactive revisability of naturalization procedures completed since 1974 – one of 70 measures proposed to solve the 'migrant' problem (see Dewinter 1992). After his remark that 'it has to be possible to revise' such naturalizations, his interlocutor Jaak Gabriëls, at that time the outgoing VU chairman, emotionally asks the question: 'Also for people who have adapted themselves?' This reply contains the essence of the package of measures supported by most of those who would not be willing to follow a return policy *vis-à-vis* 'migrants'. It implies minimally that different treatment is justified for different groups of 'migrants' depending on their degree of 'adaptedness' to our society. The fundamental *motive* for this attitude does *not* differ from what underlies proposals for repatriation: *since the core of the problem is the emergence of too much diversity (i.e. diversity which crosses the threshold of tolerance either in quantitative or in qualitative terms), the solution is obviously to be found in a restoration of as much homogeneity as possible*, allowing for just enough diversity in 'less essential' areas for the majority to be able to maintain its illusion of pluralism.

Not everyone will use the term *aanpassing* ('adaptation') as Jaak Gabriëls did. In many circles it is not acceptable because of its association with far-reaching forms of *assimilatie* ('assimilation'), a notion that is objectionable to many tolerant Flemings because the merging into mainstream society which it suggests is not compatible with explicit claims to openness and pluralism or with the unshakeable value of cultural identity. In contrast to 'assimilation', then, the ideal of *integratie* ('integration') is posited. As will be demonstrated in Chapter 4, there is absolutely no uniform interpretation of that concept. To illustrate the issue, let us dwell for a while on a definition offered by one of the most visible spokesmen of the tolerant majority, Ludo Abicht:

> From my studies of the Jewish community in Antwerp I have first of all learnt to make a sharp distinction between 'assimilation' and 'integration': while in an open democratic society one can of course not deny the individual the right to opt for full assimilation, that choice is for understandable reasons rejected by the vast majority of Jewish Flemings.
>
> As a result of assimilation, the individual disappears from the ethnic, religious or cultural minority group and adapts to the majority in such a way that the entire group-specific tradition gets lost, and this also counts as a loss for the majority which may be enriched culturally, philosophically and, why not, culinarily by this Jewish presence.
>
> But the majority of Jews in Flanders opt for 'integration', which means that they preserve and vigorously protect their Jewish identity while at the same time they occupy their rightful place in the wider Flemish community, because that is the only true content of the term 'integration'.[105]

Though many would be inclined to give literally the same definition, we wonder how many Flemings would accept the Jewish community as a good example of what they mean by 'integration' – as will be clear very soon from what we will say about the content of that notion when applied to 'migrants'. A significant Hassidic segment of the Jewish community forms a closed population group, living closely together and barely interacting with the autochthonous majority. Their knowledge of Dutch is variable in quality, from poor to absolutely perfect. The community has a high degree of visibility as a result of its dressing code. It maintains its own separate schooling network all through high school, after which many continue their studies abroad. Proportionally speaking there must be as many synagogues as there are mosques. The diamond trade is conducted in a quite traditional fashion, using hardly any written contracts and thus deviating significantly from the current societal norm. Etcetera. Compare this with the dominant idea of 'integration' in relation to Moroccan and Turkish 'migrants' and we must conclude that, when applying the same norms, the Jewish community could not be regarded as 'integrated'. For 'migrants' the notion of 'integration' involves that the formation of ghettos or 'concentration areas' is avoided, that a good knowledge of Dutch can simply be demanded, that young girls do not appear at school wearing *chadors*, that the development of an Islamic schooling network should be 'discouraged', that there should not be too high a concentration of mosques, and that elements of Islamic customary law should not penetrate the society in any way.

Maybe it is because of the ambiguity and the many divergent ways of giving meaning to the concept, that 'new' proposals for 'integration' show the tendency to introduce new terms. Royal commissioner for 'migrant' affairs Paula D'Hondt (KCM 1989) introduced *inpassing*, which literally means 'fitting into' the surrounding society (a term which almost necessarily has an assimilationist ring to it while avoiding and even rejecting the term 'assimilation'). Similarly, VLD chairman Guy Verhofstadt (1992) coined the term *inburgering*, which normally means 'settling down' but which in this context (because, needless to say, most 'migrants' have already settled down) plays heavily on *burger* ('citizen', a concept that is generally celebrated in VLD rhetoric) and acquires a meaning such as 'becoming a citizen among citizens'; more about this term, which has meanwhile gained wider currency, partly as a result of its popularity in The Netherlands, will be said in Chapter 4. Whatever the terminology, all recent proposals (made by members of the tolerant majority) share an emphasis on *what the majority may demand of foreigners* in exchange for *the rights they enjoy*. As a result, the 'migrant' debate takes on a reproachful overtone, as in the following example:

> The presence of large groups of non-Belgians in and around the capital of Europe [Brussels] is a fact. When politicians and the public opinion realized at a certain moment that our city centres were full of Moroccan and Turkish migrants, this was talked about as if their very presence was still under debate. What is now at stake is to regulate this living together and to make it happen peacefully.
>
> The same reasoning must count for the other groups of foreigners. They are here to stay. They are welcome. *But it is not asking too much that they, too, who are our guests, take into account the environment they end up in and show respect and interest for the culture, our culture. That means they had rather leave aside ghetto formation, condescension and narrow clannishness to take active steps in the direction of a liveable society.*[106] (italics ours).

The reproachfulness is not equally sharp on all occasions, but its content is a favourite refrain. Another example of the rights-and-duties discourse, combined with the idea of a threshold of tolerance, rests on KCM authority. The introductory paragraph to an article entitled 'The Netherlands follows Belgian integration model' (subtitle: 'There is a limit to tolerance') says:

> BRUSSELS/THE HAGUE – The Dutch Ministry of the Interior will follow the advice of 75 experts to 'clarify and sharpen' its *minority policies*

and to 'impose more compulsory measures'. The velvet glove [i.e. the soft approach] has not yielded much for the minorities, they say in The Hague. 'This means that The Netherlands is finally following our Belgian integration concept', according to Johan Leman, *chef de cabinet* of Royal Commissioner for Migrant Affairs Paula D'Hondt. 'Already in her first report Paula D'Hondt emphasized that migrants do not only have rights, but also duties. The Netherlands has now also discovered that there are limits to tolerance and individual freedom'.[107]

This is front-page news. If not outright judgemental, the spirit of this kind of discourse is at least paternalistic and based on evolutionistic ideas. 'Migrants' have come from a Third World country to a highly civilized Western European society, where the benefits of prosperity and development can be enjoyed, but only when behaving more responsibly and fulfilling stricter duties than would be dictated by the habits they have brought with them. Therefore, 'migrants' have to be educated to responsibility for their own good. If the 'velvet glove' does not yield enough 'for the migrant', then a more authoritarian approach is needed, as for unruly children. One cannot exercise patience eternally. Mutual rights and duties have to be determined unambiguously.

However vaguely formulated, there seems to be a wide consensus on *what can be demanded of foreigners*. In the Belgian 'migrant' debate the tone for this has been set by the KCM reports. The earliest version (KCM 1989) distinguishes three levels of social action – to be discussed further in Chapters 4 and 5 – to which the notion of *inpassing* ('fitting in') is related in specific ways:

- the level of the values and principles protected by the concept of *'public order'* and hence enforceable by law;
- the level of some *guiding social principles* about which an autochthonous majority seems to agree implicitly;
- the level of the many *cultural expressions* which threaten neither the public order nor the social principles of the host country.[108]

In relation to the third level, there should be an 'unambiguous respect for cultural diversity as mutual enrichment'.[109] It is very unclear what areas are touched by this 'unambiguous respect' for diversity, except for art, folklore and culinary matters. This is a direct result of the incredible and dangerous vagueness of the second level: *guiding* (literally *richting gevend*, 'giving direction' or 'orienting') social principles about which a *majority seems* to agree *implicitly*. The 'direction' or 'orientation' in question is called 'modernity' (where again an evolutionistic perspective surfaces), and typical examples of the 'principles' are 'emancipation' (of women) and 'true pluralism'. But how big is the 'majority' referred to? Who decides what this majority 'seems' to agree on? And if it seems to agree only 'implicitly', how do we know? Could this mean that the consensus would disappear when the principles would be made explicit? If so, then those principles could not be translated into laws, and if more or less unambiguous legislation is not possible, then deviations neither on the side of autochthons nor on the side of allochthons can be sanctioned. The obvious risk is that demands can be made of 'migrants' which *cannot* even be imposed on the autochthonous majority. The vagueness of the principle makes it possible for the majority to keep declaring minority members 'unintegrated'. The only clear criterion is to be found on the first level. Yet the political world, the press and public opinion tend to remain faithful to the vaguer packages of demands.

For full *integratie* ('integration'), *inpassing* ('fitting in') is supposed to go hand in hand with 'a promotion of the structural involvement of the minorities in the activities and goals of the government'.[110] As will be seen later, this unidirectional formulation, with the *overheid* ('government', or the 'authorities' in general) as final standard of societal involvement, results mostly in the appointment of token 'migrants' in visible positions. In later reformulations of integration policies, this specific objective often comes up as a fourth element in a list of ingredients of 'integration', added to the three corresponding to the levels of 'fitting in' (see Blommaert 1997). One such reformulation, casting further light on the content of the integration concept, was offered by Paula D'Hondt herself:

We have defined the integration of migrants into our society as *inpassing* ['fitting in']. We have given concrete substance to that concept in four points. The four points are already to be found in our first report of November 1989: in the first two points we adopt a demanding attitude towards the migrants, in the other two we are open towards them:

1   We demand assimilation where the public order is concerned. This means that migrants have to respect Belgian laws, without any exceptions, all of them, just like every Belgian.
2   We demand that the fundamental social principles of our society are respected by everyone, hence also by all migrants: women's emancipation, as we understand it; mutual tolerance; our language; etc.
3   In addition to those two very important demands which we make of the migrants – and it is not possible to demand more of people in a constitutional state, whether migrants or Belgians – we are open towards what those people can contribute: in artistic, culinary, linguistic, cultural and other domains. There our position is that mutual enrichment is not only possible but even desirable, a precondition for progress.
4   We also say that enough qualified people from migrant circles have to be involved in the goals and activities of the government, because that is the only real way to emancipation, just like it has been for women.[111]

Note that the only point that ends in 'etc.' is point 2. The vagueness does not disappear in this formulation; on the contrary, the open-endedness of the package of potential demands is emphasized. Also, it is not clear in what way 'our language' can count as 'a fundamental social principle' (to be respected unconditionally, while on the other hand linguistic enrichment is admitted in point 3). 'Respect' for 'our language', moreover, is in practice usually turned into 'full command of the language' – an issue which concerns skills rather than values. Further, it is somewhat mysterious to find a demand for 'mutual tolerance' in a package of demands which demonstrates how limited our own tolerance is, and which is even legitimated on the assumption that there is a threshold of tolerance. The limitations are all the more painful because they consist in a refusal to let the minorities keep or develop their own 'fundamental social principles', which are probably the more fundamental aspects of their own identity. To top it all off, every possibility of discussion is taken away by the unobtrusive but extremely important phrase *zoals wij die verstaan* ('as we understand it') with reference to women's emancipation. Indeed, it is a stable characteristic of the entire 'migrant' debate that it is conducted among members of the autochthonous majority; the demands are imposed unidirectionally, without any form of discussion or negotiation.

In the comparison between points 2 and 3, what strikes the most is the noncommittal formulation in point 3: we are open to the exotic in much the same way as good tourists are. The wording itself is equally vague, so that – with the exception of the culinary and the artistic – a strict dividing line between the scopes of points 2 and 3 cannot be drawn. Key notions in the further policy-making related to point 3 are *onderwijsvoorrangsgebieden* ('areas for preferential treatment in education', referring, e.g., to the special attention that goes to the teaching of the local language for 'migrant' children), *zelforganisaties* ('self-organizations', i.e. organizations for 'migrants' run by 'migrants' – but which the authorities frantically try to regulate from above), and *intercultureel kunstencentrum* ('intercultural arts centre'). In all these areas money is spent, but only on condition that the supported activities can be shown to be *integratiebevorderend* ('promoting integration'). Thus a circle of power surrounding the 'migrant' already closes itself within the confines of the exercise of defining integration. The unambiguous granting of fundamental rights paralleling the imposition of demands does not enter the picture at all. The harmonious nature of the envisaged multicultural society boils down to our granting 'migrants' the right to do anything that does not bother us, as long as it does not bother us, i.e. until we declare that a certain form of behaviour no longer fits in with our fundamental social principles so that the threshold of tolerance is crossed.

The added fourth element of the described integration policy does not form part of the original definition (KCM 1989) of the *concept* of 'fitting in'. It was presented originally as a concrete political option that, to make 'integration' complete, should go hand in hand with the more fundamental 'fitting in'. In its own right, its importance would be beyond doubt. We should point out, however, that in order to have true emancipatory power (the link being made explicitly with 'emancipation', a link which we will come back to later) point 4 should have stressed the goal of full involvement of minorities at every level of social and political life. Instead, only involvement in 'the goals and activities of the government (or authorities)' is mentioned. Moreover, participation is restricted to *bekwame mensen* ('qualified people') from 'migrant' circles, where judgements about being *bekwaam* (a term with a much more general connotation of 'being fit' than its translation as 'qualified' would suggest) remains in the hands of the autochthonous authorities who base their decision on criteria derived from their interpretation of points 2 and 3. Thus the circularity is complete, and no doubts are left as to where the power lies. It is not surprising, then, that for the satisfaction of point 4 the appointment of token 'migrants' has usually been enough.

The addition of point 4 marks a minor modification in the integration concept, designed by KCM officials to avert criticism to the 1989 version. Figure 3.2 presents the two consecutive templates. By promoting I (b) to an aspect of 'integration' on a par with I (a) (i)–(iii), it was believed that an emancipatory meaning could be given to the integration concept. From the way in which the 1989 version of 'integration' is handled as an instrument of power (see Chapter 5), and from the way in which the 1989 criteria are handled to judge migrants' suitability for 'structural involvement' (as already explained briefly, and as will be further illustrated in Chapter 5), it should be clear that the shift served a cosmetic purpose only (see Blommaert 1997).

At any rate, a 'consistent promotion of the best possible *inpassing* according to

---

I. *1989 version*
>   INTEGRATIE ('integration')
>
>   (a) INPASSING ('fitting in', 'insertion')
>
>   (i)   the law
>   (ii) guiding social principles
>   (iii) cultural expressions
>
>   (b) structural involvement

II. *Amended version*
>   INTEGRATIE/INPASSING
>
>   (a) the law
>
>   (b) guiding social principles
>
>   (c) cultural expressions
>
>   (d) structural involvement

Figure 3.2 Modifications to the integration concept

the orienting fundamental social principles'[112] is the guideline of political action. Most political parties in the tolerant majority share this idea or produce a version of their own. A concise rendition is the VU slogan 'Migrants must become Flemish'.[113] This is the ultimate translation of *a policy aimed at the preservation or restoration of homogeneity*. Hence the central role that is accorded to the learning of Dutch (or of French in Wallonia) as a remedy *par excellence* for the integration problem. Unaware of the more subtle aspects of communicative style which may continue to hamper inter-ethnic communication long after the acquisition of a common language (just as they may form obstacles in communication between men and women, or between different social classes in the same ethnic group), policy-makers and commentators alike regard 'the language' as one of the most crucial factors of adaptation. Consequently, a poor knowledge of the local language is a consistent ingredient of problem diagnoses, as in an article on a 76-year-old woman of Italian descent who has been living in Flanders quite contentedly for forty-two years:

> She is able to help herself, she gets a cleaning woman once every two weeks, her daughter Lina and her daughter-in-law Tina live nearby and visit regularly. *Still Teresa is stuck with a problem: she does not know Dutch*.[114]

Not only do most proposals contain measures related to the teaching of Dutch (the practical value of which we certainly do not doubt), but policy documents have a tendency to present proficiency in the local language as a *condition* for full membership in the society. When this is absent at the implicit level, it is usually presupposed. This tendency does not only exist at the political level. Social scientists usually agree with it. Once we heard a social scientist making a plea for immediate, automatic and *unconditional* naturalization for all 'migrants' so that they would be able to participate fully in social and political life without restrictions.[115] When questioned about this, he admitted that he had forgotten to mention the obvious condition that knowledge of 'the language' was of course required. For the media, social scientists and politicians this is indeed the most 'obvious' aspect of the entire 'migrant' debate. We will have to come back to this issue in later chapters.

Language teaching as part of the proposals for a solution to the 'problem' is symptomatic of a general call for *practical measures* which do not lack *clarity*, rather than to stick to programmatic statements. It is not enough, so the story goes, to study the problem: action is needed. Or, in Paula D'Hondt's words, 'Fitting in migrants requires drastic and quick measures'.[116] This appeal contrasts sharply with the underdefined nature of the general goal called 'integration' or 'fitting in'. Seemingly inevitable questions are carefully avoided. How is it possible to develop concrete measures to reach a goal that has not been precisely defined? Are such measures not bound to be simplistic, in total neglect of real socio-cultural processes (as we have already hinted in connection with 'the language')? The need for practical measures is satisfied by declaring war on juvenile delinquency, gang formation, urban decay, unemployment and – in general – the realities covered by the notion *kansarmoede* ('deprivation', literally 'poverty of opportunities'). Needless to say, none of these are unimportant. But for a better understanding of how they fit into the ideology guiding the 'migrant' debate, we first have to concentrate on some of the central concepts informing the rhetoric.

4

THE CENTRAL CONCEPTS

The tone of the migrant debate, as conducted by the tolerant majority, is set by a number of central concepts which the argumentation relies upon directly or indirectly and in varying combinations. These concepts share a couple of common characteristics. First, they are barely defined explicitly, or not at all. And where definitions appear, as for instance in official reports, we see that they are carefully adapted to specific rhetorical goals. Second, there is often a significant discrepancy between the 'semantic core' of some of the surfacing terms (i.e. what one would call their 'dictionary meaning') and the associative or derived meanings assigned to them in the rhetorical practice of the migrant debate. To give just one example at this stage, the notion of 'democracy' is often called upon to justify proposals or measures related to minorities. Royal commissioner for 'migrant' affairs Paula D'Hondt used to demonstrate her democratic inclinations by saying that, of course 'migrants' should have the right to vote, at least at the municipal level. She added, however, that there was no need to make this into a hot political issue because the problem would solve itself naturally: by facilitating the acquisition of Belgian nationality, the younger generations would automatically get the right to vote; the older generation, on the other hand, would eventually disappear. The right to political participation, i.e. the essence of democracy, is thus transformed from a political issue which can be decided on freely and democratically at any time, to a matter to be left to the course of nature.

In this chapter, we will discuss four concepts or conceptual constructs underlying the rhetoric of tolerance. These are culture, nation and state, democracy and human rights, and integration. In each case we will provide a contextual reading of the meanings which they receive in actual use.

Culture

Culture and identity

Cultuur ('culture') is a key concept in the migrant debate. 'Migrants' are defined on the basis of their 'otherness', their different cultural background. The problems of living together with them are partly explained with recourse to so-called cultural incompatibilities. And the official goal of current migrant policies is a 'multicultural' society, in which every community – the autochthonous majority as well as the allochthonous minorities – can fully preserve and develop their own *eigenheid* (literally 'own-ness', and suggesting 'uniqueness') or *identiteit* ('identity'), as dictated by the European pluralist model.

However, the concept of 'culture' hardly ever receives an explicit definition. This observation stretches far beyond the migrant debate. But this does not prevent the notion from being used profusely as a trope, to frame the discussion of certain phenomena, or to construct arguments. Thus we encounter an abundance of implicit, fairly *ad hoc* conceptual constructs which sometimes associate 'culture' with the assumed set of values and beliefs of a certain group, sometimes with a particular religious culture (especially of the Islamic type, contrasted with Christian cultural traditions perceived to be pan-European), and sometimes simply with the sum of everyday forms of behaviour. Two aspects of this thinking about 'culture' attract immediate attention. First, a conceptual distinction is drawn (but seldom made explicit) between *profound cultural features* and *cultural surface phenomena*. The profound features include values and beliefs, religion, so-called guiding social principles, but also language and law. Artistic forms, dressing code, eating habits and the like belong to the surface phenomena. Second, there is *an asymmetrical relationship between these two groups of features and the 'cultural identity' of communities*. This asymmetry is absent only from the reasoning of the non-pluralistic Fleming. Peter de Roover, voicing the position of the nationalistic *Vlaamse Volksbeweging* ('Flemish People's Movement'; henceforth VVB) says:

> What are culture and identity? A lot has already been written about that, but no one will deny that at least language and law belong there. Logically speaking, all ethnic groups would keep their language and judicial system in a multicultural society, as these are essential ingredients of their identity.[1]

As appears from this quotation, De Roover assigns identity-constituting values to the same cultural features for all groups of the population. By adding to this that a society with more than one language of general use and more than one judicial system cannot exist, he can conclude that the idea of a multicultural society is a mistake. The tolerant antipode of this position – the one which for the time being still seems to be able to control the debate – lacks such consistency. Ludo Abicht states in his repartee:

> Indeed, it is true that language and law are core ingredients of a culture, and that, therefore, it clashes with elementary political wisdom to give the same status to different judicial systems and languages within one small society.[2]

'Therefore' only makes sense if one wants to defend the same conclusion as

De Roover, unless – and here comes the *asymmetry* – the kinds of features that make up the core of one culture are not necessarily of the same importance for a different culture. Tolerant voices in the migrant debate systematically use the same conceptual grid. They defend the minorities' 'right to develop their own cultural identity',[3] but *to preserve the cultural identity of those minorities it is sufficient to cherish superficial phenomena, while the identity of the Flemish majority can only be maintained if the profound features remain untouched and are even adopted by the minorities.* In other words, what counts as essential to us is treated as marginal for others, and what is marginal for us suffices for them and hence becomes essential. Figure 4.1 is an attempt to capture this asymmetry.

This asymmetry makes it possible to upgrade features such as the dressing code (for instance, the *chador*), music, the noise of playing children, the kind of cars one likes to drive, to the status of important, culture-specific characteristics of Turks and Moroccans. But our own cultural identity is not defined nor affected by the way we dress, the music we listen to, the noise our children make or the kind of cars we buy. In relation to this, the increase in socio-scientific research on migrants has had at least one unpleasant side-effect (already noted by Balibar 1988). As a consequence of highly mediatized studies of 'their' culture, they are becoming more and more 'different', and more and more elements of their appearance and behaviour start counting as manifestations of this difference. Nobody seemed to mind the *chador* until the connection with Islam (read: fundamentalism) was highlighted. From that moment onwards the *chador* gained the status of the expression of an essential cultural trait, indexing religious intolerance. In the same move, the *chador* also became indexical of an assumed relation between Moslem minorities and the Belgian majority: what could be seen as a simple custom suddenly became loaded with the suggestion of deliberate resistance to the values of Belgian society. Note how this indexicality automatically triggers suggestions of intentionality. The meaning of the *chador* is seen as a *willful* expression of the rejection of Belgian values and social order by Moslems. Subsequently, the *chador* became the target of racist measures, which, in turn, effectively invested it with a symbolic value even for some migrants who were not in the habit of wearing one (thus making it in some cases effectively an object of intentional anti-Belgian symbolism). Vagueness about the migrant communities' 'cultures' has produced an unscrupulous and often totally unfounded use of the term. *Whatever the migrant may be or do, it is always getting culturalized, a process which contributes significantly to the abnormalization of the foreigner.*

	MAJORITY	MINORITIES
DEEP CULTURE	necessary	dispensable
SURFACE CULTURE	marginal	sufficient

Figure 4.1 Cultural asymmetry

In the tangled web of *ad hoc* descriptions of 'culture' we can nevertheless distinguish three general characteristics of the concept as it is handled in the migrant debate. The first one is the idea that cultures have clear-cut boundaries, and that, because of this, a cultural gap can develop between members of different cultures. Second, there is the continuous equation of 'culture' with a set of differences between 'us' and 'them' which are perceived as dangerous. A third characteristic is the occurrence of an evolutionistic and historicizing perspective on 'culture', in the sense that 'their' culture is a culture of the past when compared to ours. But whatever the labels evolutionism and historicization may suggest, the image is always *static* (i.e., each group is assumed to preserve its cultural traditions, because these are constitutive of its 'identity') and *generalized* ('the' migrant, 'the' Belgian, 'the' Moroccan, etc.).

The culture gap

In our data, culture is always associated with *borders*. Witness the frequent occurrence of makeshift terms such as 'culture gap', 'culture shock' and 'cultural barrier'. Time and again the image is created of migrants confronted with the laborious task of overcoming cultural differences between themselves and the autochthonous Belgian or Flemish population. The differences are seen as unbridgeable, because innate. Any 'cultural trait' can be used in this process: language differences, religious beliefs and experience, dress, customs, social status, and as we have seen in the case of Peter De Roover, even law. Nevertheless, there seems to be a gradation from narrower to wider cultural gaps.

Apparently, European Mediterraneans (Italians, Spaniards), and until recently also Eastern European immigrants (Poles, Hungarians), are often presented as less susceptible to the cultural shock. Because of the recently growing stream of immigrants from Eastern Europe, the attitude towards this latter group is beginning to change to their disadvantage. Still, they remain less 'different' than, for instance, Turks. There could be various reasons for this: (a) European Mediterranean groups usually come from EU countries, so that they belong administratively to the newly-created 'we', the Europeans; (b) European Mediterranean and Eastern European groups belonged to the first waves of immigrant workers; (c) a cultural familiarity is presupposed between Flemings and other European peoples, especially the 'Germanized' Eastern Europeans; (d) finally, racial considerations may enter the picture. It is striking that vague notions of cultural history, like the supposed familiarity between Poles and Flemings, are used as an argument not so much in favour of the Poles but against other groups of 'migrants'. It is assumed that 'our people' have had more contacts historically with 'related' groups such as the Poles, and much less or none at all with other foreigners. However, at the level of historical fact, these views can easily be undermined by, for instance, making a comparison between Poles and Congolese (formerly Zaïreans). In the course of the twentieth century, Belgians have had more intense contact with Congolese than with Poles. While the interaction with Poles was fairly limited, large groups of Belgians had extensive and long-standing, inter-ethnic contacts with the colonized Congolese. So, adopting the above line of reasoning, Belgians should have a better 'knowledge' of and more 'affinity' with the Congolese. After all, one of their official languages is French, and an important portion of their population has been converted to Christianity. Are these two features not generally accepted as central to Belgian 'culture'? The fact that Polish workers have contributed to the prosperity of Belgian industry by working in the coalmines and steel mills does not distinguish them from the black workers in the copper mines of Shaba, the agro-industrial companies and in the Congolese ports. What then does this affection for Polish culture or the observable aversion to Central African culture stem from? How can it be that, despite three-quarters of a century of intense, deep contacts of which the impact is still visible, Belgians still approach Congolese culture with the greatest exoticism, while unconditionally accepting our ties with groups that, certainly since World War Two, have lived in a literally separate world? The thesis that the colonial period did not succeed in generating affinity, while the Iron Curtain was not able to disrupt an existing affinity, is hard to substantiate.

Further removed from us than non-EU Europeans are the North African communities. What strikes the eye is the ease with which we classify them as 'Arab' cultures (as we already noted before), which entails gross generalizations. Additionally, their culture is almost entirely reduced to religion and its associated traditions. Other intercultural differences (and similarities) disappear out of sight, or receive attention only to the extent that they can be used as auxiliary arguments. Elements from Islam, in particular, serve as indices of important cultural difference. In this context, two phenomena are highlighted: (a) religious fundamentalism, considered to be incompatible with the pluralistic basis of Belgian society; and (b) the social position of women. Both aspects feature in a kind of prototypical Islam, constituted by images of Ayatollahs, frantic masses, and archaic, rural societies. Despite the fact that by looking at the 'central' Islam (of Egypt, Saudi Arabia, etc.) one can shed some light on the practices of the 'periphery' (as found in Moslem communities in Western Europe), it is hard to justify the gratuitous projection of associative and often strongly prejudiced images on to Moslem groups in our region. (For further support of this critique, see Maxime Rodinson 1993.)

On top of these stereotyped representations, during the past decade Islam has clearly come to be seen as an identifiable enemy of the West. This explains why claims to that effect could even be voiced publicly by Willy Claes, then Secretary-General of NATO. It also explains why, after a car bomb destroyed a federal building in Oklahoma City killing dozens of people on 20 April 1995, even the progressive Flemish newspaper De Morgen published a raving editorial, 'Ideals and children's corpses',[4] the upshot of which was that only Moslem fundamentalists could have been responsible for this act of brutality. After arguing that Jihad and Hamas had access to well-organized networks in the US, that one of the organizations with which they collaborated recently held a meeting in Oklahoma, and that people with a Middle Eastern appearance had been sighted, the argument goes as follows:

> The strongest evidence pointing in the direction of the fundamentalists is the act itself. They are the only ones with brains sick enough to plan a multiple child murder. A psychopath, even a serial killer running amuck, would not even think of using a car bomb.
>
> The sickening idea of realizing one's social or religious ideals by means of a cold-blooded and cowardly attack on a day-care centre, can only originate in the perverted mind of a religious maniac.[5]

The next day, the same paper carried a cartoon depicting a family scene with a young man asking his seated father, wearing a Palestinian headdress, 'May I have the bomb car tonight?' The author of the editorial never apologized, even after the bombers were identified as being white, middle-class, Christian Americans.

At a more principled level, questions have to be asked about the acceptability of a conceptual overlap between religion and culture. One can seriously call into doubt the reality of a 'Moslem culture' that would be so constitutive of the daily life of Moslems in Belgium as to create numerous problems with Belgian neighbours. Such a Moslem culture would, furthermore, have to be so all-encompassing and dominant that it would justify a common approach to Turks and Maghrebians (not to speak of Pakistanis, Saudis, Bosnians, Afghans and Senegalese). Authors like Balagangadhara and Erkens (1990) exhaust themselves in the construction of a cognitive-anthropological hypothesis to prove the reality of a Moslem culture. They point to the role of religion and kinship in Christian and Moslem societies. In Moslem culture, the family is supposed to function as a kind of basic heuristic device which shapes the way in which the 'other' is looked at. In Christian culture, on the other hand, there would be external familiarization through the Church. This difference would then be responsible for the failure of inter-ethnic interaction strategies between Moslems and Christians, thus leading to ghetto formation and hence to the 'migrant problem'. In the eyes of Balagangadhara and Erkens, therefore, ghetto formation is not in itself a *problem* for migrants, but rather the *solution* sought by Moslems for the frustrations of failing interaction. Needless to say, this hypothesis is based on such a generalizing view of inter-ethnic interaction that it is difficult to take its suggestions seriously. The authors take on board a transcendental view of cultural contact, in which each member of a culture (here equated with religion) is seen as an 'ideal bearer' of that culture. The result is the classical determinism according to which all forms of intercultural contact are doomed to failure. What's more, an *a posteriori* interpretation is at play here: that Moslems are a problem is accepted as a fact, just as there is the unshakeable conviction that essential cultural-religious differences are responsible for problems between Belgians and Moslem migrants. We do not hear anything about the possible influences of socio-economic factors, or power relations, and nothing is said about any possible cultural features other than religion.

Though framed in anthropological terms, this reading only reinforces the commonly held view of a situation, defined as problematic, in which Belgians (equated here with Christians, Europeans, even 'Western man') are diametrically opposed to Moslem migrants (seen as members of a homogeneous, monolithic Islamic bloc). That the Belgian 'problem' would be the migrants' 'solution' is not a solid anthropological conclusion, but a poorly disguised version of a commonplace. The assumption that culture and religion simply coincide, and that just a few identifiable principles of socialization in countries as diverse as those in the Islamic world could explain the failure of inter-ethnic contacts with members of other groups, is utterly naive. The reality of intercultural communication is much more complex than is suggested in this kind of approach (which, one suspects, substitutes 'religion' for that other dubious concept, *Volk*).

Throughout our corpus, elements from *Islam* are listed as important *cultural* differences between 'us' and North Africans or Turks (who are, for most purposes, lumped together into one category). The *chador*, for instance, gets associated with Moslem fundamentalism, and is therefore often condemned as inappropriate, disturbing, and unacceptable in our society. The supposedly religion-dependent position of Moslem women is seen as the cause of their high rate of unemployment, unequal opportunities (manifested, e.g., in a higher percentage of illiteracy), and discrimination. Many committees and working groups devote themselves to the emancipation of migrant women. These ideas about the fundamentalist inclinations of migrants and the socially inferior position of women in the migrant communities are stereotypical. They provide the undercurrent to much reporting, as in the following example from an article on a migrant youth movement in the Ghent area:

> The Rifboys do not limit membership to migrant boys, for Said Buimejene [who is in charge] is aware of the problems of migrant girls [...][6]

In this seemingly innocent excerpt, it is presupposed (a) that the social situation in which migrant girls (here a synonym for Moslem girls) find themselves is distressing, and (b) that the majority of migrants, unlike Said Buimejene, are unaware of this. Naturally, this prompts the question of how an initiative, which appears to deviate from the (implicitly attributed) social norms in migrant communities, could have any chance of success within those same communities. The Rifboys are clearly 'emancipated': they adhere to Belgian norms (equal opportunities for men and women) and therefore they are presented favourably by the newspaper. But this positive evaluation carries along an implicit negative judgement about the dominant norms within the migrant community (read: Moslem community), as it is presupposed that others in the community are insensitive to the problems of migrant girls.

In the culture gap framework, some groups may be even more remote from us than the Moslem communities originating in North Africa and Turkey. The list includes gypsies, some South East Asians, and Africans. The first group is not even sedentary, so that they cannot be moulded into the frame of some kind of 'national culture' (in terms of the dominant 'nation' concept that will be discussed below); therefore, they count as exceptionally 'strange'. They become associated with deceit and crime, a conceptual frame which surrounds them in every controversy on the tolerability of caravan camps. Asians and Africans are prototypical 'refugee' categories. Their identity is embedded in a network of stereotypes of 'development', rather than 'integration'. Outside the migrant debate, they also constitute the object of another hot topic, that of development aid.

There are also minority groups which fall almost completely outside the rhetorical patterns of the culture gap logic, despite their display of 'problematic' behavioural patterns similar to those focused on in the case of 'migrants': a concentration in certain districts or municipalities, their poor knowledge of Dutch (or French), social isolation, a concern with their own traditions and customs, etc. These are usually more affluent groups such as Jews, Japanese, Americans, Scandinavians. At one point a news reader on BRTN Radio 1 managed to refer to districts in Brussels with a high concentration of (problematic) migrants as 'the so-called *risk areas*', while in a following news item in the space of the same programme he called those districts with a high concentration of better-off foreigners 'the *better districts*'. In both cases, the districts concerned are those that are inhabited by foreign groups perceived as badly 'integrated' and as causes of irritation for the autochthonous population. The presence of one group apparently carries an intrinsic risk. Although the exact nature of this risk is seldom clear, there is a recurrent association with crime and safety problems. By contrast, the presence of the other group imbues an area with privilege or, at the very least, does not in any way harm a district's status. Thus, though this is often denied, foreigners are only problematized when their socio-economic position is weak. Only then do so-called 'objective' cultural differences enter the picture as explanations for social conflict. The *threshold of tolerance*, invoked so often to explain the trauma of confrontation with the so-called Islamic culture, appears to be far from absolute. Given the right circumstances, and especially the right actors, its effects may be cancelled.

Difference and danger

The culture gap logic views 'cultures' as bounded entities separated by differences which are dangerous. In this framework, culture defines somebody's 'identity', i.e. what makes people what they are and what makes the other different. A confrontation between cultures is seen as threatening to the identity and a near-necessary cause of conflicts. It is in the danger that justifications are found for demanding adaptation or 'integration'.

The concept of culture that occurs most frequently in the debate is known in the literature by names such as 'essentialism', 'primordialism', 'particularism' or 'differentialism': culture viewed as a complex of deep-rooted and essential features of (particular groups of) human beings. Culture is treated as something clear-cut and transparent, despite the near-total absence of more or less precise definitions ('everybody *knows* what our culture is'). Thus culture becomes the object of utterances such as 'we should protect our culture', suggesting a precise idea about what it is that should be protected. This essentialist-primordialist-particularistic-differentialist concept of culture is a key part of the folk-theoretical apparatus dominating the migrant debate.

This conceptual pattern is not only to be found in popular speech and in the media, but also in more serious anthropological work. By means of observation and description, the anthropologist often moulds the differences between him/herself and the people he or she is investigating into something that becomes their 'culture'. Similarities between two cultures tend to be experienced as natural and free of problems; hence they almost automatically become 'culture-free aspects' or even 'universal features'. The intensification of contacts between two groups increases the 'otherness' of the other group, as more differences are being discovered. At the same time, the discovery of more similarities (which necessarily goes hand in hand with noticing differences) is not deemed very relevant, as they are a source of agreement and not of conflict. This is a somewhat unpleasant side-effect of intensified socio-scientific research on 'migrants'. The inventory of real or imagined differences between 'us' and 'them' is growing continuously. This creates an impression of insuperable barriers, and minor details hardly important in daily life turn into pegs on which to hang supposedly fundamental intercultural misunderstandings. The more the other becomes different, the more he or she is construed as a source of potential conflicts. *The culturalization of foreigners, despite noble intentions, abnormalizes them more and more.* Such culturalization contributes to a confrontational attitude towards the 'migrant'. The official and commendable thesis that cultural differences are an enrichment to our society remains a dead letter as a result.

From the concept of 'culture' as a collection of intercultural differences and as a source of conflict, the image of an *homogeneous community as the norm* emerges again. According to the compelling logic of this culture concept, an 'harmonious community' is one with marginal differences, if any. The result of this *culturalization of the problem* is an integration policy which is inevitably oriented at the *de-culturalization of the 'migrant'*, the removal of any fundamental intercultural differences between autochthons and foreigners.

Evolutionism and history

Invariably the migrant debate frames culture in an *evolutionistic and historicizing perspective*. The approach is characterized by some remarkable notions of time and temporal dynamics, and has been located at the heart of anthropological practice by Johannes Fabian (1983) under the label 'the denial of coevalness'.[7]

'Other' cultures, in particular the assumed culture of Moslem migrants, are situated in the past. Aspects of their society, like their proverbial fundamentalism or the social position of women, are compared to elements from our history and seen as features of our society in the past. The prototypical 'migrants' are depicted as a traditional people, with one foot in the late Middle Ages when – as in our regions – irrational group formation, religious intolerance and patriarchy flourished. They do not care to adapt, and their culture is static and deterministic. They do not succeed in throwing off this yoke. This is the content of the rhetoric that characterizes first-generation migrants, who are seen to represent not only their own present but also (in the more benevolent versions of the story) our past. Consider the following passage from Royal Commissioner for Migrant Policies, Paula D'Hondt (1991):

> Then such a [Turkish or Moroccan] girl arrives here, from some country village, so to speak light-years removed from civilization. She ends up in the tight embrace of the family, unable to escape, unless she shows enormous strength of character. Or, unless we can create facilities to take care of her. [. . .]
>
> It is my conviction that the emancipation of the migrant will have to happen largely through the emancipation of migrant *women*. This means in the first place stamping out arranged marriages. That was also part and parcel of the liberation struggle of Belgian women. What did farmers do in the past? They married off their daughters among each other and gave them a certain amount of land as dowry. In that respect, contrary to what some people think, there is nothing new under the sun.[8]

The second generation is captured in a more hybrid kind of rhetoric. Partly belonging to the archaic home culture, they have already experienced 'modern' Belgian society through schooling and leisure. The 1989 annual report of the Provincial Integration Centre for Migrants in Ghent summarizes the problem as follows:

> Here young people are faced with different norms and values. Inevitably, this leads to serious tensions at home. In response to this, parents tighten up traditional norms and values and impose them more strictly on their children. The feeling that their children are slipping away from them is familiar to many migrant parents. Migrant youngsters find it difficult to strike a balance living with their parents in the context of a Western culture.[9]

Here, intergenerational conflict becomes a metaphor for the collision between 'modern' culture, of which youngsters have had a taste, and the norms and values of the 'home' country, which are labelled 'traditional'. In other words, the young people live (partly) in the present, while their parents are still in a past comparable to the Flemish peasant life of old. In Chapter 6 we will adduce one extensive example of how strongly this evolutionistic vision determines perspectives on policy-making.

We discern a two-pronged movement. Although the 'migrant' question is situated in the present, as a contemporary societal problem *to be approached synchronically*, the solution to the problem, the repair work, is defined as a *diachronic gesture*, aimed at bringing 'migrants' from the past into the present. They have to adapt to a society which, unlike their 'home' culture, is part of the late twentieth century. The historical metaphor is present throughout the migrant debate. Sometimes it is expressed explicitly, as in the comparison with earlier stages of our own society. Sometimes it is implied by little words and innocent phrases such as *nog steeds* ('still'), *vervallen in* ('lapse into'), *blijven* ('remain'), etc. Although this may seem like an analytical detail, the consequences are far-reaching. By placing the problematic people outside our own temporal space, they lose every chance of doing something *themselves* about their situation. Naturally, only people who have reached a higher step on the ladder of civilization (i.e. 'modernity') can possibly recognize a temporal gap or, at the very least, would know what to do about it. The denial of fundamental 'simultaneity' (or 'coevalness') amounts to a denial of power for the target group of migrant policy-making. A real dialogue between minorities and majority is ruled out. As illustrated in the words of Paula D'Hondt, the dominant rhetoric situates the only hope for emancipation in exceptional (i.e. abnormal) individual strength of character, or – and this seems more likely – in an emancipatory intervention initiated by the majority.[10]

Almost completely absent from the migrant debate is a view of *cultural dynamics*, the aspect of *change* within the culture of those who migrate. The only reference we find to change of any sort is in accounts of generation conflicts between second-generation youngsters and their parents. There is no sign of recognizing that migration in itself is a fundamental process of cultural change. Yet 'typical' members of a 'stable' culture do not migrate. Moreover, some forms of 'cultural' behaviour are automatically ruled out by moving into a new environment. Still, the first generation of migrants gets conceptualized as located in the 'typical home culture', i.e. the agrarian rural societies of the Maghreb and Turkey. Two crucial factors are overlooked in this process: (a) these 'migrants' now live in an industrialized urban environment, the 'reverse' as it were of their 'home' country; and (b) most of them have been living here for decades. One can reasonably assume that both factors must have had some influence on their behaviour and on their cultural life. Traces of the 'home' culture may still be there, but they are only partly relevant. This, however, rarely emerges as an issue in discussions, as Rob van Dijk (1991) establishes for the comparable debate in The Netherlands:

> In general reflections on the culture of the migrant, it is striking that the actual conditions of the migrants' existence are not taken into account as an influencing factor. Although the contrary is paid lip-service to, the real starting-point is that of a culture frozen at the moment of migration. The culture of the migrant as a replica of the original village culture in the home country.[11]

But if the second generation is supposed to have lost or actively rejected part of 'traditional' culture, people of Maghrebian or Turkish descent must after all be capable of some sort of adaptation. Such adaptation, however, is instantly related to an evolutionistic value scale or to opportunism. The young change because our culture is superior, or because they expect more prosperity from adaptation. Real cultural dynamics is not at issue. In this way we end up, somewhat paradoxically, with an evolutionistic perspective that is deeply static.

This non-dynamic but nevertheless evolutionistic and historicizing approach to migrant culture is probably the worst imaginable resource for explaining societal conflicts. The conflicts are essentially synchronic, but not static: they represent a *dynamic process which takes place now*, a prime object of investigations into the life of migrant communities in Belgium *here and now*. It is clear that we should inform ourselves urgently about the cultural transformation processes taking place within those communities (as in some studies of Italian immigrants conducted by Marco Martiniello; see Martiniello 1992). Probably we would then realize that they have already largely adapted culturally, and that their problems have less to do with their origins than we are inclined to assume.

An equally non-dynamic, and yet evolutionistic, view of our own culture emerges: an advanced form of human civilization, the outcome of a favourable evolution. Because the level that has been reached is perceived as advanced and therefore as 'good', nobody asks questions about its potential and desirable dynamics, i.e. the transformation processes which the autochthonous majority can or should undergo in the course of a normal confrontation with 'foreign' elements. This possibility is always blocked, rhetorically, by situating the others in a primitive past as long as they have not yet accepted the essential principles of our socio-cultural system. The validity and value of our own social principles (whether we live in accordance with them or not), our law, our language, are regarded as self-evident and unquestionable. It seems as if our social principles have reached a stage of universally valid perfection, as if our laws are inalienable elements of nature that were not created on the basis of simple (in the best case, democratic) agreements, and as if 'language' (in our case, 'Dutch') is not an abstraction but an objective and unchangeable monolithic reality which occupies so much living space that it leaves only marginal room for other languages. Here we touch upon the most fundamental problem in the discourse of 'culture and identity': *while culture is essentially a human product, the concept of identity allows some cultural features to be upgraded (or downgraded) to unchangeable nature*. When changing these features, we betray our very nature; we are, so to speak, no longer ourselves.

Nation and state

It is striking how compellingly the migrant debate moves along 'national' lines: Moroccans, Tunisians, Turks, Poles and Italians, rather than Rif-Berbers, Anatolians or Toscans. Furthermore, these national units are effortlessly associated with 'cultures'. The units in the migrant debate are thus 'national cultures' (Belgian, Turkish, Moroccan), even though these are occasionally seen as exemplary for wider cultural units (e.g. Moroccan culture as an instance of Arab or even Moslem culture). Generalizations and reductions abound, and there is little doubt that the current migrant debate offers a poor diagnosis of social problems because it continues to rely on a nineteenth-century concept of the nation state. Here we will briefly clarify this idea; further details will follow in Chapter 5.

In its Germanic form, clearly dominant in Flanders, the nation state is conceived as *a linguistically and culturally homogeneous community ('volk': 'nation', 'people'), which lives within the borders of an autonomous territory or sovereign state.* The members of such a community have their roots in a common history, and they share all important basic values. In political Flanders, VB and VU traditionally represent this ideal in its purest form.

> Annemans [a leading VB figure] writes that the concepts of nation and state must coincide, and that state borders are best defined ethnically. The concept of nation refers to notions such as community formation, culture and language. A state is only an administrative-territorial concept. Therefore, separatists are modern 'because they want to apply the principle of one state, one culture, or rather one state, one people'.[12]

The same kind of reasoning inspires the new radicalism of VU chairman Bert Anciaux when he speaks about 'nationalism, a very useful instrument in Flanders as well as in Europe'.[13] Since the early 1990s, a consensus about this has been spreading to all major parties and to a diversity of social key areas such as education. Signals in that direction are abundant: a VB proposal to introduce the 'History of the Low Countries'[14] as a new subject in education was backed by prominent members of other parties like CVP senator Herman Suykerbuyk (DS, 8 July 1992, p. 2); Flemish Minister-President Luc Van den Brande, member of the CVP, just stopping short of calling for separatism, openly declares that federalism in Belgium is not enough and that a confederate model needs to be developed – an idea recently subscribed to by SP politicians such as Norbert De Batselier; Van den Brande's idea of 'anchoring' the Flemish economy (seen as overly dependent on France in some of its strategic sectors) in Flanders, is assimilated by the Flemish Teachers' Association (*Vereniging Vlaamse Leerkrachten*) and publicized in a school-oriented pamphlet 'Anchoring for beginners' (*Verankering voor beginners*), the formulation of which benefited from the advice of such professed Flemish nationalists as Robert Senelle and Peter De Roover; a proposal by VU representative and history professor Chris Vandenbroeke to make the 'spontaneous manifestation of Flemish awareness' into a teaching goal was met with widespread sympathy, and its ultimate rejection was compensated for by reviving the old VB proposal concerning patriotic history teaching; on 9 July 1992 a VB proposal to restrict the political rights of francophones in Flanders was carried by a large majority in the Flemish Regional Council; similarly, SP member Lode de Witte, governor of the province of Flemish Brabant, openly advocated the abolishment of language facilities for francophones in the municipalities surrounding Brussel (steps towards which were recently taken in a policy guideline by the Flemish Minister of the Interior, SP – politician Leo Peeters) as well as a ban on foreign languages in signs on Flemish streets (a suggestion already implemented in road signs on Flemish territory in the Brussels area, e.g., by means of a black 'chastity' sticker on the 'o' of 'Luxembourg'). This could have been the nineteenth century, when nationalistic thinking was massively encouraged by the construction of 'national' histories, and vigorously practised in the suppression of linguistic diversity. It is strange that Flanders would have forgotten this process, as it was once its victim.

There are close links, not only between nationalistic thinking and a radical repatriation policy as a method for restoring homogeneity, but also between nationalistic thinking and the current idea of integration. Just consider the following excerpt from a report on an internal opinion poll among CVP members, bearing the telling title *Uitgesproken Vlaams* ('Distinctly Flemish'):

> The CVP turns out to be a very Flemish party. Only very few interviewees believe that 'the federalization process is going too far and makes the country ungovernable'. Quite the contrary, a large majority feels that 'social security should be federalized' and that 'Flanders should go to great lengths, all the way to independence if necessary, in order to be able to make fully autonomous decisions'.
>
> CVP executives appear to be absolutely opposed to voting rights for migrants. On the contrary, they believe that foreigners should not only adopt our language, but also our customs and habits.[15]

Except for the issue of voting rights, which has recently been declared 'debatable' again (in the context of European integration), the overall attitude has not changed since 1992. The juxtaposition expressed in the above quote between a separatist attitude (even if it concerns 'separatism if necessary'), and an uncompromising demand for integration, is not an arbitrary one. There is a clear ideological link between the two.

The nationalists' 'ideal' of the homogeneous nation state has not been fully realized anywhere, and it is demonstrably a recent historical invention (see Hobsbawm 1990). Nevertheless, the clustering of state, nation, people and culture has acquired a 'reality' status in the minds of many participants in the migrant debate. The mixing of ethnic or cultural identity with country (i.e., state) of origin, as expressed even in the core definitions of official reports, is symptomatic of this process:

> *Allochthons* are people with a different *socio-cultural origin*, going back to a different *country of origin*. [. . .]

Ethnic minorities are groups of allochthons, going back to one particular *country of origin*.[16] (italics ours)

On the basis of these definitions, it becomes possible to speak of a Turkish, a
Spanish, a Chinese and (until recently) a Soviet ethnic minority. The fact that
'countries of origin' like Turkey, Spain, China or the former Soviet Union are
mosaics of ethnic diversity in their own right is never denied when the subject is
raised explicitly, but it evaporates completely when definitions are given – definitions being crystallizations of what one believes to be 'normal' or 'typical' even
against all observable evidence. Official policies, as well as publicly expressed
opinions and attitudes, rely on figures and stereotypes which are nation- and
state-bound, despite the realization that a Basque or a Catalan may not willingly
be labelled a Spaniard, and despite the realization that many state borders outside
of Europe were drawn by means of the colonial pen and ruler (so that, e.g., the
concept 'Nigerian' may be strange, if not hostile, to many Nigerians). As a result,
important aspects of the migrants' backgrounds are lost to the debate, even
though both media and policy-makers are in theory aware of their importance.
For instance, the fact that many Moroccan migrants in Belgium are of Berber
origin, a local minority that is often perceived as problematic, did not stop Paula
D'Hondt from spending days 'negotiating' her migrant policies with the
Moroccan government. Nor did it stop *De Standaard* from reporting, as if with a
sigh of relief, that 'Morocco agrees with Belgian migrant policies'.[17] Negotiations
between states are deemed to be extremely relevant. Thus the reality of a gap in
authority between Moroccans in Belgium and the Moroccan government disappears out of sight, though it may well be just as wide as that between Moroccan
migrants and Belgians – and, in the case of second- and third-generation
migrants, even wider.

Real ethnic classifications free from national identification are intuitively
reserved for refugees. Often the explanation for their 'flight', at the same time a
frequent prerequisite for accepting the legitimacy of a request for asylum, is based
on a recognition of their position as a minority in their country of origin. When
using labels such as 'Tamils' or 'Kurds' we refer to groups of refugees, as distinct
from groups of (problematic) migrants.

The conceptual unity of nation and state exercises a serious influence on the
migrant debate. Conversely, the debate itself and its prominence in collective
consciousness may be partly responsible for a renewed and strengthened sense of
'national identity'. Thus, as an expression of national awareness, the VB slogan
Eigen volk eerst ('Our own people first') could surface only in the context of opposition to diversity.

An expression of the influence of nation-state thinking on the debate is found
in the conviction that 'naturalization' (i.e. obtaining Belgian nationality, seen by
some as an inevitable but hopefully temporary alternative to Flemish citizenship)
is not only a meaningful but also a necessary step towards 'integration'. The
concept and process of naturalization date back to long before the invention of

the nation state. But within the context of a nation-state ideology of the Germanic type, emphasizing bloodlines and ethno-cultural homogeneity, naturalization necessarily fails to take away the sources of resentment found in inter-ethnic differences. Thus Belgians of foreign descent are just as easily targets of racism and xenophobia as non-naturalized foreigners. Nor would this be typical for Belgium. Pakistanis who automatically received British citizenship on the basis of the Commonwealth Act did not escape racist reactions either; Dutch citizens born in or descending from Surinam or former Dutch Indonesia undergo similar ordeals, and even the German 'Ossies' (despite their official and much-acclaimed 'one-ness' with the 'Wessies') complain about their status as second-class citizens. Martin Luther King and Malcolm X were full-blown American citizens; Nelson Mandela and his fellow inmates at Robben Island were South African citizens.[18] Racism is not a matter of paperwork, and it would be an illusion to think that administrative measures can remove those problems of living together that have their sources in ways of thinking. Facilitating the naturalization procedure is, no doubt, a step in the right direction, if only because forms of political participation such as the right to vote *cannot* be denied to those who have been 'naturalized'. Yet, those who believe that with 'naturalization' they have discovered a magical cure, which makes it possible to avoid a debate on political rights for non-naturalized 'migrants', are in for an unpleasant surprise, as such thinking ignores the essence of the nationalistic ideal of homogeneity, as well as the presence of xenophobia and racism as real components of the migrant debate. Thus the VB migrant programme does not stop short of proposing the revision of all naturalization procedures completed since 1974. Nor does the ongoing naturalization process prevent the KCM in its final report (1993) from offering demographic projections all the way to 2010, in which *original* nationality is handled as the relevant parameter to measure the growing degree of foreignness in our society: naturalized foreigners will remain *allochthons* forever.

The same fate is hovering over all other magic formulae for restoring homogeneity as the ultimate solution to the 'migrant problem', such as the demand that they should learn 'our' language. A common language is certainly useful, but it does not remove the often cited 'cultural' differences. It is likely that 'they' will remain Moslems, that 'they' will continue living close together in poor neighbourhoods, that 'they' will still suffer a higher degree of unemployment, that 'their' children will continue having more difficulties in school and will spend a lot of time on the streets. The literature on intercultural communication teaches us that more frequent and apparently easier intercultural contact, by means of a common language, often creates new kinds of communication problems. These tend to be harder to detect and may therefore lead to a perpetuation of mutual misunderstanding. Communicative diversity persists, even when one language is used.

A nationalist ideology is a formidable obstacle in the migrant debate, because it does not tolerate fundamental forms of diversity, so that it excludes the 'integration' of non-members in advance. This problem haunts the entire debate, from VB to KCM, even though the open goals of parties such as VB and institutions such as KCM are diametrically opposed to each other. The alternative should, in principle, be relatively simple: taking as a unit of action the *state*, comprising a multitude of communities, for which parameters such as socio-economic status would no doubt have far more relevance than the concept of 'people' or 'country of origin'. But the reigning ideological atmosphere, despite audible voices of dissent, does not allow for that kind of framework.

Democracy and human rights

We have already pointed out how fond Europeans are of describing themselves as truly democratic, fostering a deep respect for others and, therefore, for human rights. Both concepts, *democracy* and *human rights*, are constantly associated with each other in the rhetoric of migrant policies. While they define the general willingness to accommodate others within a 'better' system, they also draw – as will be shown – the limits for integration and accommodation.

This conceptual phenomenon is not specifically Belgian or Flemish. Consider the following telling passage from the *Eurobarometer* of November 1989:

> The respect for human rights and fundamental liberties is part of the common heritage of the Europeans' political ideals and traditions. For 78% of the European population, democracy remains the best political system, whatever happens. And for 60% the respect for human rights is one of the important issues 'worth taking risks or sacrificing something for'.[19]

A pragmatic reading of this statement poses various problems. First, the two concepts of 'democracy' and 'human rights' get culturalized: they are presented as part of a European *cultural heritage*. Europeans are thus depicted – and here we consciously follow the transformation from culture to nature that is so typical for the dominant culture concept – as *democratic by nature*, and respect for human rights becomes an essential feature of their cultural identity. We only have to refer to Nazism and colonialism, as products of European minds, to demonstrate that this is again a highly one-sided account of history. Democracy and human rights form a *rhetorical* part of the European cultural heritage, but in reality they are mainly the names for a noble intention and a commendable objective about which it is believed that they have been approached more closely in contemporary Western Europe than ever before.

Second, if Europeans are so fundamentally democratic and full of respect for human rights, then how can we explain the rather high negative scores in the reported opinion polls? For 22 per cent of the informants, democracy is not seen as the best political system under all circumstances, and for 40 per cent the respect for human rights is not so vitally important. It appears, then, that a substantial group of Europeans seems to adhere to a fairly un-European value system. It is possible that the above claim in *Eurobarometer* would have been more accurate if it had been formulated more modestly. The statistics simply show that a considerable majority among Europeans would not want to live in a different kind of society. This involves a practical social and political positioning which may, in itself, have little to do with innate cultural values.

Third, the apparently unshakeable association between democracy and human rights is conceptually and semantically blurred, so that it forms a potential resource for rhetorical manipulation. The term 'human rights' refers to the rights of the *individual*. 'Democracy', however, is a political system and must therefore be situated at a *collective* level. Even for the most important decisions, it hardly ever requires absolute unanimity, so that the wishes of minorities and individuals have to give way, in principle, to those of the majority. Although the ideal democracy does not take majority decisions which go against the fundamental rights of any members of the society, a democracy can – and usually does – directly and quite legitimately curtail individual human rights. The rhetoric of democracy, however, creates a conceptual pattern in which a democratic system automatically and without exception safeguards the rights of the individual. Semantically, this automatic association does not make sense, but it dominates political thought to such an extent that resistance to 'democracy' as a political system is easily curbed (see Obermeier 1986). Non-democratic regimes (a category which includes, in the rhetoric of democracy, all one-party states, formerly mainly of the Marxist–Leninist type) are seen, from this perspective, as not only capable of violating human rights, but as *being* an infringement on the rights of their subjects. Mere oblivion surrounds the fact that every democratic regime also has the actual power to restrict the rights of the individual, and that every annual report by Amnesty International testifies to the occasional, if not systematic, exercise of such power. Thus 'the right to a democratic system' is seen as the human right *par excellence*. This kind of rhetoric is strongly present in statements about regimes in Eastern Europe and in the Third World. For instance, the BRTN news said of Ethiopian president Mengistu Haile Mariam that he had '*forced* Marxism upon his people'. The Ethiopian population, the story goes, subjected to a non-democratic ideology in a one-party state ruled by an enlightened despot, revolted and thus initiated a process of 'democratization'. It was, however, the same kind of process that put Mengistu in power. The earlier regime of Haile Selassie was not exactly a showcase for democracy. Still, Haile Selassie's over-throw by Mengistu in the 1970s is now described as the 'imposition of an unwanted ideology', while the structurally comparable fall of Mengistu is described as 'democratization'. The shift in reporting testifies to the contingent nature of qualifications such as 'democratic'. Yet these are invariably used as if motivated by an *absolute* yardstick. The rhetoric of democracy always carries overtones of universalism, objectivity and maximum clarity.

The common undercurrent, reconnecting political discourse to the evolutionistic culture concept, is the idea that our 'democratic' socio-political model is – of all the models tested in the course of history – the one that corresponds best to the natural, almost biological, characteristics of humanity. This conviction is strongly expressed by the new liberal-democratic theories of Fukuyama (1992), and, in

Flanders, Guy Verhofstadt (1991, 1992). In addition to the incredibly ethnocentric bias of this thesis, democracy has come to stand for literally everything that is pleasing to human beings, and for everything one is willing to defend openly. Thus the concept has lost much of its meaning, covering even very undemocratic realities (see Jacob Mey 1985). A BRTN newsreel on political problems in Uzbekistan was introduced as follows: 'The transition from Communism to *a form of* democracy turns out to be a difficult process'. Then images were shown of a group of armed men besieging the Uzbek parliament. The almost absurd relativism in the news coverage is striking: democracy is presented as multiform, to the extent that a military assault on parliament and the law of the street can count as expressions of 'a form of' democracy. When this scene was repeated on a grander scale in Moscow, with Yeltsin settling a political dispute by opening fire on the parliament building, this was not presented as undemocratic, as those inside the building were just Communists anyway. (Nor was the image itself made intertextual with earlier images of *Panzerkommunismus*, the Soviet tanks in the streets of Prague in 1968, for instance, or the Chinese tanks in Tienanmen square.) If all this can still be called 'democracy', then the term is a clear victim of semantic erosion.

Reference to neo-liberalism, in this context, is not accidental. The international recognition of new states in Eastern Europe and the former Soviet Union in the early 1990s was primarily a function of their democratic quality measured in terms of adherence to the principles of the free market economy. Any regime replacing an earlier Communist one and adopting free trade principles was easily recognized, even if – as in the case of Croatia – there was (or is) no really free press.

While, on the one hand, the concepts of 'democracy' and 'human rights' symbolize a favourable self-perception, on the other hand they carry a significant potential for defining restrictions on granting 'others' entry into our paradise. Foreigners are allowed to enter and to stay on condition that they do not threaten or even question the existing democracy or the recognized rights of the individual. A warning finger is raised at Islam, which is implicitly and explicitly depicted as a repressive, anti-democratic religion. In the following quotation, political commentator Manu Ruys touches on the consequences of the Gulf War for the Middle East, alluding, in the process, to what he perceives as properties of Moslem communities:

> The Islamic world is powerless and torn. The feverish attacks of nationalism do not stimulate a development towards a more open and free society. The feudal regimes have to deal with tendencies towards democratization, which feed on the victory of the American ally, but are they prepared to give up their fortune and power?[20]

In other words, Islamic communities are not open, they lack freedom, and they are undemocratic to the point of being feudal. The dream of a favourable development in the Islamic world is only kept alive by looking up to 'the American ally', the epitome of democracy. But probably the dream will not come true as a result of powerlessness, divisiveness, 'feverish attacks of nationalism' and the feudal rulers' longing for fortune and power. Such a lack of openness and freedom, perceived as an inherent property of Islam rather than of the states that make up the 'Islamic world', is felt to be threatening to our society, which professes the opposite values: openness, freedom, pluralism, equality, emancipation of women, etc. Therefore, we have to make sure that our Moslems adjust in time so that our advanced stage of socio-political development does not run the risk of regression.

There seems to be a paradox in maintaining an open attitude towards others, defined and justified in terms of democracy (as a group system) and human rights (at an individual level), while imposing restrictions on the same others in the name of these very concepts. Yet there is a conciliatory trope with great demagogic potential. *The rhetorical bridge between the collectivity of democracy and the individuality of human rights is the concept of 'self-determination'*. Although self-determination is essentially the right of every *individual* to take charge of his or her own destiny, it is invariably accorded as a right to the collectivity of a *people*. Pleas for democracy are easily equated with guarantees for a people's right to self-determination. However, because the logic of the nation state defines a 'people' as a linguistically, historically and culturally homogeneous population entitled to autonomy within the borders of a territory (or better still, a state of its own), the rights of the autochthonous majority are always the first to be safeguarded. The full enjoyment of democracy and human rights is, via the notion of self-determination, primarily the privilege of the 'own people'. (See Sigurd D'hondt *et al.* 1995.) Migrants have given up their own full-bodied 'peopleness' by moving out of their own territory, so that they cannot claim the right to any real form of 'self-determination'. They have surrendered themselves to us, and have to live accordingly, a demand which can be formulated in the name of democracy. The 'democratic' defence of the identity of the Fleming and of the Flemish population's right to self-determination (read: the right to a homogeneous polity, preferably a state of its own) leads, for instance, to the perception of the territoriality principle (defining a strict territorial separation between the different language communities in Belgium) as 'a democratic right' rather than as a nationalistic demand. But it also implies that anyone who wants to settle in Flanders *can be asked to conform*. When migrants (are assumed to) refuse to behave in accordance with existing norms (as we see them!), they are viewed as revolting against our democratic achievements. In other words, *it is their democratic duty to adapt, while our democratic pluralism consists in granting them the permission to stay on condition that they adapt.*

The ambiguities that follow from this are clearly reflected in the opinions about the 'migrant riots' of May 1991 in Brussels. On the one hand, the riots were interpreted as final proof of a diseased atmosphere of insecurity supposed to be created by the presence of migrants in Brussels. Neighbourhoods with a high concentration of migrants being called 'risk areas', it is immediately clear who ought to be held responsible for the riots (hence the significance of the identity of the victim, a drugs dealer of Moroccan origin, during the autumn 1997 riots). The migrants' behaviour is readily taken as proof of the *a priori* acceptance of their presence as a risk. On the other hand, systematically repressive police actions such as high-frequency identity checks, cited by migrants as reasons for their dissatisfaction, were considered the democratic right of an autochthonous population which is free to decide who can or cannot inhabit its territory. Apart from a number of intolerable 'excesses', this is seen as a principle which migrants just have to accept. Their protest is interpreted as protest against our social structures (primarily the concept of 'public order'), and it is therefore supposed to justify stepping up repressive action. No attention is paid, for instance, to the denial of voting rights, which renders migrants voiceless, leaving them with 'ventriloquism' (speaking through the voice of somebody else, usually a Belgian representative)[21] or 'illegal' protest as their only forms of political expression. This systematic neglect of the opinions, grievances and problems of what is after all an important minority, is hard to reconcile with the basic principles of a democracy which prides itself on the emancipation of other minorities (special needs groups, the elderly, women). The simple fact that migrant groups 'claim the street' – a democratic right when it comes to other interest groups that are powerful enough or that get enough backing from powerful groups – becomes an expression of resistance to the state, even though the very state system is responsible for ruling out other channels. Again, it seems that one is only entitled to enjoy democracy or human rights when belonging to the *eigen volk* ('one's own people'). Their universality is thereby seriously undermined. As Mey (1985) and Obermeier (1986) note, democracy and human rights are all too often *arguments*, rather than *contents*.

Integration

From the point of view of the 'tolerant majority', those voices in the migrant debate that accept the permanent presence of foreigners, 'integration' is the key to the solution of the 'problem', as we have already indicated in Chapter 3. On the one hand, this concept defines the *goals* of the government's *policies*, migrants ultimately becoming 'integrated' into Belgian society. On the other hand, it crystallizes the *philosophy* of Belgian migrant *politics*. In other words, 'integration' refers both to the political goodwill of the Belgians to accommodate foreigners, and to the position which migrants should eventually occupy in society.

This is only one aspect of the *semantic vagueness* which, predictably, is characteristic of the term 'integration'. Uses of the term include 'to integrate', 'to integrate oneself', 'to resist integration', 'not wanting to integrate', '(not) being integrated', etc. Lexicalizations of this kind are used in a multitude of contexts, and every time, it would seem, with exceptional rhetorical power. 'Integration' or '(not) being integrated' is what defines the limits of the migrant debate. The terminology may imply an accusation, it evaluates cultural similarities and differences, and it always points at a condition for acceptance, i.e. the *absolute* condition which migrants have to fulfil in order rightfully to enjoy the benefits of Belgian society. Despite the *absoluteness* of 'integration' *as a condition*, we never encounter a precise description of the state it is supposed to refer to. Even after a detailed reading of migrant reports, political green and white papers, research and media reports, one is left with the question: when is a migrant 'integrated'? What criteria does he or she have to meet in order to be qualified as an 'integrated migrant'? There is, however, a profusion of *ad hoc* answers, situated either on the anecdotal level (e.g., not wearing a *chador*, not slaughtering sheep at home, not making too much noise, sending the children to school punctually, and so on), or on the abstract level (e.g., adapting to the prevailing norms and values of Belgian society, really taking part in Belgian communal life, etc.). We have already pointed out earlier that attempts at providing an explicit definition, such as the one in Paula D'Hondt's first migrant report (KCM 1989), preserve an unacceptable margin of vagueness. Though the concept has undergone various kinds of rhetorical modifications since (see Blommaert 1997), the core has remained remarkably stable and vague at the same time, and a more precise definition of 'integration' (or of the state of 'being integrated') is not forthcoming.

Nevertheless, a lot can be said about the meaning of the word *integratie*, 'integration'. Some semantic-pragmatic reflections are in place here. First, *integratie* is a nominalization of the verb *integreren*, 'to integrate'. The verb is transitive, i.e. it is used with a subject which is the agent that makes a direct object, the patient, undergo an action. On the basis of grammatical expectations, a typical type of possible usage would then be 'Jan integrates Mohammed', 'Jan is integrating Mohammed', or 'Jan has integrated Mohammed'. But utterances like these never occur. A blurring of the concept appears from the use of mainly plural, more generalized, subjects and direct objects, usually in combination with an emphasis on intentionality rather than factuality, as in 'We want to integrate the migrants'. This confirms the programmatic nature of the concept of integration. 'Integrating' appears to be an action that cannot be said to be taking place during any given time span in a specified environment.

Second, the concept incorporates a clearly spatial connotation: *integreren*, 'to integrate', is to bring something *inside* from the *outside*. Although this is a departure from the etymological meaning (Latin *integer* meaning 'complete'), the spatial connotation is a salient element in the meaning of the term, further strengthened by the KCM's introduction of the notion *inpassing* ('insertion', 'fitting into'). This turns 'integration' into a boundary concept. 'Migrants' are implicitly characterized as *outsiders*, even if they have been living in the country for decades, or were born and raised there. The only valid *entry* into the society is through a process of integration, controlled (and imposed) by Belgians. Note that this also implies a rather unrealistic view of Belgian society as a well-defined, unproblematic unit with carefully defined boundaries.

Third, *integreren* is a process verb, describing a patient's transition from one state (non-integrated, 'outside') to another (integrated, 'inside'). The agent–patient structure, combined with the spatial positioning of agent (the autochthonous majority of insiders) and patient (the minority of outsiders), indicates that it is the majority of native Belgians which decides how and when the process takes place. Jan is the one who can 'integrate' Mohammed. Migrants, as outsiders, cannot even know precisely where the border lies between inside and outside. They can only see the outer wall. They do not know the criteria to be fulfilled for making the transition from being outsiders to becoming fully-fledged members of Belgian society. What is worse, as is shown above, policy texts hardly ever provide any help. While outlining an integration *policy* is unmistakably an attempt to control the process, keeping the criteria underdetermined guarantees that the majority cannot lose that control. As objects of the majority's integration policies, with that majority deciding autonomously and almost arbitrarily where the endpoint of the integration process is to be situated, 'migrants' do not have the power to integrate *themselves*. Nevertheless, the verb *integreren* is mostly used reflexively, especially in three types of context: in stipulating conditions of acceptance (*Als zij zich maar willen integreren . . .* , 'If only they were willing to integrate *themselves*'), in the assignment of duties (*Zij moeten zich integreren*, 'They have to integrate *themselves*'), or in reproaches (*Zij willen zich niet integreren*, 'They don't want to integrate *themselves*').[22] Thus the responsibility for social problems is shifted from Belgians to migrants. Whether this shift is performed thoughtlessly or deliberately, it is at least unfair to hold migrants responsible for the successful completion of a process that is entirely controlled by the Belgian majority.

The explicit pursuit of equality (or at least similarity) to be achieved by way of 'integration' thus emphasizes, paradoxically, the inequality (or the difference). By proposing an integration policy, it is assumed that the target group is not yet integrated, ignoring that they have been part of the host society for a long time and that they have undergone various forms of adaptation. At the same time, they are denied the right to co-determine the process of becoming part of the society, while being held responsible for possible failure. In this way, 'integration' spells out *the present power relationship between Belgians and migrants*, the *status quo*, rather than the process that should change or improve that relationship.

Criteria and convincing arguments are absent from the discourse on integration. It is not stated clearly why migrants would not *be* 'integrated', despite a long presence here, and despite the fact that they live a life vastly different from that of their ancestors and relatives in their 'home' country. We do not find information on when or on what basis, precisely, migrants will ever be regarded as 'integrated'. In other words, there is no clear destination for the integration process. The concept becomes even vaguer because (just like the notions of democracy and human rights) it carries connotations of *volksverbondenheid* (literally 'people-connectedness'). Paula D'Hondt articulates the consequences:

> In the Belgian context this probably means that every autochthonous cultural tradition, both Flemish and Walloon, to some extent has to develop its own *cultural* integration concept, without detracting from the value of the neighbour's traditions.[23]

Aggravated by such allowance for community-based variability in the very integration concept that serves as a cornerstone for official policies (which further underscores the culturalist bias in the integration concept), the lack of clarity carries along an enormous manipulative potential. If those in power had formulated clear-cut criteria for 'integration', part of the power would have moved to the migrants who could, under such circumstances, at a certain moment step forward and declare themselves integrated. But as long as the criteria remain vague, all power rests in the hands of the Belgian majority.

The main cause of worry is that, in spite of its vagueness, the concept of 'integration' is itself handled as a decisive criterion in dealing with migrant-related issues. Thus the naturalization procedure involves a stage at which an official needs to judge the applicant's *integratiewil* (the 'will to integrate'). Needless to say, given the hollow nature of the concept, applicants are at the officials' mercy, sometimes having to answer questions ranging from the irrelevant (such as 'What language do you speak at home?') to unprecedented levels of absurdity (as in 'Do you still eat with your hands?'). Similarly, migrant organizations are not entitled to any form of subsidy unless they can show that they are *integratiegericht* ('oriented towards integration'); by definition, a religious (read: Islamic) orientation will disqualify any organization. The way in which the integration concept was applied in naturalization procedures has been under attack for a few years, so that a standardized questionnaire was designed, parts of which remain dubiously open to manipulation, the other parts bearing little or no relation to any imaginable integration concept and resembling more closely a police inquiry. Instead of admitting the bankruptcy of the notion altogether, there are recent new attempts to escape from the problem in the form of proposals – following a Dutch example – to introduce an *inburgeringsproef* (freely translated, 'a test of having become a proper citizen'; more about this will be said below). Such a test (including a language test) is then supposed to evaluate the minimal skills and knowledge required to function properly in Belgian society. This is all too reminiscent of the *Carte d'Immatriculation* which the colonized Congolese were granted after successfully performing a number of practical and theoretical tasks to prove their having advanced on the scale of civilization (see Michael Meeuwis 1997: 59).

Because of its popular appeal, the concept of integration does not seem to need any operationalizable content to be used in defence of practical measures, including a return policy. Thus even Guy Verhofstadt, then VLD chairman, could say that 'Migrants are welcome provided that they are willing to integrate, but those who do not want to would do better to return to their countries of origin'. It did not seem to bother him that this type of policy would demand clear-cut, legally enforceable, criteria which would distinguish between an 'integrated' migrant allowed to stay and a 'not-integrated' one to be given an aeroplane ticket. Assuming that it is no longer possible for a Western democracy to pass laws which are explicitly racist or discriminatory, the criteria for inclusion would have to be applicable to all autochthonous Belgians. If Belgians were to fail them, they would also have to be treated as 'not-integrated', thus creating a rather annoying paradox. Even though many intellectuals have pointed this out, and though the common sense of many ordinary Belgians draws the same conclusions, that has not stopped further developments in the direction of 'testing for integratedness' at the policy level.

The conclusion can only be disturbing. 'Integration' as a notion, and as the core of a conceptual framework for migrant policies, is deeply *alienating* and it offers few chances for the construction of an harmonious society. How can one ever bring about 'integration' if the members of the target group are fundamentally considered as outsiders, are subjected to a process that the majority controls by imposing a general package of norms without clearly specifying them, and nevertheless remain responsible for a successful outcome? How can harmony be reached if inequality is inscribed into the process which migrants have to go through in order to become full-grown members of the society? And how can one achieve harmony if migrants are not granted any power to control their own destiny or to speak out legitimately on what should be their relationship with other Belgians? By the compelling logic of the public rhetoric, migrants are doomed to remain 'non-integrated', simply because they will always remain 'different' along one parameter or another. They are caught up in a neverending process that is completely taken out of their hands. Of course, some will escape from this fate: a small 'integrated' (elite) group of migrants who have either booked commercial successes or who have been given token functions. The existence of such an elite can then be used (and has indeed been used) rhetorically as proof that there is no real discrimination but only widespread 'unwillingness' to integrate.

During the last few years, the 'integration' concept has been criticised from various corners, often along the lines of the foregoing analysis which caused quite a shock when it was first published (as Blommaert and Verschueren 1992a). Independently, it was pointed out by sociologist Albert Martens (1993) that the concept was an insult to people's intelligence, a dogma formulated when the KCM started its work in 1989 and to be found completely unaltered four years later in the KCM's final report, as if immune to any real debate, whether conducted by autochthons or allochthons – the latter category not having been heard at all. (See also Andrea Réa 1993.) Among the migrant population, the imposition of the concept is no longer accepted, if it ever was. As a result, the term has adopted a lower profile. But the underlying world of ideas is as alive as ever. Hence the growing popularity of new terms such as *inburgering*, a word which normally means 'settling down' or 'having begun to feel at home', but which in the context of the migrant debate relies heavily on its central root, *burger* ('citizen'), thus assuming a meaning that can be paraphrased as 'achieving the status of a true citizen'. Its acceptance was first restricted to VLD circles, but it spread rapidly after its popularity in The Netherlands penetrated the Flemish media. In the Belgian context, however, it has the same loading as 'integration', with the same pitfalls. The only new element it helped to introduce into the debate is the idea of an *inburgeringsproef*, a test to find out who has and who has not become a proper citizen. In that capacity, the newly dressed-up concept has produced what may be the most alarming development of the last few years. The idea of testing the worthiness of Belgian citizenship could be almost literally copied in the latest version of the extreme right VB migrant plan (Dewinter 1996), which calls for a *burgerschapsproef* ('citizenship test') to be used for deciding who is sufficiently assimilated to be allowed to stay in Belgium, a process also to be applied to all those who were naturalized since 1974. Though the immediate policy goals are very different, the underlying conceptual unity is more frightening than ever. We have passed the stage where the 'tolerant majority', to counteract VB popularity, visibly incorporated VB rhetoric and policy positions. In spite of all the protests and warnings against this desperate strategy, we have now come full circle, with the tolerant majority generating concepts and ideas that are sufficiently acceptable for the extreme right to be incorporated, with some inevitable modifications, into their own programme.

5

HOMOGENEISM

The analyses in the foregoing two chapters demonstrate that the 'migrant debate' rests on *the idea that the ideal society should be as uniform or homogeneous as possible*. Homogeneity is not only seen as desirable, but also as the *norm*, i.e. as the most *normal* manifestation of a human society. Most of the time this view remains implicit, but it is nevertheless dominantly and systematically present in the images Belgians have of themselves and of others, in definitions of 'the migrant problem', in the proposals for a solution and in the most important components of the conceptual apparatus to cope with all of this. We will provide the overall ideological picture with the label *homogeneism*.

In this chapter we will first summarize what we have already discovered in relation to homogeneism in the Belgian migrant debate. Then more substance will be added by expanding on attitudes towards diversity. A separate section will be devoted to the role of language amongst other parameters of both diversity and homogeneity, extending the discussion briefly to a wider European context. Returning to the specifics of homogeneism in Belgium, symptoms of the ideology's hegemony will pass the review. Finally, the establishment's reaction to criticism will be described.

Homogeneism in the migrant debate: a summary

The picture that emerges from the systematic pragmatic study of the 'migrant debate' in Belgium, and especially in Flanders, is one in which the non-acceptance of fundamental forms of diversity predominates, even among the majority which tends to view itself as the embodiment of openness and tolerance. An homogeneous society, implicitly defined in terms of the vague and largely imaginary feature cluster of history, descent, ethnicity, religion, language and territory, is seen as the norm and as a condition for social harmony, yielding 'natural groups' with a self-evident right to self-determination. In this context, homogeneism abnormalizes the presence of foreigners while normalizing the autochthonous population's negative reactions to their presence, and leads to logical solutions to 'the migrant problem' formulated in terms of a discriminatory and repressive notion of integration aimed at a (partial or complete) rehomogenization of society. Let us briefly recapitulate the different dimensions of this picture.

In spite of some faint attempts at brushing up the rhetorical surface, migrants are consistently subjected to a process of *abnormalization* in a variety of ways. First of all, an essentialist and evolutionistic view of culture dominates the debate. Not only are migrants (a category which is rather systematically reserved for North African and Turkish Moslem immigrants, though it is subject to various processes of semantic reduction and associative expansion) supposed to be years behind in matters of civilization, an account of culture and lifestyles in their mostly rural areas of origin is generally treated as a primordial source of understanding their present predicaments. Migrant men are seen as the conservative forces perpetuating the backwardness of which mostly migrant women are regarded as the victims in need of protection by the progressive and emancipatory character of our advanced modern society. Islam is consistently associated with fundamentalism and fanaticism. Meanwhile, serious ethnographic studies of present-day urban lifestyles among migrants and the ways in which they practise their religion are not undertaken on a wide enough scale to counteract these stereotypes – nor are the responsible authorities convinced that such studies are needed.

A second aspect of abnormalization bears on the process of migration itself. 'Migrant policies' are shifting more and more towards 'migration policies'. Migration towards Western Europe is presented as dramatic and exceptional, to such an extent that a political commentator such as Manu Ruys can say without blushing that 'The European is in danger of becoming an extinct race'. A similar concern was observable during a prestigious conference organized in late 1992 by the *Koning Boudewijnstichting* (King Baudouin Foundation – henceforth KBS) on the subject of migration towards Western Europe. The only question seemed to be: How can we stop the flow? Present migration patterns were presented as the most fundamental challenge we have to face today, comparable to the rebuilding of Europe after World War Two. What is completely lost from sight is, for instance, that Europe has never known more massive migration than precisely the period following World War Two.[1] Yet the need for a dramatization of the present situation – sometimes naively called 'unique in history' – seems to be deeply felt. It is for that reason that 'the migrant problem' is invariably associated with the recent flow of political and economic refugees (and hence with the problem of 'illegal aliens'), incorrectly turning the refugee problem into a European issue (while 90 per cent of the world's refugees are wandering about Africa and Asia; see Dumont 1995 for facts and figures). In this context, it was interpreted as part of the KCM mandate to make proposals for 'humane' curbs on migration. Such curbs are systematically seen as a prerequisite for the success of 'integration'.

Not only is present-day migration dramatized, it is also presented as an aberrant form of human behaviour. Since the unquestioned peacefulness of an homogeneous society is seen as the norm, the very presence of foreigners, as such, is a problematic deviation from a natural state of affairs. Diversity breaks the norm. Therefore migration has to be halted as much as possible. In this context, the Belgian migrant debate has taken an interesting turn towards the problem of development. Development is seen as a means to keep potential migrants at home, and therefore as a way of avoiding an escalation of 'our problem'. In other words, as a form of pre-emptive action. In this context it is difficult to resist the temptation to point out that the link with development is also foregrounded in the rhetoric of the Flemish extreme right (VB). Given the premisses that the presence of foreigners is problematic and that migration waves can be prevented by development, the most efficient remedy for all ills so far has been offered in the VB proposal to send migrants home as development workers.

The observation that different forms of sometimes subtle, sometimes extreme diversity, always susceptible to metamorphoses under the influence of weaker or stronger migration flows and the related processes of cultural convergence and divergence, determine the character of every society, in spite of attempts at homogenization in the construction of nation states, is no match for the ideology of homogeneism. Therefore all well-intentioned documents issued by the tolerant majority start with the observation that 'No one can deny that the presence of foreigners in our country causes problems'. Note that it is not deemed necessary to make the fully explicit claim that 'The presence of foreigners in our country causes problems'. This claim is simply presupposed as common knowledge about which it is said that no one can disagree. Little does one realize that the statement is true only at the most trivial level, the level at which life itself is a problem. And little does one realize that such a position vis-à-vis diversity, enshrined in implicit meaning and thus protected against disagreement, inevitably represents a confrontational stance, a recipe for conflict.

A direct corollary to the abnormalization of the foreigner is the *normalization* of autochthonous reactions. If homogeneity is the norm, then a reaction of reservation or even exclusion in relation to foreigners is perfectly normal. Though loudly sounding the attack, official rhetoric restricts itself to a fight against unacceptable 'outgrowths' of these 'normal' reactions which, to make things worse, are usually glossed over or explained away on the basis of socio-economic insecurity or manipulation at the hands of rightist movements. The widespread occurrence of forms of real and everyday racism is either ignored or denied. The substitution of the term 'racism' by 'xenophobia' whenever the reaction of ordinary people, in contrast to the representatives of suspect political movements, are at stake, is symptomatic for this process.

Anti-racist mass demonstrations notwithstanding, racism is played down to the point of disappearance. Sometimes, the most extreme examples even come from the least suspect tolerant corners. Thus a major figure in the Flemish green party, AGALEV, says:

'Racism and nationalism are not characteristic of specific persons, groups, parties, nations or peoples. They are the business of the human race. They are always and everywhere latently present. No one can resist them'.[2]

In an exceedingly charitable article aimed at demonstrating the degree of racial comparability between people, the vanishing point of racism is reached by defining it in such general terms that it becomes a potential characteristic of every individual; an actualization of the potential is in this case not attributed to economic poverty but to psychological compensation mechanisms.

The question that arises is the following: how can racism be fought if the premises of a racist discourse are accepted, in particular the idea that homogeneity and resistance against heterogeneity are normal? Does it not follow logically from the structure of the discourse itself that a party such as the VB represents an eminently democratic movement which, on a political level, simply takes into account normal and legitimate feelings? Laws against racism cannot be adequately implemented unless one changes patterns of thinking and talking about racism; otherwise their only function can be to soothe the public conscience. The basic problem, then, seems to be that the tolerant majority only *imagines* its own tolerance.[3]

Central to the rhetoric of tolerance is the concept of integration. If homogeneity is the norm, the natural solution to problems caused by diversity is a policy of rehomogenization. While the extreme right proposes to rehomogenize society by removing all foreign elements, the tolerant majority envisages a rehomogenization based on 'integration' or the removal of disturbing differences. This interpretation of integration is of course violently objected to by its adherents who, at the explicit level, claim full respect for diversity and profess a belief in absolute equality (as in the title of the final KCM report, *Tekenen voor gelijkwaardigheid*, 'Opting for equality').

The official, and widely accepted, Belgian concept of integration hinges, as explained at length in Chapter 3, on a threefold distinction between levels of social action and principles governing social behaviour: (a) 'values and principles protected by the concept of "public order"'; (b) 'guiding social principles about which an autochthonous majority seems to agree implicitly'; and (c) 'the level of the many cultural expressions which threaten neither the public order nor the social principles of the host country'. While (a) relates to the law, (b) bears on a vague set of attitudes related to aspects of modernity, women's emancipation, a pluralist respect for all world views, and language. Migrants have to obey the law and adapt to our guiding social principles, 'as we understand them'. The only locus of tolerated difference is (c), the domain of art and music, folk dance, cuisine, home language (as long it does not penetrate public life), and religion (as long as it is not 'fundamentalist'). For the tolerant majority, which was said to believe in the salutary nature of homogeneity, this represents an extremely open attitude. However, this integration concept is discriminatory and repressive in various ways.

First, it discriminates because of its asymmetrical use of the notion of 'identity' (see p. 93). Not only are migrants requested to live according to the local law (a quite acceptable demand as long as one does not see the law as a natural fact but as an adaptable construct), but they have to adapt to the values and socio-cultural accomplishments of our society. This demand is motivated on the basis of the idea that these values and accomplishments are so fundamental to our identity that we cannot accept their being questioned by people in our midst who would not share them. It is assumed that, by accepting deviations from our 'guiding social principles', however vaguely defined, we would become the victims of our own tolerance: the foundations of our society would be at risk. This is why the 'threat' to society, as a motivation for the demand, is indirectly introduced in the formulation of (c). On the other hand, the tolerant discourse emphasizes that we do by no means want to curtail the others' identity. But in that claim, 'identity' is restricted to those domains of social action which, in the definition of our own identity, we would accord a marginal role at best. This asymmetric use of identity deculturalizes the migrant to the point of assimilation (though this will not prevent the majority from culturalizing any social problems that may involve migrants).[4]

The formulated package of demands is also discriminatory in the sense that only one (albeit poorly defined) population group, consisting mainly of Moslems from North Africa and Turkey, is subject to it. In spite of explicit claims to the contrary, not everyone is equal for the integration concept. Moslems are not regarded as fully acceptable members of Belgian society unless they accept the principle of equality between men and women, as we understand it; but no one asks the question as to how many Belgians would have to be denied full member-ship of the society on the same count. Similarly, Islamic schools are discouraged because they are seen as a danger to the integration process; but no one asks any questions about the well-developed Jewish schooling system (or, *a fortiori*, about the vast network of Catholic schools). It is already questionable whether it is at all justified to isolate a category of 'migrants' from the population as an object of special policies. Group formation is indeed a universal phenomenon, but atti-tudes and measures based on a belief in the 'naturalness' of certain groups (which can and should therefore be treated differently) lead inevitably to discrimination.

Under the (often sincere) guise of humanitarian concern for their fate, the autochthonous majority imposes integration on one (partly imaginary) minority group. This does not only happen without serious democratic involvement of this minority itself (the existence of which, for the sake of argumentation, we will not call into doubt), but the package of demands remains extremely vague. What happens, then, is the following: we impose demands unilaterally; we refrain from specifying the demands clearly enough so that migrants would be able to declare themselves 'integrated' at a certain moment; yet we hold them responsible for the integration process ('They must integrate themselves'). If it were the intention to develop a concept that would enable us to exert everlasting power over a segment of the population, we could not dream of a better one. That is why the dominant integration concept is not only discriminatory but even repressive, a judgement which does not necessarily bear on intentions, but simply on the essence of the concept.

That the integration concept functions as an instrument of power becomes clear over and over again. A recent example is to be found in regulations designed for so-called 'self-organizations' in migrant communities. In order to be acceptable to the majority as a migrant self-organization (a Kafkaesque contrivance in itself), candidate organizations have to demonstrate that they are integration-oriented – of course, in the sense in which this is understood by the tolerant majority. Recognition can be revoked if an organization undertakes any form of action (say, the establishment of an Islamic school) of which the authorities disapprove.

Diversity as pollution

The implicit nature of homogeneous thinking creates serious paradoxes. Nobody is so naive as to believe that perfectly homogeneous societies would exist in reality. Even VB spokespersons will not contradict Mark Deweerdt when he says that migration is 'of all times and places' (DS, 21–2 March 1992, p. 9) or Mia Doornaert when she states that '"Pure" cultures do not exist' (DS, 13 January 1992, p. 5).[5] Everybody knows that diversity in society is the rule rather than the exception and that mixtures of all kinds have determined the course of history. Sometimes the longing for homogeneity is talked about somewhat reproachfully and ironically:

> [. . .] we want a homogeneous society, with the people who have always lived here, gathered cosily around our church towers and in our neighbourhoods. (From a text by five Flemish Jesuits)[6]

Opinions like these usually feature in explicit pleas for openness and tolerance, or they are seen as an expression of realism and common sense. But in the same breath, a politics of integration is defended, aimed at erasing differences which are *too* big. We cite the same Mark Deweerdt, in the same article:

> Fitting in is the only solution. Migrants can be expected to learn the language of the host country, and to respect its culture and laws.[7]

Similarly, Mia Doornaert continues in her article:

> That is why contact with 'others' is not more of a threat to our culture, than it would be an assault on the 'identity' or 'culture' of immigrants to expect them to accept the rights and duties of a democratic society, i.e. to 'integrate' themselves into it.
>
> There is no doubt that adaptation can be difficult for people coming from a very different model of society. But sympathy for this does not

entail that our societies should abandon their democratic achievements.[8]

Finally, the same five Flemish Jesuits go on to say:

> What remains of social 'strangeness' or barriers, has to be overcome
> gradually in a process of fitting in.[9]

A fundamental acceptance of far-ranging and possibly lasting diversity remains
out of sight. The existing diversity is problematized; it is seen as having disrupted
a balance in need of being restored. Of particular interest is the article by Mia
Doornaert, which presents a more subtle view than is commonly found in the
media. She opposes what she calls 'progressive' paternalism, an attitude which
will invoke 'culture' in defence of any custom and as an argument for the claim
that there are 'Western values' such as tolerance and pluralism which immigrants
'cannot or don't have to understand'. Quite correctly she regards this position as
humiliating and rather useless for migrants. But she does not escape from this
other form of paternalism, assigning to migrants the task of 'integrating themselves' in relation to certain higher values, on the assumption that they have not
yet acquired them in one way or another, and that the values in question are
deeply entrenched in the Belgian social model. The questions this raises should
be clear from our analysis of the discourse on democracy and human rights.
Briefly, Doornaert fails to get away from the more general paradoxes which
underlie the concept of integration.

A fundamentally homogeneous image of Flemish society is preserved in the
debate at all costs. The persistence of this idea, in the face of abundant counter-
evidence, leads to interesting rhetorical twists. Thus the Flemish weekly *Knack*
devoted its 25th anniversary issue to *De onbekende Vlaming* ('The unknown
Fleming'). Having been hard-pressed to come forward with a conclusive definition of Flemish identity, intellectuals (even those with nationalistic tendencies)
now admit that it can hardly be given. In his contribution to *De onbekende
Vlaming*, then, Sus van Elzen observes:

> Who are the Flemings, and where do they come from? In fact they lack so
> many specific properties that they have become very specific as a result.[10]

Van Elzen knows that Flanders does not have natural borders, that it does not
have a demarcated culture of its own, nor a distinct history, and not even its own
exclusive language. Still he believes in 'identity', even if it is to be found in the
consistent absence of the expected properties. What we witness here is the
perversion of an enlightened spirit who knows all the arguments against the
concept of 'identity', but still cannot live without it.

It is in the maintenance of a fundamentally homogeneous image of society
– even if homogeneity is to be found in the systematic absence of common

properties – that the structural and conceptual affinity between the migrant debate and nationalist discourse manifests itself most clearly. But there is one small difference between the two. In the migrant debate, strictly homogeneistic claims about a 'multicultural mistake' and calls for a corresponding course of action easily give rise to accusations of racism and intolerance. On the other hand, defending the creation or maintenance of a closed, homogeneous territory, on nationalistic grounds, is seen by many as completely respectable. The call for abolishing or seriously limiting language facilities for francophones on Flemish territory – a very explicit expression of homogeneism – is widespread. We already mentioned governor Lode De Witte who does not want to see foreign languages in the streets of his province, Flemish Brabant. This wish, and the measures needed to implement it, are fully acceptable to many moderate Flemings, from dignitaries to ordinary people. The underlying pattern is the same as the one that problematizes the lasting presence of migrants. But its voicing is much more open and radical. In relation to nationalistic demands, quality newspapers and mainstream politicians go as far as VB or VVB pamphlets. Thus Robert Senelle, emeritus law professor of the University of Ghent, repeatedly advocated the abolishment of the existing language facilities, which is approvingly reported in the papers:

A brilliant Prof. Senelle invoked 'serious mitigating circumstances for the Belgian politicians', because they are tackling an enormous assignment: the replacement of a Napoleonic state structure with a federal one. He emphasized the importance of defining the language areas, and said that the introduction of [language] facilities into the constitution was a big mistake, because it violates *monolingualism*. 'A good federal structure has to be based on *fixed borders*', according to Prof. Senelle.[11] (italics ours)

Also:

Whoever settles in a certain language area must accept the consequences. Someone who does not want to adapt would do better to move out.[12]

After having established the deplorable fact that the language facilities 'have meanwhile become anchored into the constitution', and convinced that the Flemish negotiating position is unshakeable in the 'community-to-community' talks, Lou De Clerck, then chief editor of DS, observed:

Will this [strong negotiating position] be used, not only to enforce direct elections of the Flemish parliament, but also to purify the territoriality concept? If Flanders wants to become *a linguistically homogeneous country*, then now is the moment to realize the old demand 'In Flanders, Flemish'. The language border must become a true state border. At the moment it is still *polluted* by too many exceptions.[13] (italics ours)

Speaking French in Flanders, outside the private sphere, is here associated with a form of environmental pollution. Brussels used to be called an 'oil slick' in the jargon of the Flemish movement, also in moderate circles. This image still speaks to the imagination, while new threatening metaphors are entering the stage, as in 'Shadow of 120,000 francophones from the [Brussels] periphery clouds dialogue between communities'.[14] By accepting measures which affect the 'purity' of Flanders in a federal structure, one would pass a 'threshold of tolerance', as is suggested in an anonymous front-page editorial comment on the occasion of the Day of the Flemish Community:

> Concessions have been made – ranging from the constitutional reforms of 1970 to those 'petrifying' the facilities in 1988 – which have exceeded *the limits of what is acceptable.*
>
> In order to realize its autonomy, Flanders has so far opted for the federal model. Even today Flanders can support a federalist solution to the Belgian conflict of nationalities, provided it is *an honest and pure federalism.* [. . .]
>
> This means that Wallonia accepts that the language border is a state border, that the borders of the Flemish territory cannot be changed, and that francophones living in Flanders cannot get any additional facilities.[15] (italics ours)

The facilities in question are measures allowing public institutions to take into account an actual form of diversity. They are, in every sense, legally regulated and solidified expressions of tolerance and openness. Whoever wants to abolish or restrict them, does not recognize the rightful existence of diversity, is guilty of extreme homogeneism, and is therefore *intolerant* and *anti-pluralistic.* Yet, predictably, this attitude is defended in the name of 'democracy':

> Francophony is a Belgian phenomenon that could emerge because Dutch was not an official language in this state for a long time. In that sense, francophony is profoundly undemocratic.[16]

This common view is legitimated and fuelled professionally by respectable sociolinguists[17]

> The historical heritage of the language strife still greatly influences the linguistic attitude of the Flemings. The Flemings have had to fight for their language [. . .]. It is hence understandable that the Flemings are, as yet, not very tolerant in their linguistic attitude. Now that they have successfully acquired the right to their own language, they are firmly determined to defend it against any possible aggressor.
>
> (Ludo Beheydt 1995: 56)

Essentially intolerant and anti-pluralistic measures are thus defended on 'democratic' grounds. The fact that Flemish identity was once threatened by the undemocratic rule of a governing elite speaking a different language is considered a sufficient reason for demanding absolute homogeneity within present-day Flanders. No matter how loudly tolerance and openness are being professed, this attitude will only allow *temporary measures* to accommodate 'otherness' in ethnic minorities, and such measures will be aimed at rendering themselves obsolete by erasing the differences. *Lasting diversity, seen as a form of pollution within homogeneistic thought, will not be tolerated.*

Denials that the demand for migrants' 'fitting in' must be situated in the same conceptual framework as the set of nationalist goals are naive at best. Despite loud assertions to the contrary, the heart of the matter is that migrants must become Flemish in order legitimately to claim a place in the social and geographical space occupied by an homogeneous Flemish people. A lasting treatment based on differences is out of the question. They will not be given the necessary leeway to determine their own destination. The link between nationalism and an anti-multicultural attitude is surfacing more and more explicitly. Consider what Aloïs Gerlo, formerly a rector of the (Flemish) Free University of Brussels, has to say:

> The whole business of multiculturalism conflicts with the essence, the aims, and the achievements of the Flemish Movement. It is in fact directed against that movement and it is a desperate attempt at preventing it from reaching its oldest and most important goal – autonomy for Flanders. Hence the unconditional support from all francophones and advocates of Belgian unity.
>
> Apparently, many Flemish-minded politicians are not aware that their position is one big *contradiction*. One cannot advocate the preservation of one's own identity, defend the territoriality principle, speak out against additional facilities for francophones in Flemish Brabant, and *at the same time* promote a multicultural society which permits the increasing number of immigrants to maintain their own cultural identity within Flemish territory. The multicultural model of society excludes any real kind of 'fitting in'. How can one deny francophones what is readily granted to Turks and Maghrebians?[18]

This is an opinion according to which, in order to be consistent, all existing 'facilities' for the Belgian Jewish community should be questioned. A prominent defender of the rights of minorities such as Ludo Abicht apparently does not realize what treacherous waters he is swimming in when trying to reconcile his defence of a multicultural society with his Flemish nationalism:

> Now that we have finally got to the point of reaching that autonomy, which is an unquestioned fact of life for other countries and peoples, it

does not make sense to commit the Belgian mistake all over again from the vantage point of a misunderstood internationalism and cultural relativism.[19]

The 'Belgian mistake' referred to is the attempt to allow two languages and two cultural communities to live together in one state structure. Political autonomy for every linguistic and cultural community is presupposed here as the norm, with the implication of full hegemony over all deviant groups within their own territory (although in Abicht's benevolent version of homogeneism these groups are tolerated). Assaults on this basic idea are rejected as 'misunderstood internationalism and cultural relativism'. Political autonomy is 'an unquestioned fact of life for other countries and peoples'. The question is, of course, what other countries and peoples? In the contemporary world we find thousands of communities which could (and often do) identify themselves as cultures. They live together in barely two hundred states, even after the disintegration of the Soviet Union. Abicht knows this. Yet he fails to deduce from these basic mathematics that what he calls the 'Belgian mistake' is in fact the norm, and not the exception, for states worldwide.

Language and other distinctive features

The matter-of-factness with which the homogeneistic norm is upheld is symptomatic of its being anchored in a widespread European nationalist ideology. For understandable historical reasons, language has become the most important characteristic of group identity in Flanders. Now that Dutch has reached a truly advanced stage of political and institutional security in Belgium (although some would still dispute this), the struggle has not been suspended. Only the battlefield has been widened to the European context. The argumentation remains the same: we must fight for our language in order to maintain our identity in Europe, just like in Belgium before. It is not difficult to compile an anthology of statements by prominent Flemings, pointing in precisely that direction. For example:

If language is the main characteristic of our cultural identity, then all 21 million of us [speakers of Dutch] must stand united in Europe.[20]

Finally the time has come to give the highest priority, clearly and unambiguously, to an active language policy, to make sure that the neerlandophony [sic], which has shaped and moulded us all, keeps its own voice. That, precisely, will be our own contribution to Europe's multifarious culture.[21]

Flemings who would not demand of foreigners that they learn Dutch are thought of as traitors:

Intelligent people from the worlds of business, politics and culture must realize that it does not make them narrow-minded provincialists when trying to safeguard the identity of their region. The main threat to Flemish Brabant is not posed by Eurocrats, but rather by a group of Flemings (and Flemish Brabantians) who still think of their own language and culture, and therefore also of themselves, as insignificant and unimportant. According to them one cannot ask a foreigner to learn Dutch – while a Fleming abroad should use the language of the host country, preferably even immediately.[22]

Flemings are not only called upon to confront overwhelming European pressure, but also to enter European alliances: 'Dutch should form a front with, not against France'[23] in order to avert the danger of a monolithically anglophone Europe. What is more, the Flemish Movement should lead the way:

> In my opinion, the Flemish Movement can play a role here. Because it is in the best position to understand the essential difference between Europe and the USA, i.e. the linguistic diversity of Europe.
>
> Of course there are pressure groups trying to ascribe the difficulties between Walloons and Flemings to [an enumeration of political and socio-economic explanations]. But any serious person knows that the difficulties stem from the fact that Flemings and Walloons speak a different language. [. . .]
>
> The Flemish Movement is one of the few in Europe with the insight, the experience, and the passion to save Europe from an ill-fated adventure, which can, after wasting a lot of energy, only lead to chaos and conflict.
>
> Europe must assume a structure in which the linguistic groups are the building blocks.[24]

Though emphases may shift and pockets of dissent vie for public attention, within mainstream Flemish society there is little disagreement about the global pattern of argumentation. Language is seen as the essence of identity: as one of the age-old slogans of the Flemish movement has it, 'The language is the entire people'.[25] That identity must be safeguarded at all cost, which is only possible in an homogeneous linguistic region, so that the logical model for Europe is the Belgian model, with linguistic borders that coincide as strictly as possible with self-governing units. Anyone who does not agree with this is accused of historical naiveté, of having failed to learn the lessons of history.

Because linguistic homogeneity is considered so important, a heavy emphasis is placed on a *proper use* of Dutch, and on the *linguistic unity* between The Netherlands and Flanders. In connection with the proper use of language, Manu Ruys expresses his despair over 'political indifference':

> When will they [the politicians] make sure that we no longer have to be ashamed of the language of official, political Flanders?[26]

while Robert Senelle reports with great relief on an award-winning essay, 'Dutch: the official language of the Flemings(?)',[27] written by students at a high school in Ostend:

> The young Ostend language lovers are symbolic of a rising generation of Flemish youngsters for whom standard Dutch is a must [sic]. Finally we are on the right track.[28]

With regard to linguistic unity, ideological homogeneism cannot accept the factual variability of the Dutch language, except where the folkloristic level of dialects is concerned. When the socio-linguist Kas Deprez, somewhat provocatively, demands for Flanders the right to speak 'deliberately impure Dutch',[29] in the eyes of many people he is committing high treason, though all he means is that the Flemish standard language neither is nor has to be identical to the standard Dutch spoken in The Netherlands. The orthodox position, inspired by the fear that the widening European arena may smother so-called 'small language', is that there is room for only one Dutch language of culture.[30] That variability is an inevitable property of languages clearly escapes the attention. The ideology is immune to facts such as the ones mentioned by Deprez: the many varieties of English do not diminish the prestige of that language; the variants of modern Greek do not bother anybody at the EU level; the typical character of Swiss, Austrian or Bavarian German will not slow down the spread of 'German' in all its shapes and sounds throughout Central Europe. The 'ideal' of unity is no doubt more unworldly than the 'historical naiveté' it is supposed to remedy. That the reality of diversity is as manageable, and certainly as enjoyable, as the 'ideal', or, in Deprez's words, that it is 'good to undergo French influence, also in one's language', falls outside the scope of the homogeneistic potential for understanding.

What we have said so far about the Flemish language concept has unmistakable implications for migrant policies. The following newspaper headline and subtitle represent the prevailing consensus fairly accurately, and have become a leitmotif in the migrant debate:

> [Headline:] Language education is lever for integration migrants
>
> [Subtitle:] Job opportunities suffer from communication problems[31]

No doubt, communication problems diminish the chance of being hired. Similarly, a common language simplifies communication. But if a language is thought of as an homogeneous instrument, used by all speakers in similar or perfectly comparable ways, so that a common language *ensures* successful communication, then one suffers from delusions. The anthropological–linguistic literature on intercultural communication abounds with examples demonstrating that an homogeneistic lack of attention and appreciation for variation is the pre-eminent recipe for communication breakdowns. Vocabulary and grammar may be nearly identical, but the smallest differences in prosodic contextualization or information structuring may seriously impair a mutually well-intentioned attempt at interacting (see, e.g., Gumperz and Roberts 1991). Moreover, such differences sometimes create new variants of a language as soon as it is adopted by a new population group.

Furthermore, detailed analyses of inter-ethnic contacts, such as those by Ben Rampton (1995) on adolescents in Britain, demonstrate that acquiring the language of the host society does not eliminate racial-ethnic or socio-economic symbolic boundaries. On the contrary, Rampton shows how standard English becomes an element in a symbolic and stylistic boundary-making repertoire, alongside ethnic community languages and vernacular varieties of English. These linguistic elements can be used for drawing racial-ethnic and socio-economic boundaries, as well as for crossing them in an attempt to form or reinforce alliances with peers. Adoption of the language (e.g. standard English) does not automatically entail adoption of the lifestyle, world view, values or culture of its speakers. Standard English (and, *mutatis mutandis*, standard Dutch) may become loaded with new values, perceptions, associations and symbolic meaning, in ways that delude simple beliefs in 'assimilation/integration through language learning'.

It is the ideology of homogeneous languages, supposed to entail a shared world view and shared cultural meanings among their speakers, which accounts for quite a few cases of miscommunication in intercultural situations. Chris Bulcaen and Jan Blommaert (1997: 95–109) report cases of conversations between Flemish (Dutch-speaking) welfare workers and second-generation Turkish migrant young women with a *prima facie* good command of Dutch. Close analyses of the conversations, however, reveal that the perceived language proficiency of the Turkish women hides a number of less visible problems related to narrative structuring of the women's accounts, miscomprehension of idiomatic expressions, failure to pick up contextualization cues, and so on. In other words, the language proficiency is asymmetrically distributed between the welfare worker and the clients, and this asymmetry accounts for miscommunication in a number of instances. The welfare worker does not perceive this asymmetry and assumes, on the basis of the *prima facie* perception of the women's proficiency, that they 'speak fluent Dutch'. As soon as this qualification is made, two things happen. First, alongside the qualification as 'fluent speakers of Dutch', a number of other social categorizations are projected on to the young women. Their fluency in Dutch is seen as being indexical of 'Westernization' and 'integration', including imputations of a desire for modernity, rejections of Islam and the so-called 'traditional culture' of their parents, and of a desire for independence and individualism. Thus, through the ideologically guided perception of language behaviour, the young women are situated in a specific social order, one that in the discourse of social workers is usually identified as a 'culture conflict' or 'gap' between migrant parents and their children. Second, language is ruled out as a potential source of conflicts. Unlike in the case of women who do not speak Dutch and need an interpreter, the Dutch-speaking Turkish young women's communicative behaviour is perceived as being maximally transparent. Consequently, as soon as misunderstandings emerge, their cause is not sought in the communicative process, but in the women's character or initial intentions. Thus the conflict is translated into a moral and socio-cultural evaluation: they are 'difficult', 'confused' or 'unclear about their purposes'. In cases such as these, the particular homogeneistic language ideology influences institutional practices in a way which yields negative (and unintended) results for the migrant women.

A rhetorical change that has taken place over the last few years, showing the relationship between language ideology and the migrant debate in a Flemish context, is the gradual replacement of the term 'migrants' as a problematized target group in education policies with the notion *anderstaligen* ('speakers of other languages', or 'the linguistically other'). Under the guise of an objective identification of educational problems, this concept allows policy-makers to gloss over all-important issues related to the 'problem' it is supposed to show awareness of. Questions to be asked include: How much variability is there to be found among the 'linguistically other' in relation to their command of the local language? How does this relate to the need for specialized educational measures? To what extent are problems arising from being *anderstalig* (at the varying levels of proficiency in the local language) similar to or different from those related to the fact that the local language spoken in the classroom diverges (again to varying degrees) from the sociolect or dialect spoken at home by native speakers of the local language? Etcetera. But instead of asking such questions and developing policies accordingly, this new group categorization (the scope of which often coincides again with the typical 'migrant' groups) serves as an excuse for new global measures such as the territorial spreading of students. More on this will be said in Chapter 8.

The sketched ideological framework is a maze of paradoxes and unwarranted assumptions. The type of nationalism involved confronts us with a deeply rooted vision of language as an independently existing object, as an autonomous creature with its own laws, neither defined nor influenced by human beings. This view offers useful rationalizations for politically ratified attitudes and opinions along two fronts. First, there is the idea of the necessity and sensibility of language borders, delimiting the habitat of a language creature. Second, there is also the idea that acquiring the local language is the simple, necessary and sufficient condition for guaranteeing smooth communication between immigrants and autochthons. Behind the pleas for a legally defined language border one can find, on the one hand, the conviction that the autonomous linguistic creature can be pinned down to a territory, independently of the mobility of the people speaking the language. On the other hand, its justification relies on the idea of an unshakeable unity between language and the cultural identity of a population group; because of the mobility of individuals belonging to a cultural group, its region must be defended by fixing a language choice. In the belief that there is an easy linguistic remedy for inter-ethnic communication problems, then, language is again thought of as a detachable entity, a communication tool without essential links with group identities. It is thus hard to avoid the conclusion that positions are taken, underlying arguments being used at will, only in view of the protection of the identity (or is it the power?) of the majority and of (re)homogenizing society. Not a single homogeneistic measure, however, can solve the 'problem' of unrecognized but factual forms of variability, simply resulting from the fundamentally non-autonomous nature of language, which is a tool used by inevitably mobile people without fixed roots. Everyday variability constantly challenges the normative image. But this only seems to lead to an even stronger normative awareness.

This is a classical vicious circle, well-known to and forcefully addressed by linguists preoccupied with language and socio-cultural patterns in society since the days of Humboldt, Boas and Sapir. The dominant conceptual frame is Herder's world view 'composed of traditional units of language-and-culture', a world view which is, in the eyes of Dell Hymes, 'appropriate enough, perhaps, to a world pristinely peopled by hunters and gatherers and small-scale horticulturists' (Hymes 1996: 25 and 33). As a descriptive and analytical tool for understanding the relationships between language and socio-cultural patterns in contemporary societies ('modern' or not), however, this conception is hopelessly inadequate. Yet Hymes observes that:

> In Western civilization the dominant intellectual response to the existence of diversity has been to seek an original unity [. . .] The dominant practical response has been to impose unity in the form of the hegemony of one language and standard.
>
> (Hymes 1996: 28)

The emphasis on 'monoglot standards' – ideals of monolingual homogeneous communities whose culture is expressed through one shared language – is, moreover, perhaps stronger now than ever before. The Flemish case is clear, but this kind of homogeneism is by no means a typically Flemish phenomenon. In a discussion of language policies in Britain, Linda Thompson et al. (1996: 112) note that 'Britain is still not acknowledging the multilingualism of its population and this attitude is clearly reflected in the current education system' (see also Ben Rampton 1995: ch. 13). Yet Britain is a far more 'coloured' society than Belgium, and movements for multiculturalism and ethno-linguistic pluralism have a longer history there than in Belgium. In a similar vein, Michael Silverstein grimly observes about the immigrant country par excellence, the United States, that 'we live in a society with a culture of monoglot standardization underlying the constitution of our linguistic community and affecting the structure of our various and overlapping speech communities' (Silverstein 1996: 284; cf. also Ricento 1996). And Dell Hymes concludes that, when it comes to recognizing linguistic diversity within its own society, 'the United States remains a largely underdeveloped country' (1996: 63), unaware of the existence and role of different languages and language varieties within its borders, and celebrating one unchallenged hegemonic language, English.

Scrutiny of the way in which language and homogeneism are treated in a small sample of media reporting from other European countries offers further glimpses of the degree to which Herder's conception dominates the perception of ethnolinguistic and socio-linguistic affairs elsewhere, and how this sustains and fuels nationalisms.[32] In the media output of surrounding countries, the trope 'language-and-identity' surfaces less frequently as an explicit topic, even when inter-ethnic conflicts are being discussed. However, this does not mean that one cannot find a clear, popular linguistic ideology roughly based on the same premises – and including its paradoxes – as the ones that we have just sketched for Flanders. There is evidence that the issue of language is often avoided in the treatment of societal models and conflicts because of the relative normalcy of linguistic homogeneity as a property of an harmonious society. Deviations from this norm in one's own society are not easily admitted, or they become minimized, or associated with other 'problems'. Preferably, deviations are situated elsewhere, far from home. A striking example is to be found in a German article entitled 'America and immigration: melting pot or salad bowl?'[33], printed next to a report on the dispute over municipal voting rights for migrants in Germany. Although the juxtaposition was clearly based on a judgement of thematic affinity, the German issue was exclusively approached in terms of political power and the possible infringement of ethnic German rights, while language was explicitly mentioned as part of the American problem:

> Already today a hard battle is being fought over language, over the dominance of English which, for the time being, still represents an element of unity.[34]

The so-called 'Official English' movement is indeed a sufficiently interesting phenomenon to deserve the attention it gets in relation to the multi-ethnicity of the United States, even though Europeans tend to think that linguistic diversity is only found in Europe and not in America. But in this German article we find the implicit idea that societal coherence demands monolingualism. A battle over language is presented as an important disintegrating element which surfaces as a consequence of the deterioration of the economy:

> Ethnic-racial co-existence seems to succeed as long as the economy somehow flourishes.[35]

Because of the need for monolingualism, the position of German as the only language of Germany is treated as self-evident. Although linguistic diversity in Germany is as real as it is in America, it seems not to be worth mentioning.

This reduction of language to an unproblematic fact in relation to minorities in Germany shows how much is taken for granted. According to the underlying ideology, language is a unifying (or dividing) power, because it *marks identity*. Origin, history, 'culture', religion and language are treated as *a cluster of features*. The identifying function of those features implies clear distinctiveness, i.e. the existence of *natural discontinuities* in human reality. Those discontinuities are *nations* or *peoples*. As if this would reinforce their 'naturalness', these discontinuities are not uncommonly compared with 'tribes':

> During his recent visit to Germany, President Mitterand – with that French arrogance rooted more often than not in inadequate knowledge of the issues – has warned scornfully against a 'Europe of the tribes'. But whether the French head of state likes it or not, it is a fact that those 'tribes' exist, and that they demand recognition, a voice, and a place of their own in a Europe seeking unity.[36]

Nations or peoples are perceived as if they would form different biological 'species'. About an animal with feathers it is easy to predict, with a high degree of certainty, that it also has a beak, that it can lay eggs and that it can fly. In much the same way, the ideology seems to hold, a human being speaking a specific language can be assumed to carry along a distinctive history and culture (including, as the above quote suggests, a certain level of arrogance and ignorance). The features in the cluster are virtually given a genetic status, detached from time, place, individuality, and above all from a person's free will. This is why, for instance, the absence of a specific language as a distinctive feature immediately casts a shadow on a group's claims to nationhood. The dynamic nature of identities, and of the linguistic negotiations that play a role in this, disappear completely out of sight. Consider the following quotation from a newspaper article on the Ukraine, in which the 'Russianization' of this former Soviet republic is discussed:

> The poor old Ukraine has had a bad press. Both the Poles, who dominated the towns of the Western part, and the Russians, who dominated those of the East and South, looked down on the Ukrainians as peasants, speaking jargon. The language itself varied greatly from region to region – in the West quite close to Polish, in the East sometimes indistinguishable from Russian. [. . .] Politically, the Ukraine was underdeveloped [. . .]
> (*Guardian Weekly*, 4 November 1990, p. 9)

Here the absence of a clearly distinguishable language is the first in a list of symptoms of cultural poverty or erosion, underdevelopment, 'loss of identity'. The Basques, on the other hand, are pictured in quite different terms, as in an article on Spanish-Basque nationalism (entitled 'Conscious of the homeland: The Basques – hospitable but not subservient'[37]):

What is behind all this [i.e. behind Basque nationalism]? A long history of clearly militant self-determination of a people, of which the origin, just like the origin of its language, Euskara, has until today remained an enigma for ethnologues and linguists. [. . .] This protolanguage [. . .][38]

The language of the Basques, labelled a 'protolanguage' by the author (German *Ursprache*, suggesting a long uncontaminated existence), becomes the romantic focus of the identity of the Basque people in a description that is reminiscent of nineteenth-century types of scholarship. In and of itself, this provides sufficient justification for the nationalistic aspirations of the Basques. In contrast to 'the poor old Ukraine', the Basques can boast an old language, hence an old culture that is distinguishable from that of their neighbours, and one which never gave way under the pressure of cultural dominance. Therefore they deserve the title of 'a people'. This is not to say that the *Guardian* would withhold that title from the Ukrainians – but there is a clear suggestion that they have a long way to go.

Although the rhetorical premises are not always the same, there appears to be little disagreement within Europe about the reality of 'nations' or 'peoples' as natural, objective, or almost biological units that have a right to autonomy, and to the preservation or establishment of an independent homogeneous territory. To use the terminology of the German media: there is an essential difference between *das Volk* ('the people', 'the nation') and *die Bevölkerung* ('the population'); and a 'people' needs a state of its own. *Volken zonder vaderland*, 'peoples without a fatherland', as the title of a recent Flemish book (De Pauw 1992) tries to remind us, are 'marked', not because they would be exceptional, but because their conditions of existence deviate from what they are entitled to, or from what they need to be 'themselves'.

Europe and the Belgian model

To readers of this book who are unfamiliar with Belgian society it may come as a surprise that many Belgians, especially in Flanders, believe that a 'Belgian model' to deal with inter-ethnic problems (*in casu* the conflict between the Flemish and the Walloons) should be exported to prevent (further) violent conflict in places such as ex-Yugoslavia or South Africa. In the light of our analysis, which allows us to link the Belgian approach to the 'migrant problem' to wider issues related to nationalist ideologies, we do have something to say about this belief.

Let us start, though, with the common-sense question which thousands of people have been asking privately and publicly: How is it possible that the international community, or the European Union in particular, has been completely unable to prevent the war in the former Yugoslavia, which was raging until recently no more than a one-day drive away from Brussels? How can we explain the sheer impotence of all attempts to stop the fighting? The commonly used label of an 'ethnic' conflict betrays a persistent lack of analysis (though sufficient clues were provided by numerous well-informed authors, such as Detrez 1992 and

Glenny 1992, to name just two). The conflict in Bosnia was by no means ethnic: all three warring parties belonged to the same ethnicity. Nor was it linguistic by any stretch of the imagination: the attempts to emphasize differences in language between Serbs and Croats (and more recently even Bosnian Moslems) were a product rather than a source of conflict. And though religion seems to be the main marker of the group identities involved, the war was not *about* religion in any relevant sense. The concept of *group identity* seemed none the less to be crucial, which leads us directly into the realm of *ideology* since there are simply no objective parameters along which groups are naturally separable (a fact recognized by scientists in relation to biological differences between people, but even more true for the less tangible properties of culture). The centre of the conflict, moreover, was not the *existence* of self-identifying groups or 'nations' within the same geographical space as such, but the *conviction* that any such 'nation' has a right to self-governance within the confines of a territory of its own. This is the core of what we call a 'nationalist ideology'. And such an ideology serves as the ultimate legitimization for attempts to keep territorially bound nation states as homogeneous as possible – an attempt which was shown to be at the heart of 'tolerant' migrant policies and rightist anti-migrant programmes alike.

If we look closely at the Vance–Owen plan (proposing a division of Bosnia-Herzegovina into ten provinces, three of which would be under the control of each of the three 'nations', the tenth being Sarajevo to be controlled by a body representing all three national groups), or at the Owen–Stoltenberg plan (proposing a division of Bosnia-Herzegovina into three mini-states, one Croat [18 per cent of the territory], one Serbian [consisting of two severed parts, together 52 per cent], and one Moslem [two separated parts plus a few enclaves, together 30 per cent], with the two cities of Sarajevo and Mostar under the international control of the UN and the EC, respectively), or at the variations on these two incorporated in the Dayton agreement, then we see that none of the peace proposals questioned the legitimacy of the goals for which the three parties were fighting. The goals of territorially anchored nationalism were simply accepted. Only the means (war *versus* negotiated settlement) make the difference.

Once a war of this kind has erupted, that type of settlement is probably the only way open to peacemakers. But what about prevention? For this we turn to the analysis of Western European ideologies, and in particular to Belgium. Throughout the reporting on Yugoslavia, the most basic implicit (and sometimes explicit) assumption was that war was inevitable because the nationalist goals – seen as completely legitimate – had been repressed for many years by the Communist regime.[39] In other words, the goals themselves were not only seen as the only way to regain peace, but as natural aspirations which also underlie the Belgian model for the management of diversity, i.e. strict territorial divisions. In other words still, diversity has to be managed by eliminating it, the end product being homogeneous units (with minorities, to the extent that they are inevitable, kept as small and unobtrusive as possible). Recent history has invented a term for this principle: *ethnic cleansing*, a goal which, for instance, Flemish nationalists share with the warring parties in the former Yugoslavia, the difference being one of means. The Belgian peaceful means of eliminating diversity as much as possible have been the language laws. The Belgian constitution (Article 3bis) freezes four language areas (one Dutch-speaking, one French-speaking, one German-speaking, and the bilingual area of Brussels), every municipality obligatorily belonging to one and only one of these, some having the exceptional right to provide language facilities for minorities (a measure which is being challenged today), and all of this unchangeable except by law. In a new census, questions about language would not be allowed, because the language areas are fixed, irrespective of any actual future composition of the population.

The premisses of this line of reasoning and the resulting nationalist measures are not questioned. They correspond exactly to the goals of the Flemish movement which have long been incorporated by all major Flemish political parties, and which a wide cross-section of the population seems to agree upon.[40] Not only avowed nationalists take the goals for granted (as Lindemans *et al.* 1981 do in their account of the history of the Belgian language laws). But even on the political left, questions are no longer asked about the language issue. Thus, in his account of the events leading up to the forced removal of the francophone section of the University of Louvain from Louvain, and its relocation in Wallonia, former student leader Paul Goossens treats the students' demands to that effect as completely natural, not in need of explanation (though he painstakingly asserts over and over again that the Flemish student movement of the 1960s cannot be associated with the extreme nationalists with whom they marched in the attempt to assure linguistic purity for Louvain). The only passage in which a would-be explanation is volunteered goes as follows:

> It [the demand for relocation of the francophone section] was based on the idea that a university must serve its own community. Therefore, it has to be located in its own region, otherwise it turns into an elitist institution.[41]

In other words, the francophone section had to be removed from Louvain for its own good – no matter what French-speaking Belgians thought to be their own good. That there was a blatant contradiction with the cosmopolitan orientation of the international student movement as it emerged all over the Western world seems hard to admit, even twenty-five years later. Is it surprising then that, also twenty-five years later, a document (the existence of which is officially denied) circulated in Flemish government circles, entitled 'The francophone anchoring in Flanders', which opens as follows:

> One can feel endlessly irritated about the demand of francophones for more facilities in Flanders, but as long as one does not have the courage

to assess correctly their global strategy and to attack it at the roots, one can only keep negotiating and possibly giving in.

The 'roots' of the 'global strategy' in question are supposed to be situated in domains such as the economy (dominated by 'francophone' capital) or politics ('Several Flemish top politicians and business managers with a Flemish profile have a francophone wife and/or are board members of francophone companies; they are all systematically "more moderate" than their independent colleagues'). Reverence for homogeneity indeed.

Briefly, as was abundantly shown in our pragmatic analysis of the migrant debate (to be illustrated further in the remaining chapters), diversity is indeed not accepted at any fundamental level in Belgian society. These observations, many of which can be extended to other Western European countries, lead to an hypothesis concerning the inability of Western Europe to prevent war in Yugoslavia. The hypothesis is that we could not contribute to conflict prevention because we share the ideology that was at the source of the conflict. Not only could we not prevent the war, but we actively contributed to it, for instance by means of Germany's speedy recognition of the independence of Slovenia and Croatia, which made war in Bosnia virtually inevitable (see Glenny 1992). And why did Germany feel obliged to make such careless moves? If we leave opportunistic reasons of various kinds aside, we can assume that the German government thought that recognition was the right course of action. And for them it was the right course of action because ultimately it was the same ideology that ripped up Yugoslavia and that united the two Germanies. (Note that we avoid the term reunification of Germany, because that is the linguistic encoding of a falsification of history, since Germany, in its present form, has never existed before – but an encoding which serves the purpose of legitimization.)

Finally, under this hypothesis, why was there fighting in Bosnia and why has there never been a real war over language in Belgium? Belgians flatter themselves with the idea that it is in their nature to solve problems rationally. The truth is that (a) the situation is much less complex, a real mixture being found in restricted areas only, as before the implementation of the language laws; (b) Belgians have never been armed, a notorious prerequisite for waging war; and (c) the borders between the language areas are completely indefensible, since there are no mountains to retreat into and all the rivers refuse to run in the right direction.

No doubt, the time has come to stop flattering ourselves and to start questioning the ideas which we now take for granted about the management of intergroup relations, and which are encoded in the language we use to talk about these issues. Simply exporting the 'Belgian model' would be a recipe for disaster, just like, as argued by McAllister (1997), exporting the Australian model of multiculturalism to South Africa could disturb the entire society-building process there.

A note on hegemony

Returning to the Belgian migrant case, the resulting picture is not a pretty one. Briefly, though very divergent courses of action are proposed in relation to the 'migrant problem', and though the positions voiced at the discourse surface assume an air of complete incompatibility, at the level of implicit meaning we find that the basic attitude reflected in the rhetoric of the tolerant majority is roughly the same as the one put forward in the explicit position taken by the extreme right. Fundamental forms of diversity are simply not accepted. This probably explains the ease with which the extreme right manages to set the agenda, in Belgium as elsewhere in Europe.

In Belgium, the pro-foreigner anti-racist movement (to which Chapter 8 will be devoted) clearly strengthened a counterproductive attention for 'migrant problems', as if there was a definable group of migrants which, because of its special ethnic, cultural and religious character, created social problems that were more fundamental and insurmountable than the problems created by other society-structuring differences such as gender or social class. In the process, solidarity was lost, distance was reinforced, and the migrant communities were becoming more and more associated with deviance and criminality, which has resulted in the more systematic repressive attention they receive. A recent example was the announcement by the gendarmerie that they wanted to recruit allochthons.[42] This was presented by the media as quite a sign of openness, though (a) those to be hired would of course have Belgian citizenship, so that they would normally be entitled to compete equally for such law-enforcement positions without any special measures, though (b) the same reports clarified that the total number envisaged was only fifty, thus imposing restrictions on the access of allochthons to positions in the gendarmerie in spite of their Belgian citizenship, and even though (c) there was no attempt to hide that the recruits in question would be hired exclusively for deployment in 'high risk areas', i.e. areas with a high concentration of migrants. Nothing could be a sweeter victory for the extreme right, since this action has less to do with providing equal opportunities for migrants than it has with open adherence to a definition of migrant communities as prone to criminality and civil unrest and with increasing the efficiency of control and the repressive function of the gendarmerie. It is not surprising, therefore, that the Vlaams Blok was able to capitalize even further on this development by protesting this measure loudly in Parliament, claiming that migrants were now being rewarded for the fact that they were a liability for public order and safety. The only newsworthy response from members of the tolerant majority in Parliament was verbal abuse. Their actions had again, as so many times before, been dictated by a full acceptance of the premises on which anti-migrant rhetoric is based. In Germany, similar processes have led to an erosion of the most liberal refugee laws on the continent, while in France they are leading to legal infringements upon the traditional *ius soli*.

The coherence of the described patterns of thinking cuts across the different types of discourse investigated, to such an extent that it may not be exaggerated to talk about hegemonic control over the entire domain of social and political life in question. It is not difficult to understand how such hegemony is attained and maintained. In a Belgian context, the link between politics and the social sciences is a very clear one. The social sciences have been starved so dramatically that they are engaged in heavy competition for government grants. The available grant money is kept so scarce that it is spent disproportionately on contract research in the service of specific policy goals. As a result, even research questions tend to be asked on political rather than on inherently scientific grounds, and the basic premises of political discourse – themselves coming about on the basis of calculations as to which types of rhetoric can be used to avoid alienating the electorate – dominate the research and research reports. We demonstrated this process at length (in Blommaert and Verschueren 1992a: 147–89) by means of a detailed analysis of some of the most highly mediatized social science research reports of the early 1990s. Such reports usually showed open support for KCM policies, while the policies antedated the research and defined its questions, meanwhile ignoring much earlier and much more independent research (e.g. Hobin and Moulaert (eds) 1986) which was clearly incompatible with the policies. (For further illustrations of the problems of research, see Els Deslé 1993.)

The media, partly dependent for their information on both political and scientific channels, and also operating under the restrictions dictated by an attempt not to alienate the average news consumer, can hardly be expected to deviate from a common pattern of reliance on a supposedly shared background. Moreover, a disturbing link between politics and the media has on occasion been shamelessly reinforced. Thus KCM and KBS, in collaboration, created a media award to be given to a journalist or journalists whose reports 'give objective and balanced information about the presence of allochthons in our country in a manner conducive to a favourable climate for the creation of an harmonious society'. Reactions to this were remarkably absent. It should be clear, though, that public authorities are notoriously bad judges of objectivity and balanced reporting. Especially in a sensitive area such as 'the migrant question' there are few indications that the authorities – whether acting directly or through a so-called independent jury – could give any meaning to objectivity other than adherence to official policy, in this case acceptance of the dogmas of the integration rhetoric. In such a context, only desirable journalism is good journalism. Objectivity is thus reduced to expediency.

Briefly, an autochthonous circle (public opinion, politics, research, information, news reporting) surrounds the migrant communities. The structure of the *migrant debate* itself, which is almost completely polarized between those who accept the integration concept and those who would not even tolerate the presence of foreigners (with a small dissenting minority on the left), determines the nature of the *migrant problem*. And since the debate is conducted almost exclusively by members of the majority, the core of the problem is to be found in the majority itself, more specifically in the way in which diversity is regarded by the average Belgian or Flemish citizen.

The defensive reflex

The publication of *Het Belgische Migrantendebat* (Blommaert and Verschueren 1992a) – especially because of its mediatized conclusion that the extreme right and the tolerant majority, represented in their purest forms by Vlaams Blok and KCM, 'think in the same way' (a simplified way of saying that diversity, which is completely rejected by the extreme right, is not fundamentally accepted by the tolerant majority either) – caused a major controversy which then became an integral part of the debate. Let us therefore briefly look at the reactions.

The pattern of response

A clear pattern developed in responses to the book. The most encouraging favourable reactions came from migrants and people active in what has come to be called 'the migrant sector'. They consistently argued that the analysis provided them with the necessary conceptual tools to voice frustrations which they had felt for years.

Members of the autochthonous tolerant majority, on the other hand, were sharply divided over the issues. The further one moved away from centres of power and authority (i.e. among more 'marginal' political movements on the left and the publications associated with them, or social scientists with an openly critical attitude towards society) the more favourable the reactions were, the main reservation being that the analysis stayed too close to the investigated discourse and did not go deeply into socio-economic determinants of minority–majority relationships.

Most people, publications or institutions directly or indirectly associated with the authorities that have been responsible for migrant policies either avoided the issue or reacted negatively. Thus, as soon as the first press reports appeared about the book (and not before, though the book had been with them for weeks), the KCM let us know that they did not want any further contact with us, and attempts were made to put pressure on us by appealing to our academic superiors. A leading Belgian sociologist, whose work had been heavily relied on by the authorities in the justification of their policies and which had been criticised in the book, distributed a pamphlet entitled 'The words of ignorant people' (Jaak Billiet 1992), in which we were reproached for undeontological behaviour. And the main Flemish Christian-Democratic newspaper, *De Standaard*, was the only quality paper that did not publish a report on the book, though a couple of opinion articles about the issue were published; the editor in charge of migrant affairs said 'the book speaks for itself', so that he did not have to do anything about it; and when we received the *Arkprijs van het Vrije Woord* (a Flemish free speech award), the paper did not report this at all, even though, when the same award was given to KCM head Paula D'Hondt the year before, it had been front-page news.

If these gut reactions, which make an open and critical debate virtually impossible, are based on an unmistakable defensive reflex, so are the more deliberate negative judgements which centre around two strategies. First, attempts were made to associate us with the undesirable elements in society, initially VB circles (on the assumption that our plea for the acceptance of diversity was a plea for some form of apartheid), and later with the extreme left (Dutch *klein links*, literally 'the small left') 'which represents 0.4 per cent of the population'.[43] This marginalization was further underscored by the claim accompanying the transition from KCM to CGKR (in March 1993) that the debate about 'integration' was closed. According to the final KCM report (KCM 1993), the concept had been accepted 'by almost everyone', where 'everyone' stands for all major political parties and where the question was not even asked whether the subject of the concept, the migrant population, could accept it:

> In criticism voiced by the democratic opposition, we have rarely noticed fundamental contradictions of the options proposed by the Royal Commissariat. Thus, amongst other things, the integration concept of the Royal Commissariat has been accepted by almost everyone – albeit in a different formulation.[44]

In the present official rhetoric, 'integration' as defined by KCM and perpetuated by CGKR, is still presented as the only possible alternative to anti-migrant positions. Within the pro-migrant camp, further discussion – let alone disagreement and debate – is barely tolerated. Though slow shifts in orthodoxy can sometimes be observed (see Blommaert 1997), we already noted that at the end of the four-year period (1989–93) during which the KCM was functioning, its definition of 'integration' had not undergone any serious changes – a sure sign that we are dealing with a politico-ideological stance rather than the product of careful analysis or even negotiation.

Second, *Het Belgische Migrantendebat* was consistently said to be 'unscientific' or based on 'shaky grounds' or 'fragmentary data' in the negative commentaries (none of which were written by people in areas of scientific endeavour closely related to the one in which the analysis was to be situated).[45] None of these comments was supported by any real scientific argumentation, but mainly by misrepresentations of the approach. For instance, the accusation of the selective and biased use of data overlooked the demand of recurrence and coherence which was systematically made before any analysis was proposed; close and complete scrutiny of a wide range of documents (such as a KCM flier which will, by way of example, be analysed in detail in Chapter 7) led irresistibly to our conclusions, precluding the need for selectiveness or bad intentions. To the extent that facts of discourse were adduced which were said to contradict our findings, they were always explicit statements. In other words, an analysis of implicitness was countered by prime example of its object: an ideology of textualism, focused on explicit, replicable, and 'on record' discourse (cf. Collins 1996). Thus members of the tolerant majority were quoted as saying that they have 'unambiguous respect for cultural diversity as mutual enrichment', to prove that we were 'intellectually dishonest' and that we committed 'logical errors' when saying about these same people that they do not accept fundamental forms of diversity.[46] This type of comment misses the essence of our findings: often there is a clear discrepancy between what is said explicitly and the patterns of thinking that emerge from implicitly communicated meaning. In what may be one of the worst distortions of our methodology, Van Eekert and Van Herck (1993) claimed that our approach was itself responsible for the finding that the same basic ideas could be found throughout the migrant debate: our approach was supposed not to allow for differences in ideology as soon as the same language was used. Again, this misses the point completely. While using the same language, it is perfectly possible to talk about the migrant issue and even about 'problems' in a manner that reveals, at the level of implicit meaning and presuppositions, a fundamentally positive attitude towards diversity. Such a way of speaking would yield sentences such as 'The unmistakable richness and dynamics of a multicultural society is endangered by the persistence of socio-economic dividing lines which coincide with ethnic boundaries.' It is the non-occurrence of such forms of expression in mainstream discourse, and the overwhelming recurrence of negative implications, that led to our conclusions.

Widening cracks in the rhetoric of tolerance

While ignoring or rejecting the proposed analysis, the defensive reaction leaves its traces intertextually in many documents that have subsequently been distributed by the responsible authorities. But because it is not considered expedient to accept the criticism, nor to discuss it openly, the result is a widening of the cracks in the rhetoric of tolerance. Reformulations were therefore presented as mere 'clarifications' or extended reproductions of an otherwise unaltered original text. The only ambition was to *repeat* the 'correct interpretation'. Thus an attempt was made to neutralize the widening cracks with reference to an ideology of textualism. Here we shall present a few examples from the final KCM report, *Tekenen voor Gelijkwaardigheid* ('Opting for equality'; KCM 1993).

In its recapitulation of the integration concept, this document introduces two new moves to counter the accusation that the concept itself bears the seeds of discrimination. First, it is now claimed 'that this integration concept does not only count for the immigrants but also for the Belgians':

> It should be noted that this integration concept does not only count for the immigrants but also for the Belgians, who also have to respect this public order, for instance to the extent that it accords rights to the minorities, and who are also requested to respect these same basic principles which they do not always honour.[47]

143

Of course, this only begs the question. To the extent that the integration concept serves as a set of guidelines for the autochthonous population, it must be assumed that Belgians do not always live by them (which is now even admitted). To the extent that those guidelines are not such that they can be or have been converted into legislation, one cannot assume that there is a sufficient degree of consensus to be able to talk about basic social principles of the society as a whole. To the extent that a Belgian's behaviour deviates from non-legal principles, can anyone blame them, or is anyone even going to care? Would this not be a serious encroachment upon the freedom we are so proud to enjoy in our private lives? No Belgian would accept that. So, why should migrants?

Second, an attempt is made to turn our 'basic social principles' into universal norms:

> It is important in this context that one should not be blind to the fact that many of these general orienting ideas are not even so different across most societies and cultures [. . .][48]

Thus the question is begged even further. If there is universality involved, then we must assume that most migrants live up to the principles in question anyway. So, why do we need to formulate the package of demands in the first place? And if we try to justify the demands in terms of their universality, does this not imply that what is not universally accepted cannot be imposed? As always before, the core of the problem remains that some forms of cultural diversity are not regarded as 'legitimate' and acceptable. This issue is brought up literally:

> When are we concerned with a basic value? And when are we concerned with legitimate cultural diversity?[49]

To make this point convincing, the final KCM report refers to clitoridectomy (pp. 54, 163–4), even though it is admitted that this has never emerged as a problem in Belgium, and were it to do so a simple application of the laws protecting any person's physical integrity could be used against it. Thus these two defensive moves make the need for a vague notion of guiding social principles, prone to manipulation and discrimination, even less convincing now.

To counter the accusation that real equality is denied in official policy, as much as in everyday life, the final KCM report stresses that 'not more rights and duties can be given to allochthons than to the autochthonous population'. But rather than conclude that equality means *equal* rights and duties, it is said that a 'correct dosage of rights and duties' has to be found for minority and majority, implying that they are legitimately different for the two groups. And rather than conclude that migrants have to be given equal access to different areas of public life, it is said that their involvement is 'a process to be promoted and initiated by the authorities' (their own initiative apparently being unacceptable) while 'preserving the criteria mentioned in the integration concept' (thus making the acceptability of involvement conditional on the majority's concept of integration). In spite of the clear unidirectionality, this recipe is supposed to lead to 'mutual acceptance'. Or, quoted in full:

> But this mutual acceptance is difficult to realize if it is not accompanied by a second process, involving minorities actively and in a coordinated manner in the activities and goals of the authorities. Integration then stands for a process to be promoted and initiated by the authorities, preserving the criteria mentioned in the integration concept, involving minorities structurally in all activities and goals of the host country.
>
> An important condition for this mutual acceptance is the correct dosage of rights and duties both for autochthons and allochthons, and in their relation to one another. It is evident that not more rights and duties can be given to allochthons than to the autochthonous population.[50]

In a rhetorical *tour de force*, the text manages to link stringent conditions to so-called unconditional acceptance, as where it says that some public service centres 'are now able to employ *on a contractual basis, without any restrictions,* persons who do not have Belgian nationality *for non-leading functions*' (emphasis added).[51]

As a third example, a section on 'deconcentration' in the final KCM report starts with the claim that 'the threshold of tolerance' is 'a myth' (KCM 1993: 83–4). But in the same breath, measures are proposed to provide financial incentives to local authorities that could lead to a more even spread of the migrant population. And, elsewhere in the report, educational measures are presented that should help schools cope better with a multicultural context (pp. 97–102). But rather than address the issue directly in terms of problems of intercultural communication, the main pillar of the policy is again a financial incentive to promote deconcentration. This tendency developed further in the first years of operation of CGKR, to which ample attention will be devoted in Chapter 8.

These are just a few examples to show that the contradictions between the explicit and implicit levels of meaning did not disappear after they were brought to light. Nor is there reason to believe that the pattern could not perpetuate itself; it is only at the logical (as opposed to the rhetorical and social) level that, by becoming more obvious, the contradictions would become less tenable. Before leaving this topic, we would like to point at three more characteristics of the final KCM report which demonstrate how little one may be troubled by gaps between the explicit and the implicit. First, Islam is unambiguously presented as a problem. For instance, while negotiations with the 'countries of origin' are deemed necessary to relieve some educational needs related to the migrants' 'own language and culture' (KCM 1993: 100), it is presented as a major achievement that 'from now onwards it is virtually impossible to attract foreign [Islamic religion] teachers'.[52] A step in the fight against fundamentalism? Second, the entire section on youth policies (KCM 1993: 145–9) concentrates on 'alternative sanctions for petty crimes', thus reinforcing the association between migrant youth and criminality. Third, in the statistics provided to project the percentage of foreigners into the future (KCM 1993: 26–9) we see that, after naturalization, 'foreigners' (*vreemdelingen*) automatically become 'allochthons' (*allochtonen*). Thus their 'foreignness' is institutionally perpetuated, leading to further 'ethnicization'. As could be expected, the distance between minorities and majority is not narrowed by naturalization. Nor, presumably, by the natural and quite predictable processes of cultural convergence and intermarriage. But if 'migrants' are to remain a separable segment of the population, why bother about integration?

Conclusion

There is no doubt that homogeneism, the dominant ideology that directs our thinking about foreigners in our society, is far from productive. Through the abnormalization of the foreigner, it contains an *a priori* rejection or problematization of diversity. The implicit level of the migrant debate invariably entails the following central thesis: foreigners disturb the existing order, they threaten the status quo, their presence alone already turns them into a problem.[53] Homogeneism is a clear impediment to any solution for whatever societal problems might have to do with 'migrants': it has a fundamentally distancing effect on the target group. Our analysis has revealed that *the structure of the migrant debate is, therefore, a constitutive part of the migrant problem*. Bereft of ideological input from the debate, the 'problem' might dissolve into a set of sometimes complex, but usually manageable, practical issues similar to those which our socio-political apparatus has been designed to cope with because of earlier confrontations with other types of society-structuring differences between people.

The pointlessness of the current 'problem talk' derives from its fixation on (a small set of) ethnic-national division lines which are assumed to override all other sources of tension and conflict between groups. In the confrontation between the universalist heritage of the Enlightenment and the French Revolution on the one hand, and nationalist particularism on the other, general human properties and values seem to have made place for the relativity of ethnically based group identities elevated to absolute properties and values in their own right. Talk about '*the* values' or '*the* rights' of human beings (which every individual can enjoy totally), has been abandoned in favour of '*our* values' and '*our* rights' (which take precedence over those of others). Dewinter's remark that 'the rights of mankind are in our conviction subordinate to those of our own people', just about sums it up.[54] But also the official rhetoric which demands of migrants that they adapt to all kinds of social norms, *as we understand them*, fits the pattern.

While hoping that this main conclusion has been sufficiently argued and demonstrated, there is a need for further documentation, which will be offered in Part III. As was already pointed out in the Introduction, discourse-based ideology research is not immune to the risk of piecing together patterns of thought from disconnected instances of language use. Therefore, we will now demonstrate how the identified ingredients of homogeneism are at work in a specific discourse type (the language of a training programme for police officers, Chapter 6), in a single text (a widely distributed brochure educating the public in multicultural matters, Chapter 7), and in the legitimization of some typical 'anti-racist' policies (Chapter 8). Chapters 6 and 7 will bring few additional facts to light; their function is mainly illustrative and they will, therefore, be kept as brief as possible. Chapter 8, however, adds a substantial amount of information not yet contained in the foregoing.

Part III

HOMOGENEISM AT WORK

6

TRAINING FOR TOLERANCE

In the first years since its establishment in 1988, the KCM had clearly succeeded in profiling itself as the voice of tolerance, the driving force behind positive attempts at 'integrating' foreigners into Belgian society. In that capacity, the KCM did not only formulate policy advice. Nor did it shy away from efforts to contribute directly to the spread of the tolerant attitude it wanted to promote. In this chapter and the next we will analyse two such efforts: a training programme directed at the public service sector, including police officers (this chapter), and a widely distributed information leaflet (Chapter 7).

As to the training programme, its explicit goal was to provide useful and accurate cultural background information on the foreign population in Belgium in order to heighten the awareness of and appreciation for diversity among public servants. A team of trainers (including a number of people of migrant descent) was sent out all over the country almost every day and night in an attempt at improved image building. In addition, the training was also intended to provide useful practical information on how to 'deal' with migrants constructively. Thus the title of the programme was *Omgaan met migranten* (i.e. 'Interacting with migrants').

Between September 1991 and March 1992 we attended 33 hours of training (one separate 3-hour session and two full 15-hour programmes organized in five sessions of 3 hours each). The target audience in all cases consisted of police officers (but some sessions were also attended by other civil servants and welfare workers). The sessions were usually attended by two researchers. They were recorded, transcribed and analysed. Notes were taken to record audience participation. In addition to the data gathered 'in the field', the programme's syllabus (which was given to participants after completion of a full series of five sessions) was also available for scrutiny, and all the trainers were interviewed. The structure of the syllabus was analogous to the succession of training sessions, and most of the facts and viewpoints presented by the trainers were clearly analogous to those in the text.

In terms of content, the training programmes were structured as follows:

Session 1   Demography and the history of migration

Session 2   Cultural background and Islam
Session 3   A choice of topics: the second generation, or refugees
Sessions 4 and 5 Intervention techniques and practical tips

The first three of these are intended to provide general background information conceived as necessary for a better understanding of the migrant communities and of 'the migrant problem'. They were designed as an attempt to create a new conceptual framework useful to help the participants rethink and restructure their interactions with migrants in the performance of their duties. The last two sessions try to clarify practical aspects of the participants' professional routines, taking negative contact experiences as a default starting point. Throughout this structure, the classical story is being told, largely a summary of the 'problem' and its remedies as defined by the KCM. It will not be surprising, then, that an analysis reveals all the weaknesses of the dominant tolerant orthodoxy – starting with a reduction of 'migrants' to Moslems.

In the following pages, we will present a critique under four headings, the first three of which fully match the ingredients of a homogeneistic ideology as sketched in Part II. First, we will see that also in this training programme diversity is fundamentally problematized and presented as an abnormal condition. Second, it will be shown how the diagnosis of the 'problem' hinges on a set of underdefined concepts. Third, common misconceptions will be shown to be reinforced by an apologetic soothing of the tolerant conscience. Fourth – introducing a new element for the reader – communication problems are handled with the help of an untenable theoretical model which further strengthens stereotypes and prejudice.

The aberrance of diversity

At the most general level of analysis, a patent (and blatant) conflict emerges between the professed *intention* of positive image building and the overall *message* conveyed by the training. In order to pursue the intention successfully, the general emphasis would have to lead to profound respect for cultural diversity. But what the training stresses more than anything else is the set of problems and even the danger inherent in contact and communication between members of different ethnic or cultural communities. In the interaction with participants a picture is built up, in which the presence of foreigners in our society is associated with:

- disturbances of the public order and threats to safety, due in particular to the criminal activities of groups of migrant youngsters;
- a feeling of unease and distrust and a sense of insecurity on the part of autochthons in their own native neighbourhoods when there is a significant concentration of migrants;
- a culture shock on the part of migrants, and especially a near-psychotic disruption of the identity of second-generation migrant adolescents;

- a threat to a number of our own 'values' as a result of aberrant behaviour on the part of migrants: arranged marriages, different educational principles, the social position of women.

Paradoxically, ethnic and cultural diversity, which should be the essence of the multicultural society promoted by the training programme, is fundamentally *defined as a problem*, as elsewhere throughout the migrant debate.

Again, as in other instances of tolerant rhetoric, diversity is also presented as *an aberrant and recent phenomenon*. The syllabus devotes eight pages to a historical sketch of immigration into Belgium, generating the picture of a drastic influx of foreigners into a previously homogeneous territory. Those pages could serve as a perfect example of how a concatenation of well-chosen true facts can be used to communicate – even unintentionally – a completely distorted historical picture. The pivotal points in the sketch are (probably quite accurate) statistics. The 'foreigner population' of Belgium is shown to have continuously grown from about 2 per cent in 1846 to 8.6 per cent in 1986, with a significant drop from 3.5 per cent in 1910 to 2.1 per cent after World War One, and another one from about 9 per cent to 8.6 per cent in January 1985 as a result of a new naturalization law that made 54.000 foreigners 'disappear'.

The only element of interpretation is indeed this final observation, which is worded in the syllabus as follows:

> On January 1st 1985, 54,000 'foreigners' disappear administratively and almost unnoticed, as a result of the implementation of the new nationality laws. (Specifically for children from mixed marriages with a Belgian wife.)[1]

By stressing that those thousands of 'foreigners' disappear only *administratively*, this fact underscores the overall picture that is painted of the long saga of the *increasing diversification* of the Belgian population. Some explicit statements further strengthen the general message that cultural diversity is a recent aberration in Belgian (and, by extension, European) history, which therefore requires special measures. Commenting on the foreign population around the turn of the century, it is stated that the majority was Dutch, French, or German, but that there were also a few Italians:

> For the common man, the Italians really embodied the 'foreigner'. Indeed, the Belgians had not, or not much, been confronted with bearers of foreign cultures as yet.[2]

Belgium is clearly implied to have been an *homogeneous* society, gradually losing ground to the inroads made by waves of immigrants. The premise of anti-migrant rhetoric that this is a new 'revolution' with which we have to cope is thus fully confirmed. Note, in passing, the essentialist notion 'bearers of culture' (Dutch *cultuurdragers*), which pictures every individual as an ideal representative of his or her culture.

What is completely ignored in this presentation is the artificial starting point for the statistics: by definition, everyone living on Belgian soil at the time of Belgium's 'liberation' in 1830, with a very narrow margin of exception, was Belgian. As a result, only from an *administrative* point of view the starting point was nearly 0 per cent foreigners. And only from an administrative point of view could the 'Belgians' be regarded as an homogeneous 'tribe'. We do not get figures on how many people of foreign descent (in particular Dutch, French and German) resided in the country. Nor do we get information on the cultural profile and region of origin of those foreigners who vanished into thin air. Even the groups of people of German and French descent must have been extremely diversified themselves: at the end of the eighteenth century, less than 50 per cent of the people in France spoke French;[3] and the Germans had still to succeed in creating an identity of their own. In other words, diversity at the time of the Belgian Revolution was probably as impressive as it is today; only its face has changed.

Particularly noteworthy, in connection with the two foregoing paragraphs, and in view of the hidden (and probably unintentional) contradictions permeating the rhetoric of tolerance, is the way in which *administrative facts* can be foregrounded in one case and completely suppressed in another, depending on whether or not they can be used to sustain a particular world view. And all of that within the confines of a coherent piece of written discourse, within the space of a few pages.

The distortional dramatization of migration itself carries over into the wording strategies used when specific 'problems' are discussed. A case in point is the treatment given to the difficulties that second-generation migrants are confronted with. Those difficulties, especially in these young migrants' relations with their parents, are compared with 'generation conflicts' between members of the autochthonous population and their children. Such conflicts are explained in terms of differences in values and norms. At the other end of the comparison, however, the explanation remains the same, but the label shifts from 'generation conflicts' (*generatieconflict*) to 'generation gaps' (*generatiekloof*) and even 'a double generation gap'. Thus a (vaguely) quantifiable difference is introduced: their problems with shifting values and norms is much bigger than ours. Needless to say, there is no presentation of an analysis that could show exactly how 'their' problems differ from 'ours' in such a way as to justify the estimate of size. As if to compensate for this shortcoming, both syllabus and training sessions then introduce the notion of a (group-internal) '*culture* conflict':

> In addition to the generation conflict experienced by many young people while growing up, for migrant youngsters there is also the risk of a culture conflict with the parent(s).[4]

This notion of 'culture conflict' is then defined almost exclusively in terms of differences in patterns of expectation. Though this is essentially the same process as the one described earlier as 'generation conflict' – at least, nothing in the presentation could lead one to believe otherwise – the illusion of a new line of explanation is created by the introduction of the completely underdefined notion of 'culture' and cultural dynamics. It is suggested in this statement that not having spent one's youth in Morocco or Turkey, but in Belgium, automatically causes one to 'lose' part of one's home culture. Conversely, it is implied that these youths' parents, despite many years of living in Belgium, have not succeeded in changing at all. They are still living in their home culture. No real explanation is offered for the differential fates of the 'cultures' involved and their bearers. Which brings us to the way in which the central concepts of the training programme are handled.

Unmapped concepts

Throughout the KCM training programme, as in other embodiments of the migrant debate, supposedly well-understood but basically underdefined or unmapped concepts are appealed to for purposes of clarification and explanation. Their main rhetorical function is a type of *categorization* that should allow the trainers *to reduce diversity to manageable proportions without downplaying its dramatic presentation*. Their effects are, more specifically, (a) to restrict the number of contrasts, and (b) to blow up the degree of difference between the members of the restricted contrast set.

The contrast is basically reduced to *'us' versus 'them'*, where both 'us' and 'them' are overgeneralized. In the presentation of statistics, for instance, a distinction is made between 'EC foreigners' and 'non-EC foreigners'. Though such a distinction only makes sense from a purely administrative and political point of view – common European law dictating a different treatment for citizens of EC countries – it allows for the lumping together of all (Western) Europeans as a solid cultural unity founded on the pillars of democracy, Christianity ... and tolerance. Differences among EC Europeans are glossed over completely; they are treated as fundamentally unimportant.[5] By the same token, the 'them', the *migrants*, are also lumped together and defined monolithically as *Moslems from the Maghreb*:

> In this chapter, the cultural backgrounds of especially *Moslem migrants* are sketched, because they differ markedly from Western culture.[6]

The phrase 'in this chapter' understates the focus of the training programme. 'This chapter' follows a chapter devoted to Islam as a religion, and it precedes a chapter on 'intervention techniques' in which all the protagonists of the examples are (mostly Moroccan) Moslems. Foreigners of a different brand only figure in statistics, and in the optional session on political refugees. This direct association of *migrants* with *political refugees*, the treatment of which focuses strongly on *illegal aliens* and the existing administrative and judicial measures to cope with their presence, does not distract from the monolithic identification of migrants. Its main effect is to aggravate the image of the Pandora's box opened up by diversity. As pointed out earlier, Moslems from the Maghreb or Turkey and asylum seekers are the core categories of anti-integration rhetoric. Arguments against their acceptance in our society are based on the unquestioned unacceptability of patterns of behaviour among Moroccan or Turkish Moslems (the wearing of *chadors*, supposed polygamy, the expansion of the number of mosques), and on illegal entry into and residence in Belgium on the part of many other foreigners. This referential framework, constructed to legitimize intolerance, is fully adopted. A striking feature of the training sessions was that peaks of interaction between trainers and participants were usually centred around stereotypical issues related to Islam. At such moments, heated discussions emerged, used eagerly by the trainers, unable or unwilling to counter the clichés, as breathing space.

Returning first to *Islam* as the defining trait of the migrant population, the corresponding chapter of the syllabus and the training session defeat their own purpose of an 'objective' approach that could counterbalance the negative picture painted by history classes on the Crusades or by recent media coverage of certain aspects of Islam such as polygamy and the status of women. For one thing, the Arab peninsula during the pre-Islamic period is described in quite complimentary terms:

> The reigning mercantile spirit produced great religious tolerance and hospitality for all possible religions and sects.[7]

The advent of Islam under the guidance of Mohammed, to whose life – especially his wives and his feuds – much attention is paid, is coincidental with an end to tolerance. Thus a picture is presented of a dogmatic and 'rather simple' religion, differences within which are barely alluded to except in a cursory reference to Shiites (10 per cent) and Sunnis (90 per cent) (KCM 1991: Part III, 9).

As to the *Maghreb*, our migrants seem not to have left it at all. For a sketch of the non-religious cultural backgrounds, *traditional rural life in the country of origin* is described. Note that this goes under the label of 'Life in the country of origin'.[8] In keeping with the strategy of migrant lumping, the description is supposed to be equally valid for migrants from Turkey (a minority in Belgium, but too sizeable not to be mentioned) and those from the Maghreb countries. Thus *culture* is approached completely in terms of *tradition*, and more specifically tradition as it exists or is supposed to exist *in the country of origin*. The description fluctuates between hopeless overgeneralization (already apparent in the elimination of a difference between Turkey and Morocco) and the introduction of opaque nuances.

Overgeneralization we find, for instance, in the contrast that is introduced between 'we' cultures (where the social fabric is all-important) and 'I' cultures (where personal development is primary):

> The social status enjoyed within the family and the society is mainly

based on age and gender, and not so much on individual personal achievement (as in the West).[9]

Needless to say, such a statement is utterly simplistic, even with respect to what is claimed about the West.

To the extent that nuances are introduced, they are usually loaded with opacity, rendering them virtually uninterpretable:

> The opinion of the boy and the girl is taken into account *to a certain extent* in the matter of partner choice, but *in general* their say is *rather limited*.[10] (italics ours)

Nothing is added about the conditions under which, or the extent to which, partner choice is co-determined by the couple involved, let alone about the way in which these processes vary between families and change over time.

Moreover, the overall emphasis in the account of 'culture' is on *differences* in relation to a supposed Western standard of comparison, and preferably dramatic differences. To achieve this effect, subsidiary concepts – equally underdefined – are introduced. A notorious example, worthy of a longer quotation from the syllabus, is the concept of 'honour' (Dutch *eer*), which is said to be crucial for an understanding of role behaviour, which in turn is said to be of essential importance to 'we' cultures. Note that this concatenation of 'we' cultures, 'honour' and role behaviour denies the relevance of this newly introduced explanatory concept for an understanding of the West. The description goes as follows:

'Honour' can therefore be situated on two levels:

1 On a first level, honour is determined by the authority one has over *domains that should not be penetrated by outsiders*. Practically, these are the home, the family members, the possessions, the land; briefly: one's own territory. [. . .]

2 A second level is situated outside the 'domestic' domain; where the man, *in the outside world*, must be able to defend his territory and where he also has to be able to challenge others. [. . .] This boils down to being superior to others: better, stronger, richer, more religious, more generous, more courageous, etc.[11]

In addition, territorial trespassing is said to require a brave response which can lead to aggression and physical violence. All this sounds like an elementary anthropological statement about an exotic, primitive tribe (if not an ethological statement about a species in the animal kingdom).

The impression of exoticism and primitiveness is already communicated by the Dutch label *eer*, 'honour', which is used almost exclusively in collocations, and the productive use of which as an independent noun is restricted to historical texts about the social propensities of medieval knights. But the archaic connotation of the term, its association with *history*, is not accidental. It fits in with a general attempt to introduce *an evolutionary perspective*, as was discussed more fully in Chapter 4. The dramatized difference between 'us' and 'them' is placed along two axes: one geographical (Belgian society *versus* life in the country of origin), one temporal. The temporal axis is given full weight in a section which follows 'Life in the country of origin', a section dealing with 'Parallels with the Belgian (more agrarian) society around the turn of the century'. In this part of the coursebook, quotes are listed from a classical Flemish novel (*De Vlaschaard* by Stijn Streuvels) for illustration: the farm as economic unit, the farmer as patriarch, social status determined by age, honour and the loss of honour, the division between men's and women's worlds, father–son relations, arranged marriages, and the role of religion at the centre. The explicit meaning is: we were not so different a hundred years ago. But the total message says: they are a hundred years behind. Thus the description of 'our' migrants, in which no ethnography is presented at all of how they live here and now, is one more instance of denied 'coevalness'. They are the products of a spatial and temporal transplant. Hence their present predicaments can be extrapolated on the basis of a simple comparison between the culture of the country of origin and Belgian culture, as is done at length, schematically, and with full submission to the supposed clarity of the unmapped concepts, in sections dealing with 'the consequences of the cultural experience' of first-, second- and third-generation migrants.

It had not occurred to the designers of the KCM training programme that what they labelled 'honour' is just one type of manifestation of the widespread principles of face management (Brown and Levinson 1987), nor that Western notions of privacy and ambition are not too far removed from their two constituent aspects of honour.

Aspects of legitimization

Obviously, it was not the purpose of the KCM training programme just to present a problem. It was first and foremost intended to help police officers to cope with the problem. The basic rhetorical strategies to achieve this goal are *apology* and *soothing*.

Apologetic strategies are used to show innocence on the part of both migrants and Belgians. On the migrant side, two clear examples can be adduced. First, the *evolutionary perspective* on their 'culture' serves to show that there is basically nothing wrong with their intentions. If they cause societal problems, they do not do so wantonly. Nor are they aware of the adverse reactions their behaviour evokes among autochthons. They simply live in the past. And since they are the ones who are evolutionarily backward, we should do our best to understand and be patient.

Second, an element of *comparison* is introduced: the very first pages of the syllabus (as well as, usually, the first 'data' given during the training sessions) do not deal with immigration, but with Belgian emigration. An attempt is made to draw parallels between recent immigration and Belgian emigration at the beginning of the century, mostly to North America, under the pressure of poor economic conditions and in search of a better future. But the comparison is ambiguous. On the one hand it suggests a comparability of the problem: some of us have also been migrants. Therefore, again we must understand and be patient. But in the same breath, true comparability is implicitly denied. Not a word is said about the possible adaptation problems which those Belgian migrants may have had. This problemless migration contrasts sharply with the mountain of problems attributed to the settling on Belgian soil of Turks and Moroccans, who must therefore be relatively unadaptable people. Rather than using the comparison to stress the universality of the phenomenon, it underscores the exceptionality of the situation at hand. The apologetic rhetoric may backfire.

On the Belgian side, we find mainly an apology for *racism*. The only context in which the term is used is one in which 'understandable irritation' with 'problems' caused by the presence of migrants is said *not* to be racism. Anti-migrant feelings are caused by poor economic conditions and frustrations. There are only 'stereotypes' (which, incidentally, are nicely substantiated in the cultural background information provided in the training itself) and 'prejudices', and at worst 'a certain measure of xenophobia'. Real 'racism' is only to be found in some of the political propaganda on the extreme right. Thus it is not part of the societal problem to be solved. (See more on this in Chapter 8.)

Soothing strategies are used to give the trainees the feeling that the problems – though quite 'real' and deeply 'cultural' in nature – are not insurmountable, and that the understanding and patience to which the apologetic patterns of reasoning lead will be sufficient in the long run.[12] As a first example, the first session of the training programme usually starts with an experiment. The trainees are asked to estimate the *percentage* of foreigners in Belgium or in their area. If they overestimate the foreign presence (which is what the trainers hope for), the lesson is quite clear: no need for alarm, there are not as many as you think! In addition, the trainees are asked which country of origin most migrants come from. If the answer is Morocco (the desired, but wrong, response), the lesson is again quite clear: no need for alarm, most of them are in fact Italians, hence the problem is not as big as you think! The most fundamental soothing strategy, however, is directly related, once more, to the *evolutionary perspective*: the problem is basically a temporary one; migrants will change over time, just as we have changed since the beginning of this century; given time and patience, they will be able to function properly in our society; in other words, ultimately they will be integrated.

A theory of communication

The foregoing sections of this chapter are simply reminiscent of the general outline sketched in Chapters 3 and 4; the KCM training programme offered us a little extra. Though the link of a thorough ethnography of the present-day migrant population as it lives in Belgium, including a thorough ethnography of communicative patterns and styles, is completely missing, the KCM programme ventured upon 'practical advice' for police officers in their direct interaction with migrants. The chapter or session in question goes under the label 'Intervention techniques'.

The treatment of this topic is characterized by a far-reaching underestimation of its complexity. While the literature on intercultural and inter-ethnic communication shows convincingly how interaction problems are caused – if not by the exploitation of power differences – by subtle nuances in communicative style, which often boil down to different ways of anchoring discourse in the social context, and hence different ways of marking implicit information (Gumperz 1982), the issue is completely *schematized* in the course. What is worse, the presented communicative schema, attributed by the trainers to Mary Douglas,[13] is based on *misleading parameters*. One of them is the contrast between 'we' cultures and 'I' cultures, which we have already introduced. The second is a postulated opposition between cultures in which implicit communication dominates and cultures in which communication is explicit. We quote:

> It is important to know that understanding each other requires more than using the same language: indeed, one can use a language in very different ways. Typical in this respect is that we, Westerners, usually handle EXPLICIT forms of communication. This means that the emphasis is on the meaning of the words themselves, and that we do not have to look for underlying messages or a further context. (Muslim) migrants, however, handle more IMPLICIT communication codes, where it is not so much the content of the message that counts, but where especially the form or the relational aspect are decisive.[14]

Such claims hardly deserve to be refuted. If linguistic pragmatics has shown anything convincingly, it is exactly that cultures and linguistic communities do not differ according to the amount of implicit communication that takes place, but only according to the ways of marking implicit meaning.[15] As if this were not enough absurdity for one concept, implicit communication is further associated with an inability to look beyond one's own group-internal truth, while explicit communication makes it possible to take on different perspectives and to understand other people's truths. This analysis reintroduces the *evolutionary perspective* at the level of *cognitive capacities*.[16] A combination of the parameters yields the diagram shown in Figure 6.1. Not only is the schematic presentation shown in Figure 6.1 used to visualize types of communication, it is offered as an interpretative framework for distinguishing different cultural communities: A represents first-generation Moslem migrants, and B contains second-generation migrants who have already acquired the skills of explicit communication, while D is where police officers ought to be situated in the performance of their duties. C, finally, defines somewhat aberrant communicative behaviour in Western cultures, such as the sloganesque rhetoric of the political extreme right.

	'we' -culture	'I' -culture
implicit communication	A	C
explicit communication	B	D

Figure 6.1 Types of communication

This puzzle has a compelling logic of its own. During the sessions we attended, police officers volunteered at least two quite logical – but utterly false – deductions, which the trainers were unable to invalidate because they had themselves introduced the premises. First, the conclusion was drawn that the solution of the 'migrant problems' could never come from A, the members of the first generation, since they are by definition unable to adopt an 'integrated' perspective. Hence we should wait until they die, or get rid of them; but neither is feasible since new members of A are coming in all the time through (mostly arranged) marriages or illegal immigration. The logic was so compelling that it did not occur to any of the participants that the conclusion completely contradicted their own, often explicitly voiced, experience that they never had any trouble with the first generation. Second, it was concluded that, if there was this contrast between implicitly and explicitly communicating cultures, it is quite normal that we (as many Westerners indeed tend to believe) can much more readily adapt to other cultures than 'they' can. However naive and denigrating such a verdict may be, it fits in quite usefully with the art of soothing apologetically: their 'otherness' should be forgiven because they do not know any better; we, on the other hand, can understand them and should therefore be patient – since it is a matter of time or generations anyway.

The underestimation of complexity goes hand in hand with an underestimation of the importance of direct interaction. The 'problem' is cast into a generalizing mould which tries to capture societal macro-structures. Little does one realize that inter-ethnic interaction does not take place at the macro-level of social structure, that no policy can be successful without a successful implementation for which micro-level communication is invariably required (see Roberts and Sayers 1987 and Gumperz and Roberts 1991 for examples). Attention to micro-level interaction would also have forced the designers of the KCM programme to abandon the illusion of a 'typically Belgian' problem: cultural lumping would have become impossible, and the attention to detail would have revealed the importance of universal processes and their infinitely variable operation.

7

EDUCATING THE PUBLIC

A KCM-KBS flier, widely distributed by the official Belgian information bureau Inbel (through a wide range of high-exposure channels, such as the post offices), can be used to illustrate further the entire conceptual construct outlined in Part II. It was printed on one A4 sheet, folded as a triptych, thus yielding six 'pages'. The front page says:

> A good relationship starts with integration.
>
> Integration starts with a good relationship.[1]

Since this slogan, abounding in vagueness, relates the concept 'integration' to 'a good relationship' (supposedly between migrants and members of the autochthonous population), the social desirability of which is beyond dispute, it can only be seen as direct promotion for the concept itself, which is either assumed to be clear enough or a clear understanding of which should result from reading the remaining text. The text is divided into five sections separated by the following headlines:

- Not slogans, but clear language [an unintentionally ironic recommendation after launching the title slogan]
- No playing off of migrants against the underprivileged
- A good relationship starts with integration [the only part of the title slogan that comes back literally]
- The municipalities set the example
- The duties of the migrants [printed on the 'page' that forms the back of the flier when folded, so that it is the first piece of text that the reader's attention is drawn to]

Let us go through the contents systematically, section by section.

Section 1

Not slogans, but clear language

No one can deny that the presence of migrants in our country creates problems. Some want to solve these problems with simplistic, cheap slogans. 'Foreigners out', they shout loudly. These are insincere proposals which exploit the insecurity and fear of some Belgians.

Whoever uses his common sense, knows that the migrants cannot be expelled. They came to this country, partly at our request, in search of better living conditions. They had children. Their children have children. The migrants are beginning to feel at home here, they want to stay.

History has taught us that intolerance and persecution do not solve anything. No hollow and dangerous slogans then, but an efficient policy in which clear and sometimes hard language is used. In which migrants are told in no uncertain terms that each has to fulfil his duties in order to enjoy his rights.[2]

The very first paragraph of Section 1 does various things which are completely in line with the conceptual complex characterizing the Belgian migrant debate as a whole. It abnormalizes diversity by claiming that 'No one can deny that the presence of migrants in our country creates problems'. Thus the basic premiss of anti-migrant rhetoric is presented as an indisputable fact. It is highly significant that this is done by way of a semi-explicit presupposition, i.e. a structure which carries a piece of information as a presupposition while fully encoding the information in a verbal string embedded in that structure. This suggests that the presupposed information, though it functions as a real premiss for everything that follows, is not sufficiently self-evident to be left fully implicit. This means that the message is not to be interpreted at the trivial, and therefore obvious, level mentioned before (the level at which the birth of every child, or buying a new car, causes problems), but in a sense according to which the presence of migrants, as such, causes specific problems not caused by other factors in society. Yet, by embedding this in a presupposition-carrying structure, the information can be taken for granted and one can avoid making the presupposed claim more specific. At the same time, since the text is a document designed to advocate a policy, one can expect that implicit definitions of 'the problem' will be carried along by the formulation of proposals. We shall point at them as we go along. Equally unquestioned is 'the insecurity and fear of some Belgians', this normal reaction to the abnormal degree of diversity which 'creates problems'.

At once we are told what the 'slogans' are against which the section title speaks out: they are the slogans of the most radical return option proposed by the (unnamed) extreme right, which is said to 'exploit' the unquestioned, and there-fore supposedly natural, feelings of insecurity and fear. These slogans and proposals are described as 'simplistic' and 'cheap', but above all 'insincere'. The insincerity attributed to them underscores the manipulation of which the common Belgian is the victim at the hands of an unacceptable political movement, and it underlies the argumentation in Section 1. Thus the rejection of the return option is not at all based on the logical impossibility of a 'return' for those who were born here, nor primarily on a moral appeal to elements of fundamental human rights, though half-hearted reference is made to children, grandchildren, and a desire to stay, as if three generations are needed for 'beginning to feel at home'; after all, they came to this country only 'partly at our request' and in the first place 'in search of better living conditions', so that their being here is not so much a right as a privi-lege. Rather, the return option is rejected on practical grounds: 'common sense' dictates that 'the migrants cannot be expelled', and we know from history 'that intolerance and persecution do not solve anything'. It is on the basis of this prac-tical impossibility, the realization that the proposal cannot be put into practice, and on the basis of the assumption that the people behind the proposal are aware of this impracticability, that 'Foreigners out!' is qualified as an 'insincere' slogan.

If the 'slogans' in question are directed at (and against) the migrant popula-tion, so is the alternative, the 'clear language' in the section title. 'Clear and sometimes hard language' is supposed to embody a policy qualified as 'efficient', i.e. as a policy which, in contrast to the one voiced in the 'hollow and dangerous' slogans, is practical and can work. Again, the question of what is just or fair does not come up, but the focus is on what can be put into practice. If migrants cannot be told to get out, they can at least be 'told in no uncertain terms that each has to fulfil his duties in order to enjoy his rights'. In this formulation, the enjoyment of rights is presented as something to be earned, as a privilege bestowed upon migrants in return for their performance of duties. Note that the perspective, with clear focus on duties to be fulfilled, hints at their present non-fulfilment. In truly emancipatory rhetoric, the perspective could have been reversed as follows: 'Migrants must enjoy the same rights as other inhabitants of this country, because they perform the same duties (they contribute to the economy as workers, they pay taxes, etc.)'. But rather than use this strategy as a direct attack on attempts to deny migrants even the right to be here, the anti-migrant position centred around the assumption of deviance and of non-compliance with legitimate requests is accepted as a starting point. It is not surprising, then, that the rest of the docu-ment will have less to say about rights than about duties.

Section 2

No playing off of migrants against the underprivileged

Often it is said that too much is being done for migrants while the

Belgian underprivileged are forgotten. This is not true, as appears from all kinds of figures.

From 1989 onwards more than 1 billion francs per year was spent on the fight against deprivation and another 1 billion went into specific relief projects. That money was and is largely intended for disadvantaged Belgians.

Moreover, is it not unjust to play off the underprivileged against migrants?[3]

Section 2 is a brief intermezzo, a weak and mitigated response to the commonly heard complaint that too much attention is paid to migrants in comparison to the attention that goes to poorer members of the autochthonous population. Why is this response weak? First, because figures are adduced in the vaguest possible terms; comparisons with any other areas of spending are avoided, so that the reader is unable to judge whether the figures are at all impressive. Second, because the text *accepts* the false polarization in what is no more than a benevolent plea not to *use* it; no attempt is made to show that the polarization between migrants and an autochthonous class of underprivileged people is a false one because it mixes different types of society-structuring dividing lines, thus missing a chance to appeal to solidarity instead.

Section 3

A good relation starts with integration

Little can be expected from a policy of voluntary, let alone forced return. For instance, one cannot expect that the pensions of the Belgians will go up if the foreigners disappear.

Therefore, a good policy has to be directed at fitting the migrants into Belgian society. The migrant population can, amongst other things, help to expand the country's economy.

In order to stimulate integration, the Royal Commissariat for Migrant Policies has formulated a few guidelines:

1 Automatic granting of Belgian nationality to the grandchildren. A simplification of the naturalization procedure for the children. Boys who become Belgians, have to do their military service.

2 The quality of education has to improve considerably. So that everyone can feel at home in it, so that migrants and Belgians get better chances.

3   The closest possible attention for social problems in areas where many migrants live.
4   Migrants have to learn the local language.
5   The migration stop remains in place as long as the labour reserve has not been exhausted.
6   For those who want to return spontaneously to their country of origin, barriers have to be removed.
7   Integrated and capable migrants have to be able to get token functions as public servants in the municipalities.
8   There is only a place for a well-integrated Islam which respects our Western values.
9   A future-oriented policy vis-à-vis illegal aliens – a consequence of the pressure from the third world and Eastern Europe – has to be developed in a serene manner.
10   It is desirable to set up a Centre for Ethnic Equality. This will have to fight wrongful discrimination, for instance on the basis of skin colour.

The proposed measures show the importance of language and education. It should also be clear that illegal aliens are sent back without hesitation. This is not inhuman. It is inhuman to let everything take its course. So that people wander about aimlessly, end up in prostitution or are left to the mercy of illegal contractors.[4]

Section 3 picks up the anti-return rhetoric again, adding first a negative point in further support of its purely utilitarian line of argumentation (the return of migrants will *not* have the beneficial effect 'that the pensions of the Belgians will go up'), and then a positive one ('The migrant population can help to expand the country's economy'). In a typical *non sequitur*, the rejection of the return option is then opposed to what is presented as the only possible alternative, a 'good policy' which is 'directed at fitting the migrants into Belgian society', in other words 'integration'. Note two important implications. First, the formulation presupposes that migrants are not yet 'fitted into Belgian society' or 'integrated'; presumably, this is why their presence can without further qualification be presented as a problem; hence integration measures can be expected to aim primarily at changes which migrants have to undergo in order for them to qualify as fully acceptable members of our society, which is in this process regarded as a constant, unchanging entity. Second, since 'integration' is introduced as the obvious alternative, its content is supposed to be well-known and the subject of a wide consensus. The following 'guidelines' are then presented as practical measures needed to reach the goal about which agreement is presupposed once the return option has been shown to be untenable.

Implicit in the formulation of the ten measures that follow, we find a full substantiation of all the stereotypes that make up the problematization of the migrant population. In addition to the vague and general suggestion that 'social problems in areas where many migrants live' (measure 3) would be worse than and different from social problems in areas with few migrants, five more specific issues are brought to bear: education, language, unemployment, illegality, and religion.

First, though the quality of education (measure 2) is placed in the framework of what is needed for the whole population (a formulation which may be motivated by the same general concern as the intermezzo in Section 2, i.e. the common complaint that too much energy is spent on migrants), the demand that it 'has to improve considerably', put forward in such general terms in this specific context, suggests that the education problem is fundamentally related to 'the migrant problem'. The form of this relation emerges from the demand that 'integrated and capable migrants' (measure 7) should be able to get token functions: migrants are perceived, in general, as lacking in education and skills.

Second, 'Migrants have to learn the local language' (measure 4). Clearly, in order to make sense of this request, the idea must be that migrants lack the necessary language skills and are not making the necessary efforts to learn them. To the extent that this idea is based upon facts, the reality it bears on is mostly restricted to some – and by no means all – first generation immigrants. Note, further, that measure 4 is formulated as an unequivocal duty, a request which the majority has a right to make and which the minorities have to comply with. There is not even the slightest suggestion that the majority has a major responsibility in this matter. Yet, at the time when this KCM flier was distributed, migrants were on waiting lists to get into Dutch language classes. The demand on the part of the migrant population, the desire to learn, was far greater than the supply for which only the majority could be responsible. Later, funding for Dutch classes for migrants was drastically cut by the Flemish Minister of Education Luc Vandenbossche.

Third, by emphasizing that no further immigration should be allowed 'as long as the labour reserve has not been exhausted' (measure 5), again a favourite premiss of anti-migrant rhetoric is accepted: the association of the migrant community with unemployment. To use H.M. Enzensberger's (1992) term, unemployment makes migrants 'redundant': we are better off without them.

Fourth, 'the migrant problem' is associated with 'illegal aliens' (measure 9). That this is a major concern appears again from the recapitulation in the final paragraph of Section 3, where special attention is drawn to three of the five 'problems': language and education, and illegal presence in this country. In a manner reminiscent of the humanitarian motivations adduced by the extreme right in favour of the return option, a radical send-back policy is proposed vis-à-vis illegal aliens for their own protection from aimless wandering, prostitution and exploitation.

Fifth, Islam is identified as a problematic religion: it is assumed not to respect 'our Western values', and therefore it cannot be accepted unless it is 'well-integrated' (measure 8), whatever that may mean.

This problematization is even strengthened by the tendency to turn *migrant policies* into *migration policies*, the basic option being to prevent further immigration as much as possible. Two of the proposed measures serve this goal directly. First, the 'migration stop' (which only recognized political refugees and close family members of people with a residence permit can escape from) must be kept in place (measure 5). Second, 'a future-oriented policy' to keep at bay the masses ready to move in from the third world and Eastern Europe 'has to be developed in a serene manner' (measure 9). It is not so easy to interpret 'in a serene manner'. The Dutch original *in alle sereniteit* generally applies to situations in which one runs the risk of losing calm judgement. Though the appeal to serenity is praiseworthy, it emphasizes the dramatic nature which present migration flows have in popular perception, and it paves the way for harsh measures such as sending back illegal aliens 'without hesitation'. The dramatization keeps harsh measures congruent with the self-perception of openness, and makes it possible to develop and implement such measures 'in a serene manner'. As part of the same strategy, the return option is allowed to slip in through the back door in the proposal to remove any barriers that might prevent migrants from returning to their country of origin spontaneously (measure 6).

The political measures proposed in Section 3 are kept either minimal or vague. Facilitating naturalization for the second generation and making it automatic for the third (measure 1) are commendable proposals (which have meanwhile been realized), but they leave the old obstacles for first generation migrants (the only ones to which the term 'migrant' can sensibly be applied).[5] The recommendation that municipalities should employ migrants as public servants is restricted to 'token functions' and to 'integrated and capable migrants' (measure 7). And the responsibility of a Centre for Ethnic Equality is kept underspecified (measure 10).

To the extent that the tasks of a Centre for Ethnic Equality (which was later established under the name Centre for Equal Opportunities and the Fight against Racism, CGKR) are described, it has to be set up 'to fight wrongful discrimination, for instance on the basis of skin colour'. Measure 10, especially because of this task description, draws the attention for the very first time in this document to the fact that part of 'the migrant problem' might be located with the autochthonous majority in the form of racism and discrimination. But by giving 'skin colour' as the only example, a purely racial definition of racism is introduced which is virtually impossible to handle in the fight against discrimination and which overlooks the fact that skin colour is just one of the criteria used in various forms of contemporary racism (see Robert Miles 1993). Furthermore, the call for a fight against 'wrongful' discrimination (Dutch *onterecht*) hints at the existence of forms of discrimination that might be legitimate (*terecht*). That this implication is not the product of a misguided analysis or an attempt to find bad intentions in every word, is abundantly clear from what precedes. Thus measure 7 is far from being a plea for equal rights and opportunities in municipal employment. Only those can be employed who are judged by the majority to be 'integrated and capable'. While capability, if interpreted as possessing the necessary skills, is a legitimate expectation, integratedness is unidirectionally imposed (and hence the basis for institutionalized discrimination) and, as discussed earlier, it is such an intangible notion that it leaves endless possibilities of manipulation (so that it can be used to cover up forms of discrimination based on any other type of consideration, including skin colour). Similarly, measure 8 makes it possible to exclude from dialogue and decision-making any groups of Moslems defined by the authorities as 'fundamentalist' or 'non-integrated'.

Section 4

The municipalities set the example

While waiting for a Centre for Ethnic Equality to be set up, the Royal Commissariat for Migrant Policies asks the municipal councils:

1 Create an organized structure for the contacts between municipality and minorities.
2 In the domain of housing, aim at as much dispersal of the migrants as possible and prevent the decay of houses.
3 Organize the dialogue between the schooling networks at the local level and pay attention to youth policies.
4 Make absolutely sure that the foreigners fulfil their duties as subjects of the municipality and as inhabitants of the neighbourhood correctly.
5 Mosques cannot be set up indiscriminately nor in indefinite numbers.
6 Take great care of the attitude and training of municipal personnel.
7 Watch meticulously over the safety in the municipality. Any criminal behaviour is resolutely dealt with. All citizens have to feel safe at all times.
8 Put forward the emancipation of the migrant woman as a priority.
9 In principle, accept political refugees only if adequate housing and sufficient services are available.
10 Try to set up a municipal integration plan.[6]

Section 4 has the appearance of a list of duties to be performed by the autochthonous municipal councils. But apart from the positive recommendation that the attitudes and training of municipal personnel should be given due attention (measure 6), and the broad guidelines formulated in measures 1, 3 and 10, the proposed 'duties' are completely situated in the domains of repression, intervention and restriction.

Repression is the overtone in measure 4 (where the autochthonous duty consists in strict control over the way in which migrants live up to *their* duties – as imposed on them by the autochthonous population; the Dutch expression *met vaste hand* is associated with a relation of full authority), measure 5 (which gives municipalities the duty, or should we say the right, to prevent mosques from shooting up like mushrooms – a clear echo of right-wing rhetoric), and measure 7 (the duty to enforce law and order, which again, by implication, are supposed to be threatened by the mere presence of migrants). Intervention in the lives of migrants is authorized by measure 2 (which presents the prevention of the decay of houses not so much as a policy valuable in its own right, but as one of the possible aspects of an active policy aimed at 'deconcentrating' the migrant population, on the assumption that a concentration is in itself problematic, an idea captured by the notion of a 'threshold of tolerance'), and by measure 8 (which suggests that the Western ideal of gender relations can be imposed on the migrant population without any form of debate on the issue). Finally, measure 9 is formulated as a restrictive measure which can easily be used to justify the non-acceptance of political refugees by any municipality; the principle could easily have been phrased positively as a real duty: 'Adequate housing and sufficient services have to be provided for political refugees who present themselves for registration in the municipality'; it is significant that this is avoided. In the process, religion (measure 5), criminality (measure 7), and social unadaptedness (measure 8) are reintroduced as ingredients of 'the migrant problem'.

Finally, Section 5 starts with the completely misplaced adverb 'also', as if the foregoing had not yet been heavily biased towards 'a series of efforts' which the KCM 'expects from migrants'. As if to add insult to injury, the formulations of 'the duties of the migrants' imply that they do not pay enough attention to the choice of education for their children (measure 1), they do not make enough efforts to learn the local language (measure 2), they are not sufficiently oriented towards involvement in social life (measure 3), they fail to pay attention to the aesthetics of the neighbourhood (measure 4), and they are religiously and ideologically intolerant (measure 5).

Section 5

The duties of the migrants

Also from the migrants the Royal Commissariat for Migrant Policies expects a series of efforts.

1. The choice of excellent education – also for the girls – has to get priority.
2. The parents have to make a serious effort to learn the local language.
3. Youngsters have to get involved in social life and – if possible – in sports clubs.
4. Everyone has to contribute to the development of the neighbourhood and the embellishment of the streets.
5. A high degree of tolerance in matters of religion and the philosophy of life.

All measures that are listed here have ultimately one goal: a society in which everyone can advance and in which tolerance and mutual respect dominate.[7]

The sum total of the message is perfectly captured in one of the pictures included in the flier: a photograph of a migrant waiter in a restaurant taking an order from an obviously autochthonous couple, as pictured (in a more rudimentary form) in Figure 7.1. This picture is accompanied by the following sentence: 'Knowledge of the local language leads to mutual respect'.[8] A simple role reversal would have made the issue of knowledge of the local language irrelevant. Consider Figure 7.2. For the allochthonous waiter in Figure 7.1, it is indeed useful to master the language used by the restaurant guests (whether this is the local language or a language in international use). But exactly the same holds for the white waiter in Figure 7.2. The point is that *the language that is spoken is largely determined by the skills and inclinations of the guests*, who are the more powerful partners in the type of economic relationship sketched in the pictures. All this has little to do with either the local language or mutual respect. If the allochthonous guests in Figure 7.2 speak French or English, it is in the interest of the waiter to make an effort to serve them in that language. The pressure to adapt weighs strongly on everyone in a weak position. The fact that the information leaflet under investigation takes one type of linguistic adaptation for granted tells us a lot about the implicit but 'normal' relationships between allochthons and autochthons – which goes to show that the entire question revolves around patterns of power and control, and that the integration concept is a perfect tool to keep migrants 'in their place'.

Figure 7.1 'Knowledge of the local language leads to mutual respect'; version 1

Figure 7.2 'Knowledge of the local language leads to mutual respect'; version 2

8

ANTI-RACISM

Keeping pace with the growth of anti-foreigner movements, especially as embodied in electoral successes of the extreme right, the past half decade has witnessed a mushrooming of really impressive anti-racist organizations, movements, demonstrations and activities in Belgium. This anti-racism, however, is of a decidedly 'soft' kind.

Soft anti-racism uses as its main adversary Racism with a capital R, i.e. the type of political racism to be found in parties such as the Vlaams Blok. Such an adversary is easy to identify, and by defining it as the villain one can effortlessly assume the role of a non-racist, without having to go into self-criticism at the underlying level of fundamental attitudes towards diversity of which this book is intended to provide an analysis – attitudes which stretch far beyond the personal level into the domain of dominant ideologies, and are thus reflected in social and political reality. Soft anti-racism also tends to concentrate more on an individual's intentions than on the actual harm or exclusion suffered or experienced by minority members. It prefers focusing, furthermore, on 'hard racism', i.e. discriminatory behaviour directed at categories of people that are supposed to be identifiable in biological terms. As soon as other types of parameters are involved, a high degree of uncertainty arises. Soft anti-racism, finally, is based on the assumption that *tolerance* is the antidote for *racism*.

It is especially the latter property of soft anti-racism that is disturbing. 'Tolerance' is a concept to be situated at the *individual* level of attitudes and behaviour, while racism is a much broader political and ideological phenomenon, not easily confined to one corner of the political spectrum, with roots in fundamentally twisted intergroup relationships, and with forms of expression that can be either structural or personal. Pleas for individual tolerance are far from being superfluous. But an exclusive focus on tolerance, or an automatic association between racism and the remedy of tolerance, diverts the attention from the more structural societal problems which can only be addressed effectively by people in power. Thus, paradoxically, the same movement that locates the heart of racism in a political force (Racism with a capital R) fails to pay due attention to the political level of action that is needed to fight it.

The facile association between racism and tolerance as its antidote results, more often than not, in a more solid interest in anti-racist discourse in one's own tolerance and its manifold expressions than in the lack of equality and justice experienced by minority members. This phenomenon can be witnessed at a variety of levels, including news reporting. A typical example was an anti-racist demonstration in Brussels on Sunday 27 March 1994 (which, fortunately, did pay attention to one aspect of political involvement, viz. voting rights for 'migrants', though this was precisely an aspect that turned away scores of potential partici-pants). This demonstration was preceded by the most elaborate announcement campaign imaginable in a progressive newspaper such as *De Morgen*, which, by way of further support, also distributed a special Sunday edition. But in the same newspaper, no mention was made of a day of reflection organized by Belgian Moslems in Antwerp on 26 March 1994 around the theme of '20 years of recogni-tion for Islam in Belgium', which concentrated on the systematic forms of discrimination which Islam, as a religious community, is still suffering twenty years after its official recognition by the state. A show of tolerance on the part of the majority seems to carry more weight than justified expressions of frustration on the part of a minority. As a result, anti-racist movements make *themselves* into the central topic, rather than their own original goals.

Against this background, it is easy for the political authorities to join the anti-racist movement while (a) steering away from necessary courses of action that require far-reaching political decisions, and while (b) implementing measures in tune with anti-foreigner sentiments. An example of (a) would be the uninhibited laxity with which the political establishment allows violations of existing laws against racism and discrimination. On the one hand, there is the remarkable guideline to make complaints about racism the object of negotiation prior to taking legal action. This is one of the highly exceptional cases (along with massive tax fraud) in which the authorities allow negotiating in cases of unlawful behaviour. On the other hand, there is a clear absence of action against politically organized racist movements (despite the explicit claim that 'politically exploited racism' has to be fought). The VB slogan *Eigen volk eerst* ('Our own people first'), which was given practical substance ever since 1 May 1996 in the more specific *Werk voor eigen volk eerst* ('Work for our own people first'), is a clear call for discrimination, and thus in violation of the law. No one has as yet taken legal action. Clearly this would take courage, as VB is represented in parliament, has a democratic right to free speech, receives government funding, is allotted broad-casting time on public radio and television, has seats on all kinds of politically composed councils and committees, and is the single largest political party in the largest Flemish city, Antwerp. This is an uneasy mixture of status and privilege. While the privileges could be used to force a party like VB to adapt its rhetoric, the status that has led to most of the privileges prevents this.

As to (b), which goes more deeply into the heart of the problem, we will illus-trate the ongoing processes with reference to government actions in three areas: first, the functioning of the CGKR as the main symbol of participation on the part of the authorities in the fight against racism; second, special measures taken with the alleged purpose of fighting discrimination in schools; third, asylum policies.

Centre for Equal Opportunities and the Fight Against Racism (CGKR)

The CGKR, the establishment of which was anticipated in documents such as the one analysed in Chapter 7, is the official successor of the KCM since 1993. Its conception was inspired by models in other countries, such as the British *Commission for Racial Equality*. Just like the KCM, the CGKR has the status of a non-political technocratic government instrument which basically serves to keep the sensitive and hard work out of the hands of the ministerial cabinets. It contains a juridical section which has to guard against violations of the laws on racism and xenophobia and which, when deemed necessary, can provide legal support or act as plaintiff.

In 1992, when plans for its establishment were taking shape (still under the label 'Centre for Ethnic Equality'), we ventured the following prediction:

> Probably a Centre for Ethnic Equality will have to restrict itself to denouncing visible manifestations of racism, i.e. factual discrimination, or its political exploitation.[1]

We formulated this expectation on the basis of the described normalization of racism and the observed concentration on Racism with a capital R. Unfortunately, until now it has proved to be correct. In its anti-racist actions at the juridical level, the CGKR restricts itself to a number of 'test cases'. Action is taken only when there are clear instances of racist aggression, in particular when it takes the form of unlawful detention or physical violence. This limitation did not come unannounced. At her farewell as Royal Commissioner in early 1993, Paula D'Hondt declared that the CGKR would focus on exemplary cases, without following an offensive strategy in general. It may have been the intention to polish the rough edges by means of well-chosen juridical actions, hoping that in this way a moral authority could be established which would seep through to other levels of anti-racist activity.

As such, there is nothing wrong with this kind of strategy. But what are its side effects? A first one has to do with authority and power. The CGKR is a government institution with a technocratic image, profiling itself as the unchallenged authority in the field of fighting racism. The power and influence that is involved is real: CGKR representatives have seats in numerous organizations and committees which occupy themselves with various aspects of equal opportunity for minorities or with the fight against racism, and they usually have a decisive voice. CGKR Director Johan Leman also profiles himself as an authority on the *definition* of racism, as will be shown later. The Centre, therefore, occupies a central position in the entire debate and is thus in a position to judge, legitimate, or condemn the actions of other individuals, organizations or institutions. To a large extent, it has usurped the public debate and all but claims a monopoly position.

The version of racism which the CGKR accepts as 'real' racism is – as was to be expected – the limited one hinted at at the beginning of this Chapter, a version which, judging from its coherence with other discourse manifestations, matches a significant slice of public opinion (which is itself to a certain degree shaped by the rhetoric emanating from both the CGKR and its predecessor, the KCM). The theme of 'racism' is approached with the utmost caution. This already appeared from the choice of the safe and tolerant term 'equal *opportunities*' in the Centre's name, rather than the more radical and probably more appropriate alternative 'equal *rights*' (which, by the way, had at first been proposed). Complex cases are carefully avoided. Sometimes, when real scandals surface, this is not possible. But then no effort is spared to prevent the spread of blame beyond the case at hand pre-emptively. Thus, when the CGKR announced a lawsuit against police officers in a small Flemish town who had detained six Moroccan Belgians simply because 'they had no business' being in their jurisdiction and carried a cellular phone (which, to the policemen, positively identified them as drug dealers), Johan Leman judged it necessary to say:

> We absolutely want to avoid the emergence of a polarization between us [i.e. the CGKR] and the law enforcement services of this country. The fact that we file this complaint is in no way to be interpreted as an insinuation that all policemen of this country are racists.[2]

An already narrow view of racism is further confined by a heavy emphasis on juridical aspects; i.e., 'racism' is further reduced to racism *that can be prosecuted with success*, or against which punitive measures can be taken. In an interview with the daily newspaper *Gazet van Antwerpen*, Johan Leman was confronted with a number of examples to determine what precisely he would judge 'racist', and what kinds of cases the CGKR would be prepared to sue. We quote a few of the questions and answers:

GvA: Practically. I refuse to let my house to a Turkish family with six children. Am I a racist?

JL: Not necessarily. When this Turk files a complaint against you on grounds of racism, he [i.e. the home owner] is not necessarily going to be sued by us. Everything depends on the way in which he [i.e. the Turk] presents himself. I can imagine that Belgians who present themselves in the same manner are also turned down by a concerned home owner. When a *bona fide* migrant is involved who is turned down because of his skin colour, we are going to act. But it will not be simple to adduce proof. Therefore we will first try to mediate between the home owner and the candidate tenant. We are not immediately going to use the big cannons, because one should not tackle racism repressively from the start.

GvA: I'm a baker, and I'm looking for a saleswoman. A nice lady presents herself, but she is wearing an (Islamic) headdress. I refuse to employ her, because I fear that otherwise I will lose customers. Am I a racist?

JL: No. That is a professional judgement. That man can perfectly justify why he acts that way. For the reception and service to customers certain demands can be made. Sorry that I have to say this, but the same goes, e.g., for punks, and then that is not a question of skin colour.

GvA: Another nice-looking lady who speaks perfect Dutch is turned down because she is black and I am afraid to lose customers. Am I a racist?

JL: That would be racist, yes. I know that this is very delicate, and this must therefore be discussed, but here you touch racism. Though I understand of course that the shopkeeper probably acts under pressure from his customers.[3]

It is striking how this combines a narrow biological notion of racism with the reduction of racism to types of behaviour against which legal action can be taken with a certain chance of success. But in conjunction with this semantic process, the question-and-answer game is formulated in terms of the unqualified concept of 'racist', as if the reduced notion had absolute validity, so that every social practice that falls outside the scope of the incorporated criteria – no matter how unfair to individuals as members of certain groups – is brushed aside as unworthy of anti-racist attention. It is not difficult to imagine that the victims in cases described by Leman as non-racist are and feel harmed in much the same way as those in the avowed racist cases. It is at least puzzling, if not disturbing, to see the equation between attributes of a legally recognized religion (the Islamic female headdress, the *chador*) and an appearance which betrays a certain musical preference (punks). Further, it is far from clear what exactly makes the difference between a Moslem woman with a *chador* and a woman with a black skin in such a way as to provide sufficient grounds for differential treatment. With this example, Leman returns completely to a (discredited) biological view of 'race'. Note that all of this happens in an authoritative manner: statements are made by an unchallengeable personal and institutional authority, who claims great expertise, and who, moreover, has the power to make his interpretations consequential. Needless to say, the victims' experiences, the feelings of insult and harm resulting from forms of exclusion based on a type of identity, and the political and ideological embeddedness of racism, are all left out of the picture. Even the application of the laws against racism and xenophobia – about which we have already said that negotiation is preferred to litigation and that they are not being used to combat open political calls for discrimination – is subject to further constraints, as appears from another fragment in the same interview:

I want it to be clear that I do not like people who absolutely want to start a racism complaint and to get media attention as the first great victim in Belgium. I do not go for that, to be frank. The anti-racism law can even

177

feed racism if it is used in and out of season. We are not going to do that. We are, for that matter, inclined to occupy ourselves in the first place with cases of racism in public services, rather than in the private sector.[4]

The institutional and legalistic usurpation of the domain of racism leaves little space for public debate and makes it impossible to tackle just about all forms of everyday racism, which, being widespread, are major sources of resentment and intergroup tension. The legalistic stance legitimates disqualifications such as 'they're exaggerating' or 'they're just looking for racism everywhere', on the assumption that a prerequisite for racism is the demonstrable and irrefutable presence of racist intentions.

As for mediation and negotiation as a way of dealing with complaints about racism, there is no doubt that in many cases this *is* the best road to take. However, attempts at mediation become inappropriate habits if applied in cases where prosecution would be in order. Thus there was the case of a fire-bomb thrown into a house where Sikh refugees were living in a small Flemish town. In connection with this event, the town's mayor made a few remarkable statements. He suggested that the problem was simply that there were too many Sikhs, so that violent reactions from the local population were inevitable. Moreover, 'our people have to work too!' According to his words, the Sikhs did not only cause feelings of unsafety among local women, but also unemployment in the region. The mayor systematically spoke in terms of the opposition of 'our people' *versus* the Sikhs, thus turning his statements into echoes of rightist propaganda (remember 'Our own people first', its more concrete variant 'Work for our own people first', or the latter's equivalent '400,000 unemployed – why are there still foreigners?'). In line with what was becoming standard practice, Johan Leman was asked to mediate between the local authorities and the Sikh community. In a televised interview (Panorama, BRTN), he was asked to give his opinion about the mayor's comments. We quote:

JL: I think it's unhealthy. You may have your opinions about this, but you cannot simply express them as a public official.
BRTN: For instance, saying there are too many Sikhs, that's dangerous?
JL: Yes. I would not do that. Or saying there is a housing problem related exclusively or almost exclusively to the Sikhs – I would not do that. Because instead of the Sikhs you can be sure that as many Belgians have something to do with it. And second, instead of the Sikhs, there could equally be Poles or other people. And I think as PUBLIC OFFICIAL one has to be ENORMOUSLY concerned, especially in moments of crisis, with equality between people and with not trying to blame one person more than others or to insinuate that. And I think that in this case one has been a bit careless – that remains my position. Has this, therefore, been serious racism or intended as serious racism? I do not think so, but some stupid things do happen. People who are

not necessarily the worst racists but who simply do not properly assess the consequences of their acts – and THAT is more or less what happened here.[5]

A simple reformulation could run as follows: the position expressed is not neces-sarily wrong, but the 'uncivilized', careless and unqualified formulation is not acceptable. In other words, the mayor could have evaded all blame by speaking in more diplomatic terms about 'passing the threshold of tolerance'. Leman's criti-cism only touches the *style*, not the *substance*, of what he said, because that fits the official belief in the reality of thresholds of tolerance and in the problem of 'over-concentration'. Against a background where groups of youngsters shout 'Barbecue!' (a delicate metaphor for fire-bombing with human victims), under the benevolent eye of the same mayor, the soothing attitude expressed by Leman is at least suspicious. Put differently, Leman gave the mayor the licence he needed later to start vacating Sikh houses.

The carefulness and tact with which the mayor in question is being treated, rarely repeats itself where 'migrants' are concerned. During another broadcast of BRTN Panorama, Leman's opinion was asked, in connection with the 'problems' surrounding one of Brussels's ill-reputed squares in the middle of a dilapidated neighbourhood with a high degree of unemployment and a high concentration of foreigners, and where aimless gangs of migrant youngsters hang around. Again we quote:

> At a certain moment it becomes impossible to tolerate losing, as a constitutional state. You cannot tolerate that. You have to try all means. If that does not work you are – you owe it to the constitutional state to say 'Sorry, but we pick you up and take you away!' – Punishment camps, of course, have a bad reputation, don't they. The reputation is bad, but you have to, you have to, you have to somehow extract these boys from their own negative spiral in which they are trapped – that's one – and also you have to, you cannot possibly create a situation in which a couple of hundred people, in fact, have to suffer a kind of terror from a group of youngsters who have in fact lost a sense of norms – completely.[6]

Briefly, the unmistakably racist climate in the fire-bomb town, and in particular the role played by the mayor, are soothingly deproblematized. On the other hand, the behaviour of migrant youngsters, living under conditions for which the Belgian majority bears at least part of the responsibility, is dramatized and inter-preted in terms of a threatened social order (*rechtsstaat*, literally 'state of law'). Moreover, an utterly repressive suggestion is made for the solution of the problem, viz. punishment camps. Yet, also in the case of the Flemish town and its mayor, the social order was endangered. The difference is that the mayor represents that state in his town, while the migrant youngsters in Brussels live on its margins. A frontal attack on the first means that one would challenge *authority*, while an offensive against the second group does not involve the least amount of risk and is even popular in some circles. Challenging authority would be an act of dissent; a further stigmatization of a group which is already perceived in criminal terms, on the other hand, simply perpetuates an existing image, and helps the CGKR to establish a reputation of a 'neutral' and sober agent, uninfluenced by the small group of 'radically pro-migrant leftists'.

Thus the CGKR manifests itself as a 'safety fuse', the weakest point in a chain which has to take into account too many sides and which would blow as soon as the pressure became too strong – an inevitable event as soon as a definition of racism is used which is not itself embedded in power relationships. The Centre itself is, in principle, not a political institution, yet it is a policy-making body with tremendous practical influence, and at the same time it is fully dependent on political goodwill. That is why it has to navigate carefully between incompatible forces in order to survive. The CGKR serves as an alibi for the government to evade direct participation in the fight against racism. It embodies all delicate relationships and sensitivities of the Belgian political world. Thus, chiding the Vlaams Blok is permitted, since it is the official villain, but taking legal action against even that party as a party is virtually impossible, just like it turns out to be much harder to reprimand figures with authority and their services. Barring laudable exceptions, such as Leman's condemnation of some aspects of recent asylum policies (about which more is to be said below), the CGKR's carefulness is paralysing for the anti-racist movements which had high hopes for the Centre, and over which the Centre exercises true moral authority.

The non-discrimination declaration

On 15 July 1993, in the middle of the summer holidays, the different Flemish educational networks and the Flemish Ministry of Education signed a 'common declaration concerning a non-discrimination policy in education'. The original reason was no doubt the realization that education would be *the* battlefield for a change of mentality that would be needed to keep waving the banner of tolerance. This awareness was already translated by the KCM into an ambitious and wide-ranging education plan, the so-called 'education-priorities policy for migrants',[7] which was one of the few clearly developed and well-financed aspects of migrant policies. Racism and discrimination in schools, both 'in the playground' (i.e. racism during school activities) and 'at the gate' (i.e. the refusal to enrol migrants in certain schools), was also a relatively old concern of the Flemish Centre for the Integration of Migrants (*Vlaams Centrum voor de Integratie van Migranten*, henceforth VCIM). The VCIM had already issued its own 'non-discrimination manifesto', signed by roughly four hundred persons and organizations. This initiative, however, could count on little government support. Traditionally, the Belgian educational landscape is an extremely sensitive world, a world of pacts, agreements and delicate balances. A direct strategy in which all educational networks and all individual schools were asked to pay attention to what all networks and schools would doggedly deny, racism and discrimination 'in the playground' as well as 'at the gate', was most unwelcome. Especially the fact that the VCIM proposal included a kind of complaint registration, which would have led to an inductive substantiation of what precisely racism and discrimination meant in education, was experienced like a trip to the dentist. The initiative was, in true Belgian style, hidden in committees and councils.

Therefore, the news of a spontaneous agreement on a 'common declaration concerning a non-discrimination policy in education' came as a complete surprise. Suddenly, in the silence of the summer, the educational networks (i.e. the official state network *and* the Catholic network) had reached a settlement. This was received with general applause. Finally the world of education would do something about unacceptable forms of racism and discrimination. The declaration soon turned into a showpiece for the government, which felt it could now maintain that 'something had been done' to solve this problem in schools.

But what does the declaration say? The general applause was not combined with a careful reading of the text. Needless to say that little remained of the VCIM 'non-discrimination manifesto', though the name was all but copied. The cooperation between the educational networks would involve conducting 'inter-network negotiations' which should lead to common *enrollment policies* for migrant pupils. The agreements reached should be valid for a five-year period and would have to include 'procedures for the referral of target group pupils', i.e. measures to be taken when the number of 'target group pupils' (read: migrant children) would 'surpass a certain percentage'. In other words, this is a practical application of the famous concept of the 'threshold of tolerance', if there ever was one. As a result, the so-called 'non-discrimination declaration' amounts to a *spreading policy* for migrant children, put into action as soon as the concentration of migrant pupils in certain schools 'surpasses a certain percentage'. The percentage in question is not further specified. Schools, or their immediate authorities, can determine their own limitations on migrant intake. Often the criterion is the percentage of foreigners in the municipality of the school.

One positive side of the declaration cannot be denied: 'white' schools (many of them Catholic) can no longer keep their doors closed to migrants. But the only purpose of this measure is a deconcentration in other schools. Beside the enrolment or spreading policy, support for present 'concentration schools' is part of the programme. Official documents about the future of concentration schools, however, do not prevaricate when it comes to a statement of the ultimate goal: attracting more autochthonous pupils again. In other words, deconcentration once more.

In the implementation of the policy there is again a central role for the CGKR, which displays its traditional caution. Thus there are procedures for informing parents. To what extent migrant parents are involved remains most unclear. On the other hand, there is an abundance of documents directed at Belgian parents to convince them of the rationality (and ultimately of the beneficial effects for their own children) of allowing, say, 20 per cent of the children in their schools to be migrant. They are reassured, e.g., with the following words:

> Belgian parents have nothing to fear: they are not asked to make extra efforts. But we do count on their hospitality and tolerance.[8]

Moreover, the terms of the declaration were not implemented everywhere at the same time. First, a number of 'pilot projects' were developed in municipalities known for their acute 'migrant problems'. The selection of those municipalities was made in complete secrecy. After they became known, nothing was publicly released about the precise contents of the agreements, probably in view of the usual 'serene treatment' of this 'sensitive matter'. Protest is easily stifled in the absence of clarity – about which more below.

Today, a few years after the policy was launched, it is not yet clear whether schools that have violated the agreements (for instance by refusing to enrol migrant children) have suffered any sanctions. It also remains vague whether the educational networks have lived up to an additional element of the agreement, the obligation to develop network-internal 'non-discrimination codes' for practical application inside the schools. The clauses pertaining to this, however, were extremely vague from the start. For one thing, it was stated explicitly that the codes in question should take into account the 'specific pedagogical project' of the network and/or the school. This kind of qualification, rather than clarifying the overall goals, immediately introduced almost complete freedom of interpretation. Also, for this aspect of the scheme no timing was foreseen.

Let us leave these technical aspects for what they are and return to the heart of the matter. While it is deemed necessary to reassure Belgian parents that their (white) schools will not be flooded by migrants, there is, paradoxically, little good news to be communicated to migrant parents who, in the case of measures that would really be designed to fight discrimination, should be the real beneficiaries of the new policy. A spreading policy – in spite of its being reminiscent of American bussing schemes years ago – is at least a peculiar substantiation for the concept 'anti-discrimination'. Though in the long run, as said, it will prevent schools from remaining completely white, refusals to enrol migrant children because they are 'migrants' (even if they are referred to as 'target group pupils') is *not forbidden* by the new policy but simply *institutionalized and regulated*. This is a violation of a series of laws, starting with the Belgian constitution, Article 17 of which says:

> Education is free; every preventive measure is forbidden [. . .]

and goes on to say:

> The Community guarantees freedom of choice for the parents.[9]

As far as the freedom of choice is concerned, the rights of migrant parents are obviously infringed. Only migrant children are 'spread' over the schooling system, i.e. only one population group and even one subgroup of the foreigner population: no-one has proposed a proportional spreading of European non-Belgians, let alone autochthonous Belgians themselves. No other children are subject to limitations on the freedom of choice other than purely pedagogical ones. Sometimes there are, of course, attempts to hide this reality by defining the target group as the 'linguistically other' (see Chapter 5), but there are no linguistic tests to underscore the implementation practice. Quite to the contrary, the text of the non-discrimination declaration defines the 'target group pupils' on the basis of two criteria:

1   [. . .] the matrilineal grandmother was not born in Belgium and does not possess Belgian or Dutch nationality by birth [. . .] and
2   [. . .] the mother has at most enjoyed formal education until the end of the school year during which she reached the age of 18 [. . .].[10]

The first criterion is simply ethnic, and based on a view of ethnicity in which, in addition to (matrilineal) descent, language occupies a central place (hence the exception for Dutch people). The second criterion is a strange one, because eighteen years is the age limit of compulsory education in Belgium. One can hardly speak, then, of mothers with a low degree of education, unless one would define everyone who has only fulfilled the minimum requirements of compulsory education as poorly educated. On the basis of both criteria one can easily imagine a perfectly 'integrated' child, growing up in a Dutch-speaking environment and with parents who have enjoyed a decent formal education, but who would still fit the 'target group' definition. The age limit of eighteen years for the mother's degree of education, for that matter, entered the picture quite late. First fourteen years of age had been foreseen, then sixteen, but under both conditions not enough migrant children were seen to fit the criteria for the 'target group', i.e. not enough children of Turkish or Moroccan descent were made 'spreadable'. This was unacceptable, since the main criterion is the ethnic one: the entire group is seen as 'problematic'. No mention is made of specific testable criteria which could save the appearance of a purely pedagogical measure, such as earlier test scores, observable language or learning problems, etc. Hence, a child can be intelligent, score highly in school, and still be seen as an obstacle to the realization of general educational goals.[11]

Put clearly, the declaration is not strictly speaking an 'anti'- or 'non'-discrimination declaration, but rather *an instrument to regulate precisely how one should discriminate.* It is disturbing to see how one can keep selling the idea as an instrument in the fight against racism and discrimination. The declaration is unilaterally directed at migrant children, the clearly identifiable 'target group'. The idea that they should be 'spread' is based on acceptance of the classical association between the presence of migrants and the emergence of problems, and the linear association of 'many migrants' with a necessarily 'low quality of education'. The (in)adequacy of one's own 'pedagogical project' – at least a possible source of failure – is never questioned. Nothing is said, furthermore, about the way in which the measures are fundamentally related to the publicly professed *principle* that every form of exclusion needs to be fought – a principle which should also cover exclusions after a certain percentage of admissions have been granted.

The measures that should be taken, such as the development of means to tackle the didactic complications which emerge in any mixed school environment, are avoided by the attempt to render the 'problem' invisible. Whether consciously or not, spreading migrants neatly over the entire educational landscape is expected to contribute to the desired rehomogenization of society. In three words: homogeneism at work.

Since the declaration was first publicized, it has not been immune to criticism. Ever since, in September of each year, a number of children of foreign descent have had problems in finding schools that would admit them. But truly hegemonic processes have kept the criticism at bay. One strategy to guarantee that result was the way in which complaint mechanisms were installed: migrants who felt victimized by referrals received from schools were given the opportunity to complain about the implementation of the 'non-discrimination' measures; but their complaint would only be taken seriously if filed with the proper authorities – authorities installed by the same powers who invented the declaration and who installed the implementation mechanisms. Thus the victim does not get a chance. As usual, some of the prominent media also contributed to the maintenance of hegemony. We will give just one example from our personal experience. After mobilizing nine people (including five prominent members of migrant communities) for the drafting of an opinion article criticising the non-discrimination declaration, and after sending the resulting text to De Standaard, it took several weeks, many phone calls and as many revisions (mostly cuts) before it was published. Even then, the editors refused to publish it with the names of all the people involved, so that it appeared under the name of only one of the present authors (Verschueren 1994). Just three days later, the same newspaper published a response by Johan Leman, who was now in a position to attack what appeared to be the opinion of one individual, personally and professionally removed from the educational practices under debate. Thus the co-signing migrants were completely neutralized. Again: the victim does not get a chance, not even to voice an opinion and to be taken seriously.

All this does not mean that no adaptations were made under the pressure of criticism. The most noteworthy one is the explicit position taken by Minister of Education Luc Vandenbossche on the unacceptability of setting upper limits for the admission of migrants in schools – a practice which was developing rapidly and still has not been eliminated. On various occasions he has also reprimanded schools for such practices, handling the principle that freedom of choice has to be kept intact. On the other hand, however, he does not object to 'referrals' to other schools, as long as there is no real 'rejection'; nor does he object to 'target figures', as long as there are no strict 'limits'. All this leaves a lot of space for semantic manoeuvring and strategic action, so that the Minister's position has not had much effect on actual practice. The lack of clarity, for instance, results in the fact that many school supervisors still believe (quite honestly) that it is their task to limit the number of migrants in their schools. Often they have to take the blame for following guidelines imposed on them by intermediate authorities. These problems will not be solved until the entire policy is thoroughly revised, with full acceptance of diversity, no matter what numerical shape it may take. In the absence of radical policy changes, the Minister's position amounts to nothing but a manoeuvre to evade direct criticism, just like the overall legitimization process which (a) fits the non-discrimination declaration into the widely accepted goal of integration (with all its premisses), and (b) uses *anderstaligheid* ('speaking another language') as a pedagogical alibi for ethnic categorization.

Asylum policies

Government services profile themselves ever more forcefully as the defenders of 'law and order'. One of the most visible manifestations of this process is the gradual tightening of asylum policies over the last half-dozen years. In part, this is the result of decisions taken at the level of the European Union, in particular the Schengen agreements, combining a relaxation of internal border controls with a design for 'Fortress Europe'. But the way in which the agreements are put into practice, and the extent to which violence and detention enter the picture, cannot be reduced to the Schengen influence. The Belgian authorities have been developing a new, extremely repressive, stance of their own in relation to new would-be immigrants. As elsewhere in Europe, the dominant slogan is 'The boat is full'. No-one should be allowed to enter, except for the few people who, after a severe and often arbitrary selection procedure, are recognized as 'legitimate' refugees. But even those are stigmatized and distrusted.

The discrepancy between the phenomenon of migration – people leaving their country in search of a more promising horizon in the rich West – and the legal provisions is sharply illustrated by the disparity between the number of candidate asylum seekers and the number of recognitions: 95 per cent of the applications are turned down; the vast majority of people who end up at Brussels airport are immediately sent back following a cursory interview to decide whether or not they will be allowed to apply for asylum (a process during which the slightest contradiction in their statements may be used as an argument).

An interesting language game underscores the policy. An initial distinction is made between 'real refugees' and others. At the opposite end of the scale to 'real' refugees are the *illegalen*, 'illegal aliens'. Real refugees have a right to asylum, protection and solidarity; the others do not. The terms *vluchtelingen* ('refugees') and *asielzoekers* ('asylum seekers') are used alternatingly, even though 'asylum seekers' are people who have not yet been granted asylum, i.e. who are not yet recognized as 'refugees'. Further, 'refugees' are supposed to be fleeing from something. The Geneva Convention specifies five categories. Whoever is not covered by any of the categories is supposed *not* to be fleeing at all. Thus 'economic refugees' – a category which is not entitled to asylum – are not believed to be *fleeing* from poverty but to be *avonturiers* ('adventurers') or *gelukszoekers* ('fortune hunters') in search of easy money (or hard-earned money which would be better spent by employing autochthonous people). The terms 'adventurers' and 'fortune hunters' are indeed used frequently. They suggest something frivolous, almost tourist-like. The members of the category are not serious people. This suggestion is strengthened by a recurrent theme: asylum seekers are in fact the elites of their own countries. They are, following this story, not poor souls leaving all their ties and belongings in search of peace and safety, but well-educated, well-to-do citizens, who would do better staying where they are to help in the (re)development of their country. They are seen to evade their real responsibilities by looking for a haven in the West. Little does one know – or care – that many of the asylum seekers, in fact, are illiterate or semi-literate, which explains a good deal of the communication problems that arise in the treatment of their cases.

Asylum seekers are further lumped together with that other problem category, 'migrants'. The new immigration is seen as a continuation of the old (labour) immigration. 'Problems' with one group are projected on to the other. Needless to say, as a result the overall picture becomes even more negative. Young migrants of the second and third generation are now often associated with forms of criminality which may be the products of the recently opened borders between East and West. Thus the stigmatization process continues to get worse. The pernicious influence of categorial thinking in the migrant debate becomes crystal clear in this context. Since 'migrant' is already an undifferentiated (though selectively applied) categorial concept, only allowing for distinctions between men and women and generations at a secondary level, and since the category is further stuffed with the new groups of asylum seekers and economic refugees, any reasonable discourse about 'migrants' becomes virtually impossible. The concept is semantically conflated and ceases to cover any practical reality.

The language game, however, goes further. The asylum-seeker debate is dominated by a rhetoric with two central themes, *practical feasibility* and *respect for the social order*. The unaffordability of asylum seekers is a standard refrain in arguments that 'The boat is full'. They arrive uninvited to benefit from our social security system. The taxpayer has to pay the bill. For how long can this continue? The cost–benefit argument, also used elsewhere in the migrant debate, resurfaces: they cost money, without any reasonable return. Human dignity is provided with a price tag. The money to be spent, the argument continues, should go to development aid, so that potential asylum seekers could enjoy a nice future in their own country. The partial truth in this could be brought out only by heavy investment in that direction which, of course, does not happen. On the contrary, structural development programmes have been slowly replaced by disaster aid and so-called humanitarian military interventions, and even so the Belgian budget for development cooperation has been decreasing steadily over the years.

The element 'respect for the social order', which recurs over and over again in various domains of foreigner politics, equally lacks credibility. Asylum seekers are presented as a plague. Their presence is assumed to lead directly to a higher crime rate and feelings of unsafety. Few terms are as hollow as *onveiligheidsgevoel* ('feeling of unsafety'), since it hinges on the validity of stereotypes, and in particular the automatic association between crime and the presence of foreigners. Government services have the tendency to adopt the negative stereotype and to use it to legitimate their repressive policies in relation to these 'criminogenic' newcomers. Louis Tobback, then Minister of Internal Affairs, illustrates this:

> No one can tell me approximately today how many illegals run around in our country. But there are tens of thousands, and apparently they must be well-behaved people, otherwise we would have had Brixton twenty times over! All these illegals do not have any access to the normal social provisions and can, therefore, not possibly function normally in our society. A state concerned about its social order cannot keep this up. This situation can explode at any moment and that is my greatest concern.[12]

Note that a direct link is posited between the uncontrolled and supposedly massive presence of administratively unknown illegal aliens and the possibility of an explosion of violence. It is unclear who the agents behind the violence would have to be. The suggestion is made that fortunately, and perchance, those illegal aliens are well-behaved people who do not upset the local population too much. Yet they are pictured as a remaining threat, even in the absence of any incidents for which they could be blamed.

The notion of 'crime' is handled quite elastically. Rejected asylum seekers, by their very name 'illegal aliens', are placed outside the law. Their being here is a crime. It is the duty of the authorities to make people respect the law. Therefore, illegal aliens may be treated like criminals – and they are. There was the example of a well-planned and massive police raid in Louvain during which a formidable police force picked up large numbers of (mostly completely innocent) foreigners, investigating them carefully in search of the slightest breach of Belgian law – and being able to find fault with only a few. In the same line of business, illegal aliens end up in prisons among ordinary criminals, or in detention centres called *opvang-centra* ('reception centres') which pass all tests for prisons. A new 'reception centre' was built in Steenokkerzeel and opened in March 1994 after an investment of 200 million Belgian francs. It is a complex with search lights and two rows of barbed wire, four metres high. Inside, fifty guards, aided by a system of video surveillance, keep everything under control. Still, then-Minister of Interior Affairs Louis Tobback emphatically claimed that this was not a prison because – entering the language game again – 'here are no criminals', only 'illegal aliens'. Even though the daily routine has all the appearances of the prison system, according to the director it should not be interpreted that way:

Nothing is compulsory . . . Our safety guards are civil servants. They are unarmed and are not allowed to use violence.[13]

Yet the asylum seekers in the 'reception centre' are robbed of their freedom and cannot leave the centre at will. Hence this is a prison, albeit one with a relatively moderate style, from which escape is possible only for people 'with a really bad attitude' (Tobback's words). This repressive approach was further developed by Tobback's successor, Johan Van de Lanotte. It is now possible in Belgium to detain asylum seekers, even during the period when their application is being evaluated, for virtually indefinite periods.

A favourite strategy in all of this is the recourse to public opinion. It is the ordinary citizen who is opposed to the presence of foreigners. It is the ordinary citizen who could become the victim of violent conflict – or who could start voting for the Vlaams Blok. Thus a repressive admittance policy and a repressive attitude towards illegal aliens, in the hands of socialist ministers, become instruments of democracy. Tobback once more:

In a democracy there is a limit to the admittance capacity of the community. I do not claim that it has already been surpassed in Belgium, but there is really a limit![14]

In the same vein, Tobback justified the police raid in Louvain by pointing at the fact that 'the boat' was politically and psychologically full. He added that we live in a democracy, and that in a democracy one cannot dictate how people should think. In other words, if there are negative opinions about foreigners, an aggressive approach is in order. A lack of tolerance among majority members is thus not seen as a danger for democracy and human rights, while an assumed lack of pluralist tendencies among Moslems *is* a danger for democracy and warrants discriminatory treatment. Discrimination and repression can therefore be justified in two ways: by attributing a lack of tolerance to minorities, or by responding 'democratically' to the negative attitudes of members of the majority. Unfortunately, both have become standard practice. More and more, a link is being developed between integration and the need to restrict the acceptance of asylum seekers. Foreigners have to be 'integrated', and that process already proves to be so problematic for our established minorities that Belgian society is judged incapable of absorbing more diversity. This is not seen as a deficiency of Belgian society, but as a natural state of affairs. (For further demonstrations of the link between asylum policies and integration rhetoric, see Blommaert 1997.)

Briefly . . .

These three illustrations do not tell the whole story. We do not deny that some sensible initiatives have been taken by the authorities, which often also display an awareness of the dangers of racism. The laws against racism have been tightened, for instance. It has become easier to acquire Belgian nationality. And polit-ical refugees who have been waiting for an evaluation of their applications for over five years have been 'regularized'. But the illustrations are meant to show that, when it comes to concrete policy options, there is a populist tendency to go in directions that are believed to yield the best harvest of votes. The resulting policies contribute to various forms of institutionalized discrimination, a sure recipe for racism without end.

EPILOGUE

Science is always autobiographical. In that sense, the different chapters that precede this epilogue do not only provide an account of 'research', with all its connotations of detachment, neutrality and professional devotion. They also provide a story of the involvement of the authors in what they have described and analysed. Every step in our analysis was an argument exchanged between us and others, part and parcel of the migrant debate. In Chapter 5 we presented a brief sketch of the ways in which our interventions in the debate were received. But it may be wise to underscore that we do not (and did not) want to make a strict distinction between, on the one hand, a series of activities qualified as 'scientific' (with the connotations mentioned above), and public or political activities such as interventions in the debate on the other. The decision to analyse was prompted and motivated by developments in the debate. Our scientific work was our way of participating in the debate, a form of political action.

No doubt this raises problems of voice. Perhaps we have not always been able to 'describe' as neutrally and objectively as we should. We would be deluding ourselves if we were to pretend to have the voice of a neutral bystander. Our voice automatically represents a particular position within the debate. We believe that we could not have acted otherwise, both ethically and in terms of norms of 'scientific' investigation. Scientists often assume the comfortable position of uninvolved (and hence invulnerable) outsiders or 'experts'. Often this construction of 'outsiderness' is a defensive shield as well as an alibi. We cannot claim that we were never involved, nor do we wish to do so. As a consequence, there is a double 'we' in the story: 'we the authors', but also 'we, members of the majority.' Our critical, outsiders' voice can never obscure the fact that, in the picture we sketched, we bear as much guilt for the troubled relationships we analysed as anyone else.

In a recent paper commenting on the practice of pragmatic research, Charles Briggs (1997) advocates an approach in which the analysis of forms of violence and conflict in and through discourse is combined with 'reflecting on how this shift in focus reveals the need to examine and revise key assumptions that underlie work in pragmatics and related areas in general, even research that seeks to place struggle and disorder in the margins or to displace them from research on language as a whole'. In other words, being a political actor and assuming a political voice may be at the heart of what we (should) understand by scientific activity in the field of pragmatics. The epilogue to this story, therefore, cannot be a purely theoretical or methodological reflection. Rather, we prefer to vent some deeply 'unscientific' thoughts. After all, this book may be finished, but the debate continues.

In *The Rhetoric of Reaction*, Albert Hirschman (1991) investigates patterns of argumentation used by 'reactionaries' at three points in history when important social and political changes were taking place: first, the development of civil society symbolized by the American and the French revolutions, with freedom of speech, thought and religion, the right to equal justice and individual freedom; second, the acceptance of universal suffrage, or the right of citizens to take part in the exercise of political power; third, the rise of the welfare state, casting individual and political rights in a social and economic frame, with minimal guarantees for education, health and economic security. In each of those cases, Hirschman discerns three types of argument against the changes: the *perversity* argument, claiming that the actual effects of the changes are the opposite of what was intended; the *futility* argument that nothing really changes anyway; and the *jeopardy* argument, according to which the changes endanger valuable past achievements.

Today's 'reactionaries' have found a new 'revolution' to which they eagerly apply the same types of argument. The 'revolution' in question is the type of ethnic and cultural diversification taking place in European societies today. 'Progressive' acceptance of multicultural society is said not to have the intended beneficial effect on immigrants, but to condemn them to a life of estrangement outside of their natural environment: the perversity thesis. Further, attempts at 'integration' are doomed to failure because the immigrant cultures are too fundamentally different: the futility thesis. Finally, the presence of large numbers of fundamentally different ethnic and cultural communities threatens our most basic values, notably democracy and Christianity: the jeopardy thesis.

'Progressives' and other members of what we have called the 'tolerant majority' have their own version of the same patterns of reasoning. We cannot ship hundreds of thousands of people back 'home'; so we'd better accept their lasting presence; hence talk of anything but integration is a waste of energy: the futility thesis. Further, assuming that we want what's best for them (an assumption which even inhabits 'reactionary' rhetoric, as suggested above), sending them back would not improve their situation, since most of them would lead estranged lives in a country of origin where they have not lived for a long time: the perversity thesis. Finally, giving them that kind of treatment would threaten some of the constituent values of democracy and Christianity, notably hospitality, pluralism and tolerance: the jeopardy thesis.

At this surface level of argumentation, 'progressives' or the 'tolerant majority' favouring multiculturalism cannot but fail to convince their counterparts, since the debate consists entirely of claims and counterclaims juxtaposed in the same argumentational framework built on the same foundations. The foundations in question form a solid ideological construct which we have characterized as the *doctrine of homogeneism*: the belief that homogeneous societies are facts of nature which cannot be disturbed with impunity – a belief shared quite generally both by opponents and proponents of anti-migrant movements. In this book we have adduced numerous test cases. Even the clearest instances of rhetoric used to promote a positive image of migrants, or the *rhetoric of tolerance*, were shown to conform unequivocally to the doctrine, thus fully confirming our earlier suspicions – and justifying our worst fears. The basic fear is that failure to replace the premises, rather than to brush up the surface, is ultimately bound to strengthen the appeal of anti-migrant arguments. The most fundamental one of those unchallenged premises is the idea that the ethnic and cultural diversification of European societies is indeed a 'revolution' comparable to the emergence of civil society, universal suffrage and the rise of the welfare state.

Just like reactionaries and progressives before us, and after careful scrutiny of large amounts of data, as researchers we can only offer our own version of perversion, futility and jeopardy. First, within the confines of the rhetoric of tolerance as we have observed it, even clear attempts at positive image building are *futile*, not in the sense that they may not have the beneficial effect of more patience (which is a virtue, and may favourably influence interaction, even if it is there for all the wrong reasons), but in the sense that they will not convince anyone of the normality of a multi-ethnic society. Second, the achieved effect may be diagonally *opposite* to the intended one, since the overall rhetoric reinforces most of the premises of any anti-migrant movement, notably the idea that diversification is a new phenomenon which inevitably causes fundamental societal problems. Third, the cultural differences to which the most benevolent versions of the rhetoric reduce the 'problems' are utterly *dangerous* constructs because they feed all the (mostly negative) stereotypes they are supposed to combat.

Cultural differences are comparable to any other society-structuring type of difference (gender, age, class, profession, world view and religion, political conviction). They are in no way more problematic and hence they do not have to be subjected to any form of *normativeness*, neither in the sense of homogenization (as in the traditional Belgian 'integration' concept), nor in the sense of the cultivation of separate identities. Our research shows, however, that they are continuously used as arguments to hide discriminatory treatment. The fight against racism cannot possibly succeed unless a true *acceptance of diversity* is taken as the *starting point* of any perspective on society. In fact, diversity has to be taken so seriously that its locus is no longer any type of *group*, but the *individual* – where any individual can belong to many different types of rarely coinciding groups at the same time (see Chapter 2). This is the only way to escape from the dilemma, which haunts most 'multiculturalist' rhetoric, that accepting diversity also stresses diversity, so that it may cause a further distancing between groups. We emphatically reject the type of 'multiculturalism' which takes 'cultures' seriously as 'entities' that can lead juxtaposed lives, provided that the group-level diversity

– seen as a problem or challenge – is sufficiently 'managed'.[1] Group-level entities are always constructed arbitrarily and for certain purposes. Individual variability, on the other hand, is a natural aspect of the *condition humaine*, antedating any type of group formation and persisting throughout any group-formation processes. Let us briefly list some of the practical implications of this point of view.

First, an acceptance of diversity means the acceptance of true *equality*. It is not enough to *say* that one accepts the equality of migrants. There is no acceptance of equality as long as the autochthonous majority wants 'them' to become 'like us'. Therefore it is wrong to demand adaptation with respect to endlessly manipulable 'values and achievements of our society', and to allow for diversity only in the domain of 'cultural expressions' ('diversity-as-mutual-enrichment', i.e. the exchange office model of a multicultural society). On the other hand, there is no acceptance of equality, either, if migrants are denied the right to change and assimilate in any areas they choose. Spontaneous processes of adaptation have obviously operated in many domains and for many individuals. But the majority does not have the right to regulate how far these processes have to go. In that sense, the content of *Tekenen voor Gelijkwaardigheid* ('Opting for Equality', KCM 1993; see Chapter 5) is a caricature of its title.

Second, equality is an empty notion without *equal opportunities* for everyone; equal opportunities cannot be realized without *equal rights and duties*. According to CGKR Director Johan Leman, a society which offers equal opportunities is

> [. . .] a society in which capable members of the minorities, who satisfy the principles of successful integration, can fully occupy a function and obtain a status on the basis of equality with anyone in the majority.[2]

Following this definition, the right to equal opportunities can be denied anyone who does not meet the demands of 'capability' and 'successful integration'. It is the perfect basis for institutionalized discrimination.

Third, equal rights and duties are embodied in *political participation*. Hence also the right to vote is required. The sociologist Jan Vranken expresses more or less the same idea as Johan Leman when he says:

> It remains one of the major problems that members of the migrant population who know Belgian society well enough, are still not participating in decision-making.[3]

All migrants are members of this society and know aspects of it which autochthons could not even imagine. Therefore the majority has no basis to judge who can and who cannot participate in decision-making processes. This kind of attitude is denigrating, and clearly in violation of the acceptance of equality.

Fourth, for the enjoyment of equal rights and duties, the *legal system* is the *only norm*. The guidelines of the society are formulated in one legal system which has to be sufficiently adaptable and flexible to meet the needs of different members of that society, whatever their group affiliations may be. One cannot place demands on migrants that cannot be placed on members of the majority; only what is legally binding can be enforced.

Fifth, any form of *exclusion* based on membership in a subjectively defined group (on the basis of ethnicity, race, skin colour, religion, values, descent, language or language variety), the right to equal treatment of which is not protected by other laws, is definable as *racism*, and is to be situated in the domain of application of the laws against racism and xenophobia. Not only the political racism of the extreme right needs to be attacked, but also every form of everyday racism. Even when the word 'race' is carefully avoided, and when exclusion does not touch racially defined groups (which is rarely the case anyway because of the vagueness of the concept 'race'), one can adopt a 'racist' attitude.

Sixth, every practical form of implementation of the above principles has to be decided (a) *in direct negotiation with all parties involved* to the extent that the decisions to be taken require action or cooperation on the part of the autochthonous majority (as is the case with the granting of voting rights), or (b) *by the allochthons concerned* to the extent that the subject matter primarily touches their lifestyles. From this perspective, it is hard to imagine a majority regulating the 'self-organizations' of migrants – an Orwellian situation which is a reality in Belgium.

Needless to say, these recommendations go far beyond the Belgian migrant debate.

NOTES

INTRODUCTION

1 For examples from the Former Soviet Union, Asia, Africa and Latin America, see Crawford Young (ed.) (1993).
2 Quoted from a lecture given by David Hollinger at the University of Antwerp, 12 May 1995.
3 In one of the cases referred to, the Supreme Court simply declined to hear the University of Maryland's appeal against a court ruling that forced them to eliminate a scholarship programme designed specifically for black students. There is little doubt that this will set a precedent affecting race-based scholarships. The argument is that this makes American society more 'colour blind'. Whether it brings higher education closer to the goal of equal opportunities for minorities is an entirely different matter.

CHAPTER 1

1 Quoted from MOST Newsletter 1 (December 1994).
2 Quoted from the presentation of MOST objectives, structures and activities in MOST Newsletter 1 (p. 3). Note also the leading theme of MOST Newsletter 3 (June 1995), 'Cultural Pluralism and Multiculturalism: Managing Unity in Diversity'.
3 Fortunately, this 'tolerant majority' still is a majority in the Western world. But, at the time of writing, the extreme right already represents 30 per cent of the voters in Antwerp, the place where this book is being written.
4 Gérard-François Dumont (1996) offers a detailed survey of various elements influencing the face of current migration patterns. See John Rex (ed.) (1996) for a comparative overview of the way in which migrant communities have been integrated in the political process in a number of European cities.
5 There are numerous cases of this kind. Thus, recently, a foreign doctoral student accepted at a Belgian university and residing legally in another European Union country was told that he could not even apply for a visa unless he first returned to his country of origin.
6 Visa applicants are asked to sign a declaration to the effect that they have been properly warned by the consulate that they should 'abstain from taking part in Belgian politics and avoid embarrassing Belgium by taking positions in international political affairs, in particular by criticising foreign governments'. The French text runs as follows: '[. . .] reconnaît avoir été avisé de ce qu'il devra s'abstenir de prendre parti dans la politique belge et éviter de mettre la Belgique en difficulté par des prises de position en matière politique internationale, notamment en critiquant des gouvernements étrangers'.

7 For a strong theory of control over public debate, see Herman and Chomsky's (1994) 'propaganda model' of the functioning of the mass media. As for the suggestion that debates are instruments of control, this study will no doubt offer some evidence. Democratic debates can be used to redirect or silence spontaneous forms of resistance and opposition: as soon as the debate about a problem is concluded, the problem is supposed to be solved and every opposition against this solution can be qualified as marginal or even antidemocratic.

8 Most recently, 'objectivity' in general, in fields ranging from archaeology to legal argumentation, has been shown to be subject to patterns of selective vision (Goodwin 1994).

9 Present-day Belgium did not exist until 1830.

10 There is an extensive literature about these issues. See, e.g., the contributions to Blommaert and Verschueren (eds) (1991) and Hinnenkamp (1995).

11 References are to a training programme called *Going International*, produced by Copeland Griggs Productions (San Francisco), and to a fairly popular book *Culturen sterven langzaam: over interculturele communicatie* (Cultures Die Slowly: About Intercultural Communication) by the Flemish anthropologist Rik Pinxten (1994).

12 Thus there is a clear continuity between the migrant debate and colonial rhetoric, that earlier example of speaking about other cultures. When Belgian colonial historiography described 'ferocious Zande warriors', this qualification was hardly an objective characterization of the attitudes of the Zande, but rather an account of their reaction to white control and domination. The Zande did not acquiesce in the fact of colonization, and therefore entered history as fiendish brutes. Etienne Balibar (1991: 12) identifies 'two specifically racist *ideological schemas* which are likely to continue producing memory and collective-perception effects: the colonial schema, and the schema of anti-Semitism'. Balibar explains the fact that, in contemporary Europe, Muslims are a permanent target of racism by the confluence of both schemas, 'so that imagery of racial superiority and imagery of cultural and religious rivalry reinforce each other'.

CHAPTER 2

1 The parallel is a rough one indeed. Flanders is predominantly Catholic, but even though The Netherlands is perceived as a Protestant, Calvinist country, there are more Catholics than Protestants. Thus language is more of a distinctive feature than religion. On the other hand, religion is a stronger marker of identity in the distinction between Serbians and Croats: the language difference is more geographical than ethnic, so that spoken by Serbians in the Krajinait is much closer to the Croat version of Serbo-Croatian than to the version spoken in Serbia.

2 Following Bakhtin (1986), we use the term 'genre' to designate recognizable types of language usage related to diverse 'spheres' of human activity.

3 Note that in this context 'migrant worker' does not refer to a migrant who works but to someone who works in the field of migrant affairs.

4 In the linguistic literature, many divergent views are to be found of what 'pragmatics' is supposed to stand for. We opt for the widest possible interpretation, involving a necessarily interdisciplinary perspective on language in use. See Verschueren *et al.* (eds) (1995).

5 This premiss is shared by researchers involved in the analysis of ideology in discourse (e.g. Robert Hodge and Gunther Kress 1993), even if they would not label their research 'pragmatic'.

6 'Speculation' is basically the same as what Eco (1990, 1992) would call 'overinterpretation'. The only difference is that the product of speculation (interpretation which

goes beyond the limits set by an adopted methodology) may be 'true', whereas the term 'overinterpretation' already suggests a deviation from the truth.

7 The demand for 'coherence' implies that the end product of our research can never be a full description of the ideological work that goes on. It is not possible to 'make sense', scientifically, of each and every ingredient of the manifestation of an ideology. Human beings, as complex organisms, are simply not mechanical or consistent enough. The same is true, by extension, of human societies. The main challenge for the researcher is to push the limitations of an approach as far as possible, and to know where to cut off.

8 See J.J. Gumperz, T.C. Jupp and C. Roberts (1979), J.J. Gumperz (1982) and C. Roberts and P. Sayers (1987) for evidence that the implementation of policy decisions, however carefully designed and whatever the amount of goodwill on the part of the participants, may go wrong.

CHAPTER 3

1 A special issue of *Innovation* (9.1.1996) provides a number of studies of migration as an urban phenomenon in Europe. A paper by Jan Blommaert and Marco Martiniello (1996) discusses Antwerp and Liège.

2 Dutch *vreemdeling* is ambiguous between 'alien/foreigner' and 'stranger'. In the context of the present debate the ambiguity is usually cancelled in favour of 'alien/foreigner'. But even so, an associative link with 'strangeness' usually remains.

3 Henceforth, the original (usually Dutch) versions of quotations will be given in the endnotes. The title cited here goes as follows: 'Erkende politieke vluchtelingen of illegalen: Het blijven vreemdelingen' (DS, 2 April 1990, p. 7).

4 'GENT – Of een vreemdeling in ons land erkend is als politiek vluchteling, waardoor hij dus dezelfde rechten en plichten heeft als een Belg, maakt voor het gros van de bevolking niets uit. Gastarbeiders, illegaal in ons land verblijvende vreemdelingen, politieke vluchtelingen . . . Alles wordt over dezelfde kam geschoren: het zijn vreemdelingen. En ongeacht hun statuut blijven ze met dezelfde problemen kampen'. (DS, 2 April 1990, p. 7)

5 'De vreemde mutatie van Brussel'. (DS, 12–25 August 1991) Here the ambiguity of *vreemd* between 'foreign' and 'strange' is consciously played upon.

6 'BRUSSEL, De voorbije dagen stelden we diverse groepen "onbekende en rijkere" vreemdelingen in het Brusselse stadsgewest voorgesteld [sic]: Nederlanders, Fransen, Duitsers, Japanners, Skandinaven, Britten en Amerikanen, en ook Polen en Zaïrezen. Al deze groepen bleken onderling zéér te verschillen. En dan hadden we het nog niet over de vier grootste (en meeste [sic] bekende?) groepen migranten in Brussel: Italianen en Spanjaarden, en vooral Turken en Marokkanen. De vreemdelingen in Brussel kunnen dus niet onder één noemer worden gebracht, tenzij dan in de bevolkingsstatistieken. Alleen maar het onderscheid Belgen/buitenlanders maken, is duidelijk onvoldoende'. (DS, 24/25 August 1991, p. 2)

7 '[. . .] als een model van pas gearriveerde migrantengroep' (DS, 24/25 August 1991, p. 2); '[. . .] groeiende groep migranten' (DS, 22 August 1991, p. 2); 'Poolse migranten nog niet in kaart gebracht door gebrek aan gegevens' (DS, 21 August 1991, p. 2).

8 'Zweedse kolonie wil kulturele eigenheid behouden in eenwordend Europa' (DS, 22 August 1991, p. 2).

9 'Japanners niet echt op zoek naar integratie' (DS, 19 August 1991, p. 2).

10 'Japanners wonen graag dicht bijeen, en vertonen aldus alle kenmerken van nieuwe migranten: die zoeken mekaar op'. (DS, 19 August 1991, p. 2)

11 'De Polen kunnen als een zeer aparte groep van migranten worden beschouwd. Het gros van de Polen zijn zwartwerkers, die legaal het land binnenkomen, hier illegaal werken, en blijkbaar zéér vlot aan werk geraken'. (DS, 21 August 1991, p. 2)

12 'Op het Koninklijk Kommissariaat voor het Migrantenbeleid wordt de evolutie van de groep Poolse migranten nauwlettend gevolgd, voorzover er informatie over beschikbaar is'. (DS, 21 August 1991, p. 2)

13 'Financieel–economische aspecten van een migrantenbeleid in België" ' (KCM, December 1990).

14 'Culturele verscheidenheid als wederzijdse verrijking' (KCM 1992a).

15 'Het Koninklijk Commissariaat voor het Migrantenbeleid is zich bewust van de potentiële rijkdom voor het eigen samenleven in dit land van de onder ons aanwezige andere culturen'. (KCM 1992a: 5).

16 '[. . .] een verrijkend aanbod voor het culturele leven' (KCM 1992a: 4).

17 The subtitle of the report goes as follows: 'Een verenigingsleven van en met migranten, door de overheid ondersteund'. A tentative literal translation could be 'A society-life by and with migrants, supported by the government'. *Verenigingsleven* refers to formally organized, club-like social activities, which may have any focus in the realm of 'expressions of culture' (except, as will become clear later, anything related to Islam).

18 The title of the 'migrant policies' document: 'Een groene kijk op samen leven', literally 'A green perspective on living together' (AGALEV, June 1991). The Dutch text of the quotation: 'Het intense contact via migranten met een Turks [sic] of Marokkaanse kultuur is verrijkend. Deze verrijking vinden we reeds terug in onze eetkultuur, in de hedendaagse muziek . . . maar het kan ons westerlingen ook helpen bij de oplossing van onze problemen. De funktie en waardering van de ouderen in de migrantenfamilie steekt schril af tegen de wijze waarop wij ouderen uit onze samenleving bannen. In het licht van een verouderde bevolking kan samenleven met migranten leiden tot nieuwe inzichten'. (p. 7).

19 'Oudere migranten geven geen last'. (DNG, 6 June 1992, p. 3).

20 Borgerhout is a part of Antwerp with a relatively high proportion of Moroccans; it is one of the main areas that are always mentioned when 'migrant problems' are discussed. In popular parlance it is often referred to as 'Borgerocco'.

21 'Maar ik herhaal het: een uitvalsbasis voor die patrouilles is dat hier zeker niet. Pas op, ik wou soms dat zo'n burgerwacht met honden bestond, hé? 't Zou er hier rap anders uitzien. Want wat is het probleem, mijnheer? Die oudere Marokkanen geven geen last, die zijn beleefd, die gaan zelfs van het trottoir af, als ik voorbij kom. Maar die bende hier op het pleintje, wanneer gaan die ons gerust laten?' (DNG, 6 June 1992, p. 3).

22 'Het Koxplein wordt verpest door bendes: zo werd zelfs een zwangere vrouw aangepakt in een telefooncel'. (DNG, 6 June 1992, p. 3.)

23 'Ze zeggen dat het hier een Vlaams Blok-café is. Bon, ze komen hier een of twee keer per jaar vergaderen, en daarbij, 99% van de mensen van Borgerhout stemt daarvoor. Wij weten wel waarom. Van mij mogen ze nog 100.000 migranten sturen, als ze zich maar een beetje aanpassen en ons gerust laten. Maar dat horen ze bij de Stad niet'. (DNG, 6 June 1992, p. 3)

24 We are referring to the document entitled *Samenleven in de jaren '90: Inzichten van de SP over het migrantenvraagstuk* ('Living together in the 1990s: Insights of the SP regarding the migrant issue'), issued for a press conference on 2 November 1989.

25 'In bepaalde buurten wonen vooral oudere Vlaamse mensen en jonge migrantengezinnen met kleine en opgroeiende kinderen, zodat er voor die ouderen in verhouding veel drukte en lawaai is. Spanningen zijn in dergelijke situaties "normaal"'. (p. 5)

26 'Maar ook de eigen positie van vooral de Turkse of Marokkaanse vrouw maakt dat haar contactmogelijkheden en bewegingsruimte beperkt zijn, zodat ze zichzelf automatisch in een geïsoleerde positie stelt'. (p. 5)

27 This facile psychologization is supported with long articles (as, e.g., in DM, 8 June 1996, p. 3 and p. 23) and greedily underscored with quotes from members of the

'migrant' community itself, completely ignoring any questions concerning social changes that have taken or are taking place.

28 'Hun wens [de wens van de jongeren] om "ons" leefmodel over te nemen, met de welvaart die ze ervan verwachten, kunnen ze dikwijls niet waarmaken door een te laag scholingsniveau en moeilijkheden om aan werk te geraken'. (p. 6)

29 'Mijn boek is ode aan Marokkaanse vader van mijn kinderen' (DS, 4–5 January 1992, p. 12).

30 '"Vreemde grootmoeders" bekijkt Marokko open en kritisch' (DS, 4–5 January 1992, p. 12)

31 'Uitgegeven als jeugdboek, eigenlijk meer geschikt voor volwassenen, niet bepaald een hoogvlieger, maar wel interessant door *de open en warme maar ook kritische kijk van de schrijfster op een nog zeer traditioneel stukje Marokko en zijn bewoners*'. (DS, 4–5 January 1992, p. 12; our italics)

32 '*Minder prettig in het verhaal is dan weer het toch wel zeer grote overwicht van de man op de vrouw*'. And: '*Nog iets dat ons tegen de borst stuit, is het fanatiek belang dat vooral vaders hechten aan de maagdelijkheid van hun dochters, terwijl ze voor hun zonen een oogje toeknijpen*'. (DS, 4–5 January 1992, p. 12) Especially the first sentence is hard to translate into English because of the use of particles of various kinds (*dan, weer, toch, wel*) the cumulative effect of which is a strong downgrading of the positive side of the story.

33 'De Belgische taalstrijd is één van de vele tekenen die er op wijzen dat juist *verdeeldheid* het meest distinctieve kenmerk van de Europese beschaving is – datgene wat de Europese beschaving van de andere onderscheidt'. (*Nucleus*, February 1990, p. 3) The article from which this line is taken appeared in *Nucleus*, a Flemish monthly which profiles itself as 'intellectual' and Christian Democratic. Its establishment (in January 1990) was prompted by the observation that if Flemish people were asked to name Flemish intellectuals, they came up almost exclusively with the names of non-believers. Its somewhat curious goal was to demonstrate that it is possible to be both Christian and intellectual.

34 'Met veel nadruk zei hij [Gaston Geens] dat de culturele verscheidenheid een van de treffendste kenmerken is van het Europese continent en "die rijkdom moeten we ten volle benutten"'. (DS, 25 April 1990, p. 3)

35 These data were borrowed from Barbara Grimes (ed.) (1988).

36 'Het monotheïsme verklaart voor Mark Eyskens het Europese raadsel' (*Nucleus*, February 1990, p. 2).

37 'Het monotheïsme is gedurende eeuwen de hefboom geweest voor onstelpbare creativiteit en vernieuwingsdrang'. (*Nucleus*, February 1990, p. 2)

38 '[. . .] de revolutie werd gevoed door de gemeenschappelijke christelijke wortels van de Europese beschaving'. (*Nucleus*, March 1990, p. 1)

39 Title of an article from *The World in 1990* (The Economist Publications, 1989).

40 'Het liberalisme, of de *vrijheid*, is ontstaan uit *het kristelijke fundament van de westerse maatschappij*'. (*Trends*, 18 June 1992, p. 52; our italics)

41 'Kerk kiest voor multikulturele samenleving' (DS, 15–16 June 1991, p. 8).

42 '[. . .] noodzakelijk wederzijds respekt voor elkaars kultuur en godsdienst, interkulturele uitwisseling en interreligieuze dialoog' (DS, 15–16 June 1991, p. 8).

43 '*Uiteraard* wezen wij daarbij uitdrukkelijk op de gelovige motivatie van ons engagement. *Als kristenen* worden wij opgeroepen om *de gastvrijheid voor vreemdelingen* – vooral voor de armen en zwakken onder hen – te beoefenen'. (DS, 15–16 June 1991, p. 8; our italics)

44 'Bolkesteins tesis komt erop neer dat kristendom, rationalisme en humanisme de Westerse wereld waarden hebben meegegeven zoals scheiding tussen kerk en staat, vrijheid van meningsuiting, non-discriminatie en verdraagzaamheid en dat de islamitische wereld op dat vlak veel minder ver staat'. (DS, 17 September 1991, p. 4)

45 'De islamitische bom' (DS, 31 January 1992, p. 8); 'Stop kruiperigheid' (*Trends*, 23 April 1992, pp. 54–8); 'De nieuwe zuil: Islamistische vijfde kolonne' (*Trends*, 7 May 1992, pp. 118–22).

46 'Vlamingen zijn van nature een gastvrij volk, nieuwsgierig naar andere kulturen, nieuwe invalshoeken'. (DS, 24–5 August 1991, p. 2)

47 'De toestand in Antwerpen wordt veel explosiever'. (BRTN TV1, *De Zevende Dag*, 25 March 1990)

48 'En nochtans wordt op het terrein de situatie altijd maar slechter en slechter. De spanning tussen de bevolkingsgroepen in ons land in de verschillende wijken van de steden en gemeenten neemt alsmaar toe'. (PVV-Info, BRTN Radio 1, 29 March 1990)

49 'Het migranten-vraagstuk moet ook worden geplaatst in zijn geopolitieke kontekst. De Europeaan dreigt een uitstervend ras te worden. [. . .]
De doorsijpeling is begonnen kort na de Tweede Wereldoorlog. De druppels werden sinds lang waterstralen. Valt de dijkbreuk nog te vermijden? [. . .] Komt hier geen algemeen-Europese benadering, dan staat de opgroeiende generatie in de 21ste eeuw dramatische schokken te wachten'. (DS, 19 May 1990)

50 'Migranten vormen enorm reservoir' (DS, 31 March 1992, p. 2).

51 [Title:] '*Vreemdelingenprobleem* ook in Nederland tijdbom'
[Subtitle:] 'Regering wil *illegale buitenlanders* hard aanpakken' (DS, 20 June 1991, p. 10; our italics)

52 [Title:] 'Regering benoemt ambassadeur voor *migrantenzaken*'
[Subtitle:] 'Strengere aanpak arbeid *illegalen*' (DS, 25–6 April 1992, p. 1; our italics)

53 [Title:] 'Regering pakt *veiligheid* en *migranten* aan'
[Subtitle:] 'Dehaene: spoedig maatregelen' (DS, 21 April 1992, p. 1; our italics)

54 'Op de vergaderingen van de partijbureaus werd verwoed naar het waarom gezocht. Er liggen een aantal redenen voor de hand: *de migranten, de kriminaliteit en de onveiligheid*, de massale onverschilligheid van de jongeren voor alles wat naar politiek ruikt'. (DS, 26 November 1991, p. 16; our italics)

55 'Want als we iets willen doen *aan de migrantenproblematiek of aan de onveiligheid*, dan gaat dat geld kosten'. (DS, 29 November 1991, p. 3)

56 'Hoe groot de afstand was geworden tussen het beleid en de mensen, kon men nog het best meten aan het onbegrip van ministers tenoverstaan van de *toenemende onveiligheid en de moeilijkheden met migranten*'. (HLN, 23–4 November 1991, p. 2; our italics)

57 'Doordat de vorige ontslagnemende regering zeer weinig heeft gedaan om de groeiende moeilijkheden met vooral jonge en meestal in on land geboren "vreemdelingen" aan te pakken, is een toenemend gevoel van onveiligheid ontstaan dat niet alleen oudere mensen er 's avonds toe verplicht binnen te blijven (zeker in grote steden) achter de gesloten deuren van hun woning'. (HLN, 26 November 1991, p. 2)

58 'De jongeren die tot Belg worden genaturalizeerd, vervreemden van hun oorsprong. [. . .] De jeugd zit met de klassieke handicaps van de nieuwkomer: leerproblemen, de familiale spanningen, de vernauwde toegang tot de arbeidsmarkt. De sociale moeilijkheden leiden tot ontsporingen, druggebruik, straatkriminaliteit, wrijvingen met de autochtone bevolking en met de ordediensten'. (DS, 22 May 1992, p. 10)

59 'Opengebroken straten, kapotte winkelramen, vernielde auto's. Brussel was 4 nachten in de greep van het geweld. Met stokken en molotov-cocktails werd een spoor van vernieling getrokken door de hoofdstad'. This appeared in an announcement of the PVV programme 'Librado', to be broadcast by BRTN TV2, 18 June 1991; it occupied nearly half a newspaper page. Similar riots broke out in Brussels in the autumn of 1997 after an incident in which a Moroccan–Belgian drugs dealer was shot and killed by policemen. In line with earlier remarks, this incident fueled the association between migrants and crime in the eyes of members of the majority.

60 'Vorst, een jaar na de rellen' (DS, 13 May 1992, p. 2).

61 'Brusselse rellen zijn meer dan geïsoleerde incidenten', and 'Herrieschoppers verstoren integratieproces' (DS, 18 March 1992, p. 2).

62 'Het ziet ernaar uit dat Brussel de migrantenrellen heeft gekregen die al een tijd in de lucht hangen, net zoals Nederland destijds gekonfronteerd werd met Molukkersgeweld, en Groot-Brittannië gedeelten van Brighton [sic] in brand zag vliegen bij kleurlingengeweld. De rellen van Brussel kunnen niet langer als alleenstaande incidenten worden beschouwd. Zij zijn ook niet alleen maar te wijten aan de nervositeit die gewoonlijk met de ramadan gepaard gaat. Er liggen lijnen in, gevaarlijke lijnen. De overheid zal zeer snel moeten ingrijpen'. (DS, 18 March 1992, p. 2)

63 'Deze kleine groep oefent via de straat een diktatuur uit, waarvan de slachtoffers zowel de Belgen als het gros van de niet-Belgen in Brussel zijn. Het is deze kleine groep om een intifada te doen, met als inzet het verwerven van kontrole over een territorium: een gedeelte van de openbare ruimte. Op deze wijze verhinderen zij ook elke poging tot inpassing van de niet-Belgen, en berokkenen zij grote schade aan de samenleving. Tegen de leiders van deze intifada moet dan ook streng worden opgetreden'. (DS, 18 March 1992, p. 2)

64 'De recentste migrantenrellen zijn uitgelokt door kriminelen die andere jongeren meesleepten [. . .]' (DS, 31 March 1992, p. 2)

65 'De Vlaamse Liberalen en Democraten zijn tolerant, maar niet ten koste van uw veiligheid'. This slogan appeared on numerous VLD pamphlets and advertisements.

66 'Het loopt echter serieus mis wanneer vreemdelingen misbruik maken van onze spreekwoordelijke Antwerpse gastvrijheid'. (GvA, 13 May 1995; the same advertisement from which this line is taken appeared in various places on several days).

67 '[. . .] de verontrustende groei van het extreem-rechtse gedachtengoed [. . .]' (SP, November 1989).

68 'Van mij mogen ze nog 100.000 migranten sturen, als ze zich maar een beetje aanpassen en ons gerust laten'. (DNG, 6 June 1992, p. 3)

69 'Ik ben niet iemand die gekant is tegen de aanwezigheid van migranten in onze samenleving. Onder mijn leerlingen zijn een aantal Marokkanen die erg hun best doen en vast van plan zijn om een volwaardig beroep te leren. Maar het zijn die jeugdbendes die het imago schenden van de hele Marokkaanse gemeenschap'. (DS, 6 June 1992, p. 3)

70 'Ik geloof niet dat het hier om racisme gaat'. (*Knack*, 3–9 June 1992, p. 41)

71 Mehan (1996: 253): 'Proponents of various positions in conflicts waged in and through discourse attempt to capture or dominate modes of representation. [. . .] This competition over the meanings of ambiguous events, people and objects in the world has been called the "politics of representation" [. . .]. Indeed, the process of lexical labeling is itself an entextualization process. Complex, contextually nuanced discussions get summed up in (and hence, are entextualized through) a single word'.

72 '[. . .] dat een aantal groeperingen uit het Antwerpse, en niet alleen het Vlaams Blok, systematisch de – zeg maar *normale* – gevoelens van achterdocht die mensen hebben ten opzichte van mensen met een andere huidskleur en andere taal opklopt, uitbuit'. (Marc Van Peel, BRTN TV1, *De Zevende Dag*, 25 March 1990)

73 'Waarom niet toegeven dat de blijvende vestiging van islamitische families en groepen een vergissing is geweest en dat bepaalde reakties van de inheemse bevolking gegrond zijn en niets te maken hebben met rassenhaat, maar alles met het recht op een veilig en ongestoord bestaan?' (Manu Ruys, DS, 19 May 1990)

74 'Een gereserveerde houding ten opzichte van het vreemde is een konstante in het menselijk gedrag'. (*Knack*, 3–9 June 1992, p. 59)

75 'Moreels ging niet uit de weg dat xenofobe reakties in de Derde Wereld soms heftiger zijn dan bij ons'. (HN, 6 June 1992, p. 6)

76 'Zeg niet "fascist" tegen Blok-kiezer' (DS, 13 February 1992, p. 2).

77 This is front-page news (DS, 9 June 1992), with details of the reported research presented at length on p. 2.

78 '[. . .] de politieke uitbuiting van spanningen en vooroordelen [. . .]'. (SP, *Samenleven in de jaren '90*, November 1989)

79 '[. . .] de vatbaarheid van mensen voor systematische negatieve beïnvloeding zoals door het Vlaams Blok'. (SP, *Samenleven in de jaren '90*, November 1989)

80 'Ook al lijkt het mij geen racisme en zeker geen antisemitisme, toch kan een demagoog er handig misbruik van maken'. (*Knack*, 3–9 June 1992, p. 41)

81 'Vele mensen bevinden zich vandaag in zwakke sociale situaties, [. . .]'. (SP, *Samenleven in de jaren '90*, November 1989)

82 'Zeker in economisch moeilijker tijden hebben mensen uit de onderste laag, zelf de eerste slachtoffers van armoede, werkloosheid, verrotting... de neiging om, als ze gekonfronteerd worden met grote groepen vreemdelingen, deze te beschouwen als oorzaak van alle kwaad'. (AGALEV, *Een groene kijk op samen leven*, June 1991, p. 7)

83 'Uit onderzoek blijkt dat de belangrijkste oorzaak van samenlevingsconflicten en onverdraagzaamheid tegen migranten in eerste instantie niet zozeer moet gezocht worden in de culturele verschillen met daarmee gepaard gaande racistische gevoelens dan wel in de slechte materiële bestaansvoorwaarden waaraan zowel autochtonen als allochtonen zijn blootgesteld'. (from *Onderzoeksvoorstellen Buitenlandse Minderheden* ['research proposals related to foreign minorities'], presented by a working group on 'Wetenschappelijk onderzoek inzake buitenlandse minderheden in Vlaanderen– België' ['scientific research regarding foreign minorities in Flanders–Belgium'], January 1989, p. 15).

84 'Racisme en vreemdelingenhaat komen voort uit angst en onzekerheid omtrent de toekomst en worden gevoed door werkloosheid en armoede' (from *Verslag, namens de Onderzoekscommissie racisme en vreemdelingenhaat, over de bevindingen van de onder-zoekscommissie* ['Report, on behalf of the Investigation committee on racism and xenophobia, about the findings of the investigation committee], 1991, p. 3)

85 'De golf van racisme die we beleven, is volgens mij de uitdrukking van een diepgaande onzekerheid van de mensen in de maatschappij. Die onzekerheid is het resultaat van de modernizering van de wereld, die heel veel energie opslorpt. De zogenaamde prestatie- en kompetitiemaatschappij wordt als iets zeer vermoeiends ervaren. Dat boezemt angst in, want je slaagt of je slaagt niet. Ik geloof dat de mensen teleurgesteld zijn in de demokratie omdat ze de indruk hebben dat in een demokratie alles maar heel langzaam verandert. Vele mensen hebben behoefte aan duidelijk omlijnde situaties maar onze maatschappij is heel ingewikkeld geworden. Ook dat zorgt voor onzekerheid en angst.

Tijdens de jongste gemeenteraadsverkiezingen in Frankfurt hebben veel jonge mannen rechts-radikaal gestemd. Uit een onderzoek bleek dat ze moeite hadden met hun rol als man, dat ze niet goed wisten hoe ze een relatie met een vrouw moesten aangaan, dat ze in het algemeen niet met de maatschappelijke ontwikkelingen wisten om te gaan. Migranten vormen dan een gemakkelijk doelwit om stress af te reageren, ze worden zondebokken'. (*Knack*, 3–9 June 1992, p. 60)

86 'In het geval van sommige kiezers van het Vlaams Blok kan men spreken van "wanhoopsracisme" (al zal straks overduidelijk blijken dat de term "racisme" hier eigenlijk niet op zijn plaats is)'. (Bijttebiet *et al.* 1992: 31)

87 'Het sukses van Vlaams Blok en Front National wijt hij aan de frustraties van misnoegde mensen, die in hun onwetendheid de vreemdelingen met alle zonden van Israel beladen'.

88 [Title:] 'Lijdensweg van Louise leidt naar racisme'
[Subtitle:] 'Woonperikelen voedingsbodem voor wrevel tegen politieke vluchtelingen' (DS, 13–14 July 1991, p. 9)

89 'Vlaams Blok is armoedepartij' (DS, 30 March 1990).

90 'Nog een fenomeen dat in Antwerpen speelt is het *distanciëringsracisme*, waarbij rijke mensen die niet of nauwelijks met migranten te maken krijgen – tenzij in de vorm van

hun buitenlandse huispersoneel – zich toch tegen hen afzetten. Zij geloven dat als de migranten blijven én inspraak krijgen, de maatschappij zal veranderen en hun eigen positie in de maatschappij in gevaar zal komen'. (Chris Kesteloot, social scientist, quoted in the Flemish weekly *Humo*, 9 April 1996, p. 136)

91 'Vrijheid en verdraagzaamheid, hoe belangrijk ook, moeten beperkt blijven, vanwege precies die wederzijdse interactie tussen de twee. Voor de vrijheid is dat duidelijk. Onbeperkte vrijheid voor de enen leidt tot verdrukking van de anderen: dat geldt voor de politieke, culturele, de sociale en de economische verhoudingen. Maar ook verdraagzaamheid moet ingeperkt worden en mag niet ontaarden tot onderdanigheid, lijdzaamheid, onverschilligheid of tot de uiteindelijke limiet, de permissiviteit'. (Lieven Van Gerven in Herwig Arts *et al.* 1991: 7–8).

92 'De verdraagzame mens opteert echter voor een pluralistische maatschappij, waarin alle opinies aan bod kunnen komen met gelijke rechten. Toch heeft hij enkele bedenkingen tegen de excessen van de ideologische "vrije-markt-economie"'. (Herwig Arts, in Herwig Arts *et al.* 1991: 23)

93 'In werkelijkheid heeft juist de mens die vanuit een traditie leeft, iets revolutionairs. Alleen hij durft het immers aan om soms, als dat moet, tegen de stroom van zijn tijd in te zwemmen. Hij weet dat wie de tijdgeest huwt, spoedig weduwnaar wordt'. (Herwig Arts, in Herwig Arts *et al.* 1991: 27)

94 'De vraag is of de islam wel in overeenstemming te brengen is met de liberale demokratie en de vrijheid, de verdraagzaamheid, de verscheidenheid en het tegen-sprekelijk debat zonder dewelke geen open samenleving mogelijk is'. (Guy Verhofstadt 1992: 64)

95 'Van zodra de islam echter de staat en de samenleving wil ordenen overeenkomstig haar morele beginselen en haar opvatting over wat goed en kwaad is, wordt *de grens van de verdraagzaamheid* overschreden. De verdraagzaamheid in de liberale demokratie mag niet zo ver gaan, dat zij uiteindelijk uitmondt in een openlijk of zelfs maar stilzwijgend verdringen van de eigen waarden: de vrijheid van meningsuiting, de vrijheid van gods-dienstbeleving, de gelijkberechtiging van man en vrouw, het pluralisme, de scheiding van Kerk en staat. Die waarden door de islamitische gemeenschap in ons land doen aanvaarden en er naar laten leven ook is de weg van de "inburgering" die moet worden bewandeld'. (Guy Verhofstadt 1992: 66–7; our italics)

96 'Ik weet niet of het een fout was de islam te erkennen. Ik weet wél dat het een fout was het op zo'n ondoordachte manier te doen, zonder de gevolgen voor dit kleine landje in te schatten'. (Paula D'Hondt 1991: 52)

97 'Overal ter wereld is vreedzaam samenleven complex en moeilijk' (DS, 15–16 June 1991, p. 8).

98 'Meestal geven de gebeurtenissen in Amerika een voorsmaakje van wat er binnen tien of vijftien jaar bij ons zal veranderen. Dat was zo met het drugprobleem, de jeugdmis-dadigheid, de almacht van de tv, de veranderende seksuele moraal, Aids. Al die problemen manifesteerden zich eerst in Amerika en pas daarna in Europa.
De rassenrellen in Los Angeles moeten voor ons een waarschuwing zijn: een multikul-turele of multiraciale maatschappij leidt tot chaos, plundering en geweld. Willen wij binnen tien jaar dezelfde toestanden in Brussel en in Antwerpen?' (DS, 20 May 1992, p. 9, and HLN 23–4 May 1992)

99 'Laten we openlijk zeggen dat we Vlaanderen niet willen én mogen laten uitgroeien tot een multikultureel land'. (DS, 12 May 1992, p. 8)

100 'Naar een leefbare multi-kulturele gemeente' (DS, 15 December 1989).

101 'De nieuwe zuil: Islamitische vijfde kolonne', by the orientalist Koen Elst in *Trends*, 7 May 1992, pp. 118–22; and 'Van gastarbeid naar moslimzuil', by the political commentator Manu Ruys, DS, 22 May 1992, p. 10).

102 'Maar de bocht die de migrantenkwestie neemt, verandert het probleem van de

achterstelling in een fenomeen van moslim-bewustwording en radikalisering'. (Manu Ruys, DS, 22 May 1992, p. 10)

103 '[. . .] allerlei actiegroepen [werken] planmatig aan de opbouw van organizaties en instellingen die erop gericht zijn de islamitische gemeenschap blijvend te vestigen in de Westerse landen. [. . .] de oprichting van koran-scholen, islamitische jeugd-verenigingen, financiële en sociale instellingen, media-organen'. (Manu Ruys, DS, 22 May 1992, p. 10)

104 BRTN TV1, *De Zevende Dag*, 14 June 1992.

105 'Uit mijn studies over de joodse gemeenschap in Vlaanderen heb ik om te beginnen geleerd een scherp onderscheid te maken tussen "assimilatie" en "integratie": terwijl men in een open demokratische samenleving natuurlijk het individu het recht niet kan ontnemen voor volledige assimilatie te kiezen, wordt deze keuze door de overgrote meerderheid van de joodse Vlamingen om begrijpelijke redenen verworpen.

Door de assimilatie verdwijnt het individu uit de etnische, religieuze of kulturele minderheidsgroep en past zich zodanig aan de meerderheid aan dat de hele eigen traditie daarmee verloren gaat, en dit verlies geldt evenzeer voor de meerderheid die door deze joodse aanwezigheid kultureel, filozofisch en, waarom niet, culinair verrijkt kan worden.

Maar de meeste joden in Vlaanderen kiezen voor "integratie", wat betekent dat ze hun joodse eigenheid bewaren en krachtig beschermen én tegelijkertijd hun recht-matige plaats in de grotere Vlaamse gemeenschap innemen, want dat is de enige juiste inhoud van de term "integratie"'. (DS, 14 May 1992, p. 10)

106 'De aanwezigheid van grote groepen niet-Belgen in en om de hoofdstad van Europa is een feit. Toen politici en publieke opinie op een bepaald moment beseften dat onze stadskernen vol Marokkaanse en Turkse migranten zaten, werd erover gepraat alsof hun aanwezigheid zelf nog ter discussie stond. Het ordenen en vreedzaam doen verlopen van dit samenleven, daar komt het op aan.

Dezelfde redenering moet gelden voor de andere groepen van vreemdelingen. Zij zijn er, en zij blijven er. Ze zijn welkom. *Maar het is niet teveel gevraagd dat ook zij, die hier te gast zijn, rekening houden met de omgeving waarin ze terecht komen en respekt en interesse opbrengen voor de kultuur, onze kultuur. Dat betekent dat ze gettovorming, neerbuigendheid en benepen clangeest beter aan de kant laten om zelf stappen in de richting van een goed samenleven te doen'.* (from the conclusion to the article series on 'De vreemde mutatie van Brussel' ['The foreign mutation of Brussels'], DS, 24–5 August 1991, p. 2; our emphasis)

107 From 'Nederland volgt Belgisch model van integratie' (subtitled 'Er is grens aan toler-antie'): 'BRUSSEL/DEN HAAG, Het Nederlandse ministerie van Binnenlandse Zaken gaat op aanraden van 75 deskundigen haar *minderhedenbeleid* "verduidelijken en verscherpen, en meer dwingende maatregelen opleggen". De fluwelen handschoen heeft voor de minderheden niet veel opgeleverd, luidt het in Den Haag. "Daarmee volgt Nederland eindelijk ons Belgisch integratiekoncept", meent Johan Leman, kabi-netschef van Koninklijk Migrantenkommissaris Paula D'Hondt. "Al in haar eerste rapport benadrukte Paula D'Hondt dat de migranten niet alleen rechten, maar ook plichten hebben. Nederland ontdekte nu ook dat er grenzen zijn aan tolerantie en individuele vrijheid"'. (DS, 5 March 1992, p. 1)

108   • het niveau van de waarden en beginselen die door het concept '*openbare orde*' beschermd worden en derhalve juridisch afdwingbaar zijn;

      • het niveau van enkele *richting gevende sociale beginselen* waarover een autochtone meerderheid het impliciet eens lijkt te zijn;

      • het niveau van de vele *cultuur-uitingen* die noch de openbare orde noch de sociale beginselen van een gastland in het gedrang brengen.

(KCM 1989: 35–6)

109 In the following comments we refer to the literal text of the policy guidelines formulated with direct reference to the three distinguishing levels of social action. The guidelines are: '(a) assimilatie waar de "openbare orde" het vraagt; (b) consequente bevordering van een zo goed mogelijke inpassing volgens de oriënterende sociale basisbeginselen die de cultuur van het gastland schragen en die met "moderniteit", "emancipatie" en "volwaardig pluralisme" – zoals een moderne westerse staat dit verstaat – te maken hebben; en (c) ondubbelzinnig respect voor de culturele diversiteit-als-wederzijdse-verrijking op de andere vlakken' (KCM 1989: 38–9) [(a) assimilation where the 'public order' demands this; (b) consequent promotion of the best possible fitting in according to the orienting social principles which support the culture of the host country and which are related to 'modernity', 'emancipation' and 'true pluralism' – as understood by a modern western state —; and (c) unambiguous respect for the cultural diversity-as-mutual-enrichment in all other areas].

110 According to the official formulation, the integration concept starts from *inpassing* ('fitting in') in relation to the three criteria mentioned and goes hand in hand with 'een bevordering van de structurele betrokkenheid van de minderheden bij de activiteiten en de doelstellingen van de overheid' (KCM 1989: 39).

111 'Integratie van migranten in onze samenleving hebben wij omschreven als *inpassing*. Dat koncept hebben wij gekonkretiseerd in vier punten. De vier punten vindt men al in ons eerste rapport van november 1989: in de eerste twee punten stellen wij ons eisend op tegenover de migranten, in de andere twee staan wij open tegenover hen.

1 Wij eisen assimilatie waar het om de openbare orde gaat. Dit wil zeggen dat migranten de Belgische wetten moeten respekteren, zonder enige uitzondering, allemaal, zoals elke Belg.

2 Wij eisen dat de sociale basisbeginselen van onze samenleving door iedereen, en dus ook door alle migranten gerespekteerd worden: de emancipatie van de vrouw, zoals wij die verstaan; de wederzijdse verdraagzaamheid; onze taal; enzovoort.

3 Naast die twee zeer belangrijke zaken die wij van de migranten eisen – en méér kan men in een rechtsstaat van de mensen niet eisen, of ze nu migrant of Belg zijn, staan wij open voor wat die mensen ons kunnen bijbrengen: op artistiek, culinair, taalkundig, kultureel en ander gebied. Daar gaan wij ervan uit dat wederzijdse verrijking niet alleen mogelijk maar zelfs wenselijk is, een voorwaarde voor vooruitgang.

4 Wij zeggen ook dat voldoende bekwame mensen uit de migrantenkringen bij de doelstellingen en aktiviteiten van de overheid betrokken moeten worden, omdat dit de enige echte weg is tot emancipatie, zoals het dat bijvoorbeeld ook voor de vrouwen geweest is'.

(DS, 1–2 February 1992, p. 7)

112 '[. . .] consequente bevordering van een zo goed mogelijke inpassing volgens de oriënterende sociale basisbeginselen' (KCM 1992b: 3).

113 'Migranten moeten Vlaming worden'.

114 'Ze trekt zich flink uit de slag, heeft een poetsvrouw één keer om de veertien dagen, haar dochter Lina en schoondochter Tina die dichtbij wonen, springen geregeld binnen. *Toch zit Teresa met een probleem: ze kent geen Nederlands*'. (DS, 6 June 1992, p. 13; our italics)

115 During the *Studiedag buitenlandse minderheden in Vlaanderen/België: Evoluties, opinies en beleid* [Symposium foreign minorities in Flanders/Belgium: Developments, opinions and policy], Antwerp, 19 October 1990.

116 'Inpassing migranten vraagt drastische en snelle maatregelen' (title of an opinion piece by Paula D'Hondt, DS, 1–2 February 1992, p. 7).

CHAPTER 4

1 'Wat is cultuur en eigenheid? Daarover is al veel geschreven, maar dat daartoe in elk geval taal en recht horen, zal niemand ontkennen. Logischerwijze behouden alle etnische groepen in een multikulturele samenleving hun taal en rechtssysteem, wezenlijke onderdelen van hun eigenheid'. (DS, 12 May 1992, p. 8)

2 'Het klopt inderdaad dat taal en recht tot de kern van de cultuur behoren, en dat het dus indruist tegen de elementaire politieke wijsheid om binnen één kleine gemeenschap verschillende rechtssystemen en talen dezelfde status te verlenen'. (DS, 14 May 1992, p. 10)

3 '[. . .] het recht op ontwikkeling van de eigen culturele identiteit' (KCM 1992a: 5).

4 'Idealen en kinderlijkjes', written by Yves Desmet (DM, 21 April 1995, p.2).

5 'De sterkste aanwijzing in de richting van de fundamentalisten is de daad zelf. Zij zijn de enigen met voldoende verziekte breinen om een veelvoudige kindermoord te plannen. Een psychopaat, zelfs een amok makende *serial killer*, zou er nog niet aan denken zich te bedienen van een bomauto.

Het misselijk makend idee om de eigen maatschappelijke of religieuze idealen te verwezenlijken door een koelbloedige en laffe aanslag op een kinderdagverblijf, kan alleen ontstaan in de geperverteerde geest van een godsdienstwaanzinnige'. (DM, 21 April 1995, p. 2)

6 'De Rifboys richten zich niet alleen tot migrantenjongens, want Said Buimejene [de verantwoordelijke] is zich bewust van de problematiek van de migrantenmeisjes [. . .]'. (HV, 7 January 1991)

7 Fabian's definition: '[. . .] a persistent and systematic tendency to place the referent(s) on anthropology in a Time other than the present of the producer of anthropological discourse'. (1983: 31)

8 'Dan arriveert zo'n [Turks of Marokkaans] meisje hier, uit een of ander plattelandsdorp, bij wijze van spreken op een lichtjaar verwijderd van de beschaving, komt hier terecht in de omknelling van het gezin, en raakt er niet meer uit, tenzij ze van een enorme persoonlijkheid getuigt. Of tenzij wij mogelijkheden kunnen scheppen om haar op te vangen. [. . .]

Het is mijn overtuiging dat de emancipatie van de migrant voor een niet gering deel zal moeten gebeuren langs die van de migranten*vrouw* om, en dan heb ik het in de eerste plaats over het uitroeien van de gearrangeerde huwelijken. Dat heeft trouwens ook deel uitgemaakt van de ontvoogdingsstrijd van de Belgische vrouw. Wat deden boeren vroeger? Ze huwden hun dochters onder elkaar uit en gaven ze een bepaalde hoeveelheid land mee. Wat dat betreft, is er minder nieuws onder de zon dan sommigen menen'. (Paula D'Hondt 1991: 42)

9 'Jongeren worden hier met andere waarden en normen geconfronteerd. Onvermijdelijk leidt dit tot grote spanningen thuis. Uit reactie gaan de ouders de traditionele waarden en normen verscherpen en ook scherper opleggen aan hun kinderen. Het gevoel dat hun kinderen hen als zand tussen de vingers glippen, is veel migrantenouders niet vreemd. Migrantenjongeren hebben het moeilijk om een harmonie te vinden in het samenleven met hun ouders binnen een westerse cultuur'. (Oostvlaams Provinciaal Integratiecentrum voor Migranten, *Jaarverslag* 1989: 10)

10 We note, in passing, that this denial of coevalness and its consequences in the domain of power distribution are probably the clearest indications of the similarity between the rhetoric on migrants and that on colonial subjects in the past. Fabian (1983: 51–3) identifies these features as the central rhetorical instruments of colonial knowledge of the subjects overseas.

11 'In algemene bespiegelingen over de cultuur van de migrant is het opvallend dat het migrantenbestaan als beïnvloedende factor niet is verdisconteerd of ondanks dat het tegenovergestelde met de mond beleden wordt, feitelijk uitgegaan wordt van een op

het moment van migratie bevroren cultuur. De cultuur van de migrant als replica van de oorspronkelijke dorpscultuur in den vreemde'.

12 'Annemans schrijft dat de begrippen natie en staat moeten samenvallen, en dat de staatsgrenzen hierbij best etnisch worden bepaald. Het begrip natie slaat op begrippen als gemeenschapsvorming, kultuur en taal. Een staat is enkel een administratief-territoriaal begrip. Separatisten zijn dus modern, "omdat zij ook het principe één staat, één kultuur, of eerder nog één staat, één volk willen toepassen"'. (DS, 6–7 October 1990, p. 3)

13 '[. . .] het nationalisme, dat zowel in Vlaanderen als in Europa een zeer hanteerbaar instrument is' (quoted in DS, 11 June 1992, p. 3).

14 The phrasing in Dutch referred to the history of the *Nederlanden*. The literal translation would be the 'Netherlands'. Obviously, it was not the intention to introduce a course on the history of the country that is now called 'The Netherlands'. Historically, the *Nederlanden* are the 'Low Countries', corresponding more or less to present-day The Netherlands and Belgium combined. But what is meant in the present context is the combination of The Netherlands with present-day Flanders, conceived by some Flemish nationalists as a cultural unity.

15 'De CVP blijkt een zeer Vlaamse partij. Slechts zeer weinig ondervraagden vinden dat 'het federaliseringsproces te ver gaat en het land onbestuurbaar maakt'. De grote meerderheid daarentegen vindt dat 'de sociale zekerheid geregionaliseerd moet worden' en dat 'Vlaanderen tot het uiterste moet gaan, desnoods tot de onafhankelijkheid, om volledig autonoom te kunnen beslissen'.

De CVP-kaderleden blijken absoluut niet van stemrecht voor migranten te willen weten, zo leert de enquête. Integendeel, ze vinden dat buitenlanders niet alleen onze taal, maar ook onze gebruiken en gewoonten moeten overnemen'. (DS, 20–21 June 1992, p. 3)

16 '*Allochtonen* zijn mensen met een andere *socioculturele herkomst*, teruggaand op een ander *land van herkomst*. [. . .]

'*Etnische minderheden* zijn groepen van allochtonen, op één *land van herkomst* teruggaand'. (KCM 1989, part 1, p. 34; our emphasis)

17 'Marokko akkoord met Belgisch migrantenbeleid' (DS, 22 May 1991, p. 2).

18 This immediately calls into doubt the widespread belief that racism is *caused by* immigration, a proposition implicit in discussions about the threshold of tolerance and frequently used in antiracist information campaigns. In principle, there is no necessary connection between immigration and racism. Probably the worst acts of racism in history have been perpetrated against non-immigrants, be they the original populations of regions subject to conquest or colonization (the Americas, Africa and other parts of the Third World) or long-time resident groups such as the Jews in Central and Eastern Europe, the Armenians or the Tutsi. Note that Apartheid was institutional racism against 'natives'.

19 'De eerbiediging van de mensenrechten en de fundamentele vrijheden maakt deel uit van het gemeenschappelijke erfdeel van politieke idealen en tradities van de Europeanen. Voor 78% van de Europeanen blijft de democratie – wat er ook moge gebeuren – het beste politieke stelsel. En de eerbiediging van de mensenrechten is voor 60% één van de belangrijke kwesties die '"de moeite waard zijn dat men er risico's voor neemt of er iets voor opoffert"'. (*Eurobarometer*, November 1989, p. 2)

20 'De islam-wereld ligt machteloos en verscheurd. De nationalistische koortsaanvallen bevorderen de evolutie naar een opener en vrijer samenleving niet. De feodale regimes hebben af te rekenen met tendensen tot democratisering, die zich optrekken aan de zege van de Amerikaanse bondgenoot, maar zijn ze bereid afstand te doen van fortuin en heerschappij?' (DS, 1 March 1991)

21 The term was borrowed from John Sorenson (1991).

22 Note that, unlike with English 'to integrate', reflexivity with the Dutch *integreren* has to be indicated lexically (with the reflexive pronoun *zich*); the corresponding 'themselves' could be left out of the English glosses, but was kept to make explicit what happens with the Dutch examples.

23 'In de Belgische context betekent dat wellicht dat elke autochtone culturele traditie, de Vlaamse zowel als de Waalse, voor een deel haar eigen *cultureel* integratieconcept moet ontwikkelen, zonder afbreuk te doen aan de waarde van de traditie van de gebuur'. (KCM 1992a, p. 4)

CHAPTER 5

1 For figures and details, see W. Laqueur (1970).

2 'Racisme en nationalisme zijn niet de zaak van bepaalde personen, groepen, partijen, naties of volksgemeenschappen. Ze zijn de zaak van het menselijke ras. Ze zijn steeds en overal latent aanwezig. Niemand is er tegen bestand'. (DS, 7 January 1993)

3 Note that Socrates and Nietzsche both agree that imagining that one possesses a virtue which one does not possess, borders on insanity. See F. Nietzsche (1957).

4 Johan Leman (1992), the main architect of the dominant integration concept, has no problem in admitting that cultural differences do not seem to play a conflictual role when the socio-economic status of the outgroup is high (as in the case of the Japanese community in Brussels). Yet this does not lead him to the conclusion that in the first place social inequality should be dealt with; instead 'the migrant problem' is constantly placed in a cultural light, to the point where even religion is seen as an obstacle to socio-economic emancipation. In that perspective, Leman makes a distinction between forms of Islam hampering integration versus those conducive to integration (a distinction to which a different treatment of the two groups is also attached).

5 Both Deweerdt and Doornaert are high-ranking DS journalists. Doornaert's statement was hard to translate. The Dutch version says: 'Louter "volkseigen" kulturen bestaan niet', literally 'Purely "volkseigen" cultures do not exist'. The problem lies in the term *volkseigen*, freely translated as 'being the exclusive property of a people'.

6 '[. . .] wij wensen een homogene maatschappij, met de mensen die hier altijd al geleefd hebben, rond onze knusse kerktorens en buurten'. (DS, 3 April 1992, p. 10)

7 'De enige weg is die van inpassing. Van migranten mag worden verwacht dat zij de taal van het gastland leren, en zijn cultuur en zijn wetten respecteren'. (DS, 21–2 March 1992, p. 9)

8 'Vandaar dat kontakt met "anderen" net zo min een bedreiging voor onze kultuur is, als het een aanslag op de "identiteit" of "kultuur" van immigranten zou zijn van hen te verlangen dat ze de rechten en plichten van een demokratische samenleving aanvaarden, dus zich daarin "integreren".

Dat de aanpassing moeilijk kan zijn voor mensen die uit een heel ander samenlevingspatroon komen, staat vast. Maar begrip daarvoor betekent niet dat onze maatschappijen moeten afstappen van demokratische verworvenheden'. (DS, 13 January 1992, p. 5)

9 'Wat nog aan sociale "vreemdheid" of barrières overblijft, dient geleidelijk overwonnen te worden in een proces van inpassing'. (DS, 3 April 1992, p. 10)

10 'Wie zijn de Vlamingen, en waar komen zij vandaan? In feite missen ze zoveel specifieke kenmerken dat ze er heel specifiek bij geworden zijn'. (*Knack*, 14 February 1996, p. 134)

11 'Een schitterende prof. Senelle pleitte "ruime verzachtende omstandigheden voor de Belgische politici", omdat die aan een enorme opdracht bezig zijn: de vervanging van een Napoleontisch door een federaal staatsbestel. Hij legde de nadruk op het belang van de omschrijving van de taalgebieden, en zei dat de inschrijving van faciliteiten in

de grondwet een zware fout was, omdat zo afbreuk wordt gedaan aan de *ééntaligheid*. "Een goede federale structuur moet gebaseerd zijn op *vaste grenzen*", aldus prof. Senelle'. (DS, 11 May 1992, p. 2; italics ours)

12 'Wie zich in een bepaald taalgebied vestigt, moet hieruit de konklusies trekken. Wie zich niet wil aanpassen, doet er beter aan te verhuizen'. (DS, 25 March 1992, and again in DS, 30 June 1992, p. 7)

13 'Zal daar gebruik van worden gemaakt om niet alleen de rechtstreekse verkiezingen van het Vlaams parlement af te dwingen, maar ook om het territorialiteitsbegrip zuiver te stellen? Wil Vlaanderen *een taalhomogeen land* worden, dan is het nu het ogenblik om de oude eis 'In Vlaanderen Vlaams' eindelijk waar te maken. De taalgrens moet een echte staatsgrens worden. Nu is ze nog te veel met uitzonderingen *bezoedeld*'. (DS, 27 April 1992, p. 8; italics ours)

14 'Schaduw van 120.000 Franstaligen uit rand versombert dialoog tussen gemeenschappen'. (DS, 4 May 1992, p.2)

15 'Er zijn toegevingen gedaan – van de grendelgrondwet van 1970 tot de grondwettelijke "betonnering" van de faciliteiten in 1988 – die *de grens van wat aanvaardbaar is*, overschreden.

'Om zijn zelfbestuur te verwezenlijken, heeft Vlaanderen tot nog toe gekozen voor het federale model. Vlaanderen kan ook vandaag nog achter een federalistische oplossing van het Belgische nationaliteitenkonflikt staan, op voorwaarde dat het om *een eerlijk en zuiver federalisme* gaat. [. . .]

'Dat betekent dat Wallonië aanvaardt dat de taalgrens een staatsgrens is, dat de grenzen van het Vlaamse grondgebied onaantastbaar zijn, dat de Franstaligen die in Vlaanderen wonen geen bijkomende faciliteiten krijgen'. (DS, 11–12 July 1992, p. 1; italics ours)

16 'De francofonie is een Belgisch verschijnsel, dat kon ontstaan omdat het Nederlands in deze staat lang geen bestuurstaal was. In deze zin is de francofonie grondig ondemocratisch'. (Guido Fonteyn in DS, 30 June 1992, p. 7)

17 Note that homogeneistic thinking has deeply penetrated socio-linguistics in various domains, including work on language planning; see Jan Blommaert (1996).

18 'Het hele multikultureel gedoe is in strijd met de wezenheid, de doelstellingen en verworvenheden van de Vlaamse Beweging. Het is in feite tegen haar gericht en het is een wanhopige poging om te verhinderen dat ze eindelijk haar oude, voornaamste doelstelling—zelfbestuur voor Vlaanderen—bereikt. Vandaar die onvoorwaardelijke steun van alle franskiljons en Belgicisten.

Vele Vlaamsgezinde politici geven er zich blijkbaar geen rekenschap van dat hun houding één *kontradiktie* is. Men kan niet *terzelfdertijd* opkomen voor de vrijwaring van de eigen identiteit, voor het territorialiteitsbeginsel, tegen bijkomende faciliteiten voor Franstaligen in Vlaams Brabant, én voor de multikulturele samenleving die de steeds talrijker immigranten toelaat de eigen kulturele identiteit binnen het Vlaamse grondgebied te bewaren. Het multikultureel samenlevingsmodel sluit iedere echte "inpassing" uit. Hoe kan men aan Franstaligen ontzeggen wat men geredelijk toestaat aan Turken en Maghrebijnen?' (DS, 23 July 1992)

19 'Nu we eindelijk op het punt staan die autonomie te bereiken, die voor andere landen en volkeren een vanzelfsprekend gegeven is, heeft het geen zin, de Belgische vergissing vanuit een verkeerd begrepen internationalisme en kultureel relativisme nog eens over te doen'. (DS, 14 May 1992, p. 10)

20 'Als de taal het eerste kenmerk van onze kulturele eigenheid is, moeten we, met 21 miljoen samen optrekken in Europa'. (CVP senator Herman Suykerbuyk in DS, 30 April–1 May 1992, p. 9)

21 'De tijd is gekomen om eindelijk in alle duidelijkheid en alle ondubbelzinnigheid de grootste prioriteit te verlenen aan een aktieve taalpolitiek, die er zorg voor moet dragen dat de neerlandofonie [sic], die ons allen gevormd en gemodelleerd heeft, een

eigen stem blijft behouden. Juist daardoor zullen we een eigen bijdrage leveren tot de veelzijdige kultuur in Europa'. (The well-known Flemish publicist Jozef Deleu, cited in DS, 31 August–1 September 1991, p. 7)

22 'Intelligente mensen uit de wereld van ekonomie, politiek en kultuur moeten inzien dat ze geen enge provincialisten zijn wanneer ze de identiteit van hun streek willen beveiligen. Niet zozeer Eurokraten bedreigen Vlaams–Brabant, als wel een groep Vlamingen (en Vlaams–Brabanders) die hun eigen taal en kultuur en dus ook zichzelf nog steeds nietig en onbeduidend vinden. Volgens hen mag je een vreemdeling niet vragen Nederlands te leren – een Vlaming in het buitenland moet dan weer wel de taal van het gastland gebruiken, en liefst onmiddellijk'. (Hubert Swalens, member of the municipal council of Grimbergen, in DS, 9 July 1991, p. 7)

23 'Nederlands moet front vormen met, niet tegen Frankrijk' (DS, 13–14 June 1992, p.1).

24 'Het is hier dat mijns inziens de Vlaamse Beweging een rol kan spelen. Want zij is het best geplaatst om het essentiële verschil tussen Europa en de VS te begrijpen, en dat is de taalverscheidenheid in Europa.

Er zijn natuurlijk drukkingsgroepen die trachten de moeilijkheden tussen Walen en Vlamingen toe te schrijven aan [opsomming van politieke en socio-economische verklaringen]. Maar een ernstig mens weet dat de moeilijkheden voortkomen uit het feit dat Vlamingen en Walen een andere taal spreken. [. . .]

De Vlaamse Beweging is een van de weinige in Europa die het inzicht, de ervaring en de gedrevenheid heeft om Europa te behoeden voor een noodlottig avontuur, dat na zeer veel energieverspilling enkel in chaos en ruzie kan eindigen.

'Europa moet een struktuur krijgen waarin de taalgroepen de bouwstenen zijn'. (DS, 17 July 1991, p. 8)

25 In Dutch: 'De taal is gans het volk'.

26 'Wanneer zorgen zij [de politici] ervoor dat wij ons niet meer hoeven te schamen over de taal van het officiële, het politieke Vlaanderen?' (DS, 5 April 1991, p. 7)

27 'Het Nederlands: de officiële taal van de Vlamingen(?)'

28 'De jonge Oostendse taalminnaars zijn het symbool van een aantredende generatie Vlaamse jongeren voor wie algemeen Nederlands een must [sic] is. Zo zijn we eindelijk op de goede weg'. (DS, 10 July 1991, p. 7)

29 '[. . .] bewust onzuiver Nederlands [. . .]' (DS, 2 April 1992, p. 9)

30 This position is emphatically defended, e.g., by Willy Penninckx and his *Vereniging Algemeen Nederlands* (Standard Dutch Association) in articles evoking a connotation of good management or of military operations, such as 'Voor Vlamingen is taalzorg een kwestie van kwaliteitszorg geworden' (For the Flemings, language care has become a matter of quality control) or 'Vlaming, parakommando in verdediging van het Nederlands' (The Fleming, paratrooper in the defence of Dutch) (DS, 15–16 February 1992, p. 1 and p. 8).

31 Headline: 'Taalonderwijs is hefboom voor integratie migranten'. Subtitle: 'Kans op werk lijdt onder communicatieproblemen'. (HLN, 5 December 1991, p. 16)

32 For a more elaborate comparative study, with emphasis on the role of language in homogeneistic thinking, we refer to Blommaert and Verschueren (1992b); for a wider comparative perspective, we recommend Meeuwis (1993), Young (ed.) (1993), Wilmsen and McAllister (eds.) (1996) and McAllister (1997).

33 'Amerika und Einwanderung: Schmelztiegel oder Salatschüssel?' (*Die Zeit*, 9 November 1990, p. 7).

34 'Heute schon spielen sich harte Kämpfe um die Sprache, um die Dominanz des Englischen ab, das vorläufig noch eine verbindende Kraft darstellt'. (*Die Zeit*, 9 November 1990, p. 7)

35 'Die ethnisch-rassische Koexistenz scheint zu gelingen solange die Wirtschaft einigermassen floriert'. (*Die Zeit*, 9 November 1990, p. 7)

36 'Tijdens zijn jongste bezoek aan Duitsland heeft President Mitterrand met die Franse hooghartigheid die niet zelden wortelt in een gebrekkige dossierkennis, minachtend gewaarschuwd voor een "Europe des tribus". Maar of dat nu het Franse staatshoofd bevalt of niet, het is een feit dat die "volksstammen" bestààn, erkenning, zeggenschap en een eigen plaats eisen in het Europa dat naar vereniging streeft'. (DS, 27 September 1991, p. 10)

37 'Der Heimat bewusst: Die Basken – gastfreundlich aber nicht servil' (Die Zeit, 16 November 1990, p. 83).

38 'Was steckt dahinter? Eine lange Geschichte der allerdings militanten Selbtstbehauptung eines Volkes, dessen Herkunft ebenso wie die Herkunft seiner Sprache, des Euskara, den Ethnologen und Linguisten bis heute Rätsel aufgibt. [. . .] Diese Ursprache [. . .]'. (Die Zeit, 16 November 1990, p. 83)

39 A typical phrasing, in a semi-explicit form, was the cursory reference to the *opgekropte nationalistische onvrede* ('suppressed nationalist discontent') (DM, 15 January 1994, p. 23).

40 We quote:

> Voor de Vlaamse Beweging is de eenheid en de homogeniteit van het Nederlandse taalgebied steeds één van haar prioritaire doelstellingen geweest. (For the Flemish Movement, the unity and homogeneity of the Dutch-speaking language area has always been one of its most important goals.)
>
> (Alen *et al.* 1990: 211)

A brilliant historical sketch, showing that neither the fact nor the idea of present-day Flanders as a unity marked by a common language could emerge until it ended up in a unitary Belgian state, is to be found in Wils (1992), where it is also shown that the corresponding francophone nationalism was imperialist in nature (e.g., because it would never grant its own Flemish minorities any of the language rights it demanded for francophone minorities in Flanders). For an account of the resulting federalization process, see Hooghe (1991).

41 'De Vlaamse tema's, in casu de overheveling van de Franstalige universiteit uit Leuven, werden nooit uit het oog verloren. Dat was meer dan opportunisme of populisme, zoals me door uiterst links of traditioneel rechts dikwijls is verweten. *Het kaderde in een opvatting dat een universiteit in dienst van de eigen samenleving moet staan. Bijgevolg moet ze in de eigen regio gelokalizeerd zijn, zoniet wordt ze een elitaire instelling.* Overigens was het onze stellige overtuiging dat de Franstalige afdeling al veel kenmerken had van een onvervalste kastenuniversiteit'. (Goossens 1993: p. 17; translated part emphasized)

42 This was reported in the media on 11 May 1993. It was even front-page news under headlines such as 'Rijkswacht wil allochtonen werven' ('Gendarmerie wants to hire allochthons').

43 Interviews with Johan Leman, main KCM adviser and now CGKR director, in *Markant* (5 February 1993) and *Knack* (28 April 1993).

44 'In kritieken van de democratische oppositie hebben wij zelden fundamentele tegenstellingen ontwaard ten aanzien van de opties voorgesteld door het Koninklijk Commissariaat. Zo is o.a. het integratieconcept van het Koninklijk Commissariaat bijna door elkeen – zij het in een andere formulering – aanvaard'. (KCM 1993: 15)

45 E.g. Johan Leman, in the interviews mentioned before (note 43); Joan Ramaekers, DS, 25 March 1993; Van Eekert and Van Herck (1993).

46 Karl van den Broeck in DM, 26 February 1993.

47 'Opgemerkt moet worden dat dit integratieconcept niet alleen opgaat voor de immigranten maar ook voor de Belgen, die ook deze openbare orde te respecteren hebben bijvoorbeeld in de mate dat zij rechten toekent aan de minderheden, en die eveneens verzocht worden deze zelfde sociale basisbeginselen te respecteren die zij niet altijd eerbiedigen'. (KCM 1993: 51)

48 'Belangrijk daarbij is dat men er niet blind voor zou zijn dat veel van deze grote oriënterende ideeën niet eens zo verschillend zijn over de meeste samenlevingen en culturen [. . .]'. (KCM 1993: 54)

49 'Wanneer gaat het over een basiswaarde? En wanneer gaat het over rechtmatige culturele diversiteit?' (KCM 1993: 52)

50 'Maar die wederzijdse aanvaarding is moeilijk realiseerbaar als er niet tegelijk een tweede proces op gang wordt gebracht, waarbij minderheden op een actieve en gecoördineerde wijze betrokken worden bij de activiteiten en de doelstellingen van de overheid. Integratie staat dan voor een proces dat door de overheid wordt bevorderd en op gang gebracht, met behoud van de criteria vermeld bij het integratieconcept, waarbij minderheden structureel betrokken worden bij alle activiteiten en doelstellingen van het gastland.

'Een belangrijke voorwaarde voor deze wederzijdse aanvaarding is de juiste dosering van rechten en plichten zowel bij de autochtonen als bij de allochtonen, als in hun onderlinge verhouding. Het is evident dat niet méér rechten en plichten kunnen toegekend worden aan de allochtonen dan aan de autochtone bevolking'. (KCM 1993: 57)

51 '[. . .] zodat de centra in staat zijn om op contractuele basis, zonder enige beperking, personen van niet Belgische nationaliteit aan te werven voor niet-leidinggevende functies'. (KCM 1993: 62)

52 '[. . .] dat het aantrekken van buitenlandse [Islamitische] leerkrachten van nu af aan quasi onmogelijk zal zijn'. (KCM 1993: 173)

53 At this point, the reader may be reminded of Zygmunt Bauman's discussion of modernity and ambivalence. Many of the features of the Belgian migrant debate could be seen, from Bauman's perspective, as features of a typically 'modern' way of dealing with Others: the rejection of ambivalence represented by immigrants, the backdrop of nationalism, the paradoxes of 'assimilation' (see especially Bauman 1991: 141–3).

54 This refers to a statement made by VB leader Filip Dewinter during a broadcast of the television programme *De Zevende Dag* (BRTN TV1, 14 June 1992): '[. . .] de rechten van de mens staan wat ons betreft ondergeschikt aan die van ons eigen volk'.

CHAPTER 6

1 'Op 1 januari 1985 is er het vrijwel geruisloos administratief verdwijnen van 54.000 "vreemdelingen" ingevolge de toepassing van de nieuwe nationaliteitswetgeving. (Specifiek voor kinderen uit gemengde huwelijken met een Belgische vrouw.)'. (KCM 1991: Part I, 15)

2 'De Italianen belichaamden voor de gewone man volop de "vreemdeling". De Belgen waren immers nog weinig of niet met vreemde cultuurdragers geconfronteerd'. (KCM 1991: Part I, 9)

3 See F. Brunot (ed.) (1927–43) and M. de Certeau *et al.* (1975) for the basic facts. For further comments in relation to nationalism and language politics, see R.D. Grillo (1989) and E.J. Hobsbawm (1990).

4 'Naast het generatieconflict dat vele jongeren in hun opvoeding kennen, is er voor de migrantenjongeren ook nog het risico op een cultuurconflict met de ouder(s)'. (KCM 1991: Part IV, 31)

5 See Chapter 3 for an account of how this vision of unity contrasts with the European self-perception of living on the culturally and linguistically most diversified continent in the entire world.

6 'In dit hoofdstuk worden vooral culturele achtergronden van *moslim-migranten* geschetst, aangezien deze merkelijk verschillen van de Westerse cultuur'. (KCM 1991: Part IV, 1)

7 'De koopmansgeest die er heerste bracht een grote tolerantie met zich mee op religieus gebied en een gastvrijheid voor alle mogelijke godsdiensten en sekten'. (KCM 1991: Part III, 3)

8 '*Het* leven in *het* land van herkomst'. (KCM 1991: Part IV, 2; italics ours)

9 'De sociale status die men binnen de familie en de gemeenschap geniet is in hoofdzaak gebaseerd op de leeftijd en op het geslacht en niet zozeer op de individuele prestatie van de persoon (zoals in het Westen)'. (KCM 1991: Part IV, 4)

10 'Bij de partnerkeuze wordt wel *in zekere mate* rekening gehouden met de mening van de jongen en het meisje, maar *doorgaans* is hun inbreng *vrij gering*'. (KCM 1991: Part IV, 11; italics ours)

11 'De "eer" kan dus op twee niveaus worden gesitueerd:

1 Op een eerste niveau wordt de eer bepaald door het gezag dat men heeft over *domeinen waar buitenstaanders niet mogen indringen*. Concreet gesteld zijn dit het huis, de familieleden, de bezittingen, de grond, kortom: het eigen territorium. [. . .]

2 Een tweede niveau stelt zich buiten het 'huishoudelijke' terrein; waar de man *naar buiten toe* zijn terrein moet kunnen verdedigen en waarbij hij eveneens anderen moet kunnen uitdagen. [. . .] Het komt erop neer om de meerdere van de andere(n) te zijn: beter, sterker, rijker, godsdienstiger, vrijgeviger, moediger, enz. [. . .] (KCM 1991: Part IV, 4)

12 Another, quite prominent, manifestation of the same basic attitude is the title of the first KCM report issued in November 1989: *Integratie(beleid): Een werk van lange adem* ('Integration (policies): A long-term effort').

13 Though the building blocks of the communication theory presented in the KCM programme can indeed be traced back to Mary Douglas (e.g. 1970), the resulting construct can hardly be said to be hers.

14 'Het is belangrijk te weten dat elkaar begrijpen méér inhoudt dan dezelfde taal hanteren: men kan een taal immers op erg verschillende manieren gebruiken. Typisch hierbij is dat wij, als Westerlingen, doorgaans EXPLICIETE vormen van communicatie hanteren. Dit wil zeggen dat de nadruk ligt op de betekenis van de woorden zélf, zonder dat er hoeft gekeken te worden naar achterliggende boodschappen of een verdere context. (Moslim-)migranten daarentegen hanteren meer IMPLICIETE communicatiecodes, waar niet zozeer de inhoud van de boodschap telt, maar waar vooral de vorm of het relationele aspect doorslaggevend zijn'. (KCM 1991: Part V, 4)

15 Some scholars even define pragmatics as the study of language use from the perspective of implicitness; see Östman (1986).

16 Unfortunately this kind of perspective is not uncommon in debates on intercultural and international communication; for a brief case study, see Verschueren's (1984) critique of Glenn (1981).

CHAPTER 7

1 'Een goeie relatie begint bij integratie. Integratie begint bij een goeie relatie'.

2

Geen slogans, wel duidelijke taal

Niemand kan ontkennen dat de aanwezigheid van migranten in ons land problemen meebrengt. Sommigen willen die problemen oplossen met simplistische,
goedkope slogans. 'Vreemdelingen buiten', roepen ze luid. Het zijn leugen-
achtige voorstellen die inspelen op de onzekerheid en de angst bij een aantal
Belgen.

Wie zijn gezond verstand gebruikt, weet dat de migranten niet uit het land
kunnen worden gezet. Ze kwamen destijds naar ons land, deels op onze vraag,
op zoek naar betere leefomstandigheden. Ze kregen kinderen. Hun kinderen
hebben kinderen. De migranten voelen zich hier stilaan thuis, ze willen hier
blijven.

De geschiedenis heeft ons geleerd dat onverdraagzaamheid en vervolgingen
niets oplossen. Geen holle en gevaarlijke slogans dus, wel een efficiënt beleid
waarbij klare en soms harde taal wordt gesproken. Waarbij aan de migranten
duidelijk wordt gemaakt dat elk zijn plichten moet vervullen om zijn rechten te
genieten.

3

Kansarmen en migranten niet tegen elkaar uitspelen

Dikwijls wordt gezegd dat er te veel voor migranten gebeurt terwijl de Belgische
kansarmen in de kou blijven staan. Dat is niet zo, blijkt uit allerhande cijfers.

Vanaf 1989 werd per jaar telkens meer dan 1 miljard frank gebruikt voor de
bestrijding van kansarmoede en nog eens 1 miljard ging naar specifieke kansar-
moedeprojecten. Dat geld was en is grotendeels bestemd voor de Belgische
kansarmen.

Is het bovendien niet onrechtvaardig om kansarmen en migranten tegen
elkaar uit te spelen?

4

Een goeie relatie begint bij integratie

Van een beleid van vrijwillige, laat staan gedwongen terugkeer kan weinig
verwacht worden. Bijvoorbeeld niet dat het pensioen van de Belgen omhoog zal
gaan als de vreemdelingen verdwijnen.

Een goed beleid is er dan ook op gericht de migranten in te passen in de
Belgische samenleving. De migrantenbevolking kan onder meer meehelpen aan
de economische expansie van het land.

Om de integratie te bevorderen, heeft het Koninklijk Commissariaat voor het
Migrantenbeleid enkele krachtlijnen uitgestippeld.

1 Automatische toekenning van de Belgische nationaliteit aan de kleinkinderen.

Een vereenvoudiging van de toekenningsprocedure voor de kinderen. Jongens die Belg worden vervullen hun legerdienst.

2   De kwaliteit van het onderwijs moet gevoelig verbeteren. Zodat iedereen er zich in herkent, zodat migranten én Belgen er beter van worden.

3   De grootste aandacht voor samenlevingsproblemen in wijken waar veel migranten wonen.

4   De migranten moeten de streektaal aanleren.

5   De migratiestop wordt gehandhaafd zolang de arbeidsreserve niet volledig is opgebruikt.

6   Voor mensen die spontaan terugwillen naar hun land van oorsprong, moeten de drempels worden weggewerkt.

7   Geïntegreerde en bekwame migranten moeten in de gemeenten als ambtenaar een voorbeeldfunctie kunnen krijgen.

8   Er is alleen plaats voor een goed geïntegreerde islam die onze westerse waarden respecteert.

9   Een toekomstgericht beleid tegenover de clandestiene vreemdelingen – een gevolg van de druk uit de derde wereld en Oost-Europa – moet in alle sereniteit worden uitgestippeld.

10 Het is wenselijk dat er een Centrum voor Etnische Gelijkheid komt. Het moet onterechte discriminaties, ondermeer op basis van huidskleur, bestrijden.

Uit die voorgestelde maatregelen blijkt het belang van taal en onderwijs. Ook moet duidelijk zijn dat clandestiene vreemdelingen resoluut worden teruggestuurd. Dit is niet onmenselijk. Wel onmenselijk is alles laten betijen. Zodat die mensen doelloos zwerven, in de prostitutie terecht komen of in de handen van koppelbazen worden gedreven.

5   The corresponding duty for boys to do their military service is now outdated, since obligatory military service was abolished in Belgium after the KCM flier was circulated.

6

De gemeenten geven het voorbeeld

In afwachting dat er een Centrum voor Etnische Gelijkheid komt, vraagt het Koninklijk Commissariaat voor het Migrantenbeleid aan de gemeentebesturen:

1   Maak een georganiseerde structuur voor de contacten tussen gemeente en migranten.

2   Streef op het vlak van de huisvesting naar een zo groot mogelijke spreiding van de migranten en belet verkrotting van huizen.

3   Organiseer de dialoog tussen de onderwijsnetten op lokaal vlak en voer een intens jeugdbeleid.

4 Waak er met vaste hand over dat de vreemdelingen correct voldoen aan hun plichten als burgers van de gemeente en bewoners van de wijk.

5 Moskeeën kunnen niet waar dan ook noch in onbeperkt aantal worden gevestigd.

6 Maak ernstig werk van de houding en de vorming van het gemeentelijk personeel.

7 Waak nauwgezet over de veiligheid in de gemeente. Eventuele criminaliteit wordt resoluut aangepakt. Elke burger moet zich op elk moment veilig kunnen voelen.

8 Stel de emancipatie van de migrantenvrouw als een prioriteit voorop.

9 Aanvaard politieke vluchtelingen in principe alleen als er aangepaste woningen en een voldoende menselijke omkadering beschikbaar zijn.

10 Probeer een gemeentelijk integratieplan op te stellen.

7

De plichten van de migranten

Ook van de migranten verwacht het Koninklijk Commissariaat voor het Migrantenbeleid een reeks inspanningen.

1 De keuze van een uitstekend onderwijs – ook voor de meisjes – moet op de eerste plaats komen.

2 De ouders moeten een ernstige inspanning leveren om de streektaal te leren.

3 De jongeren moeten zich inschakelen in het verenigingsleven en – zo mogelijk – in de Belgische sportverenigingen.

4 Iedereen moet bijdragen tot de opbouw van de buurt en de verfraaing van het straatbeeld.

5 Een grote verdraagzaamheid inzake godsdienst en levensbeschouwing.

Alle maatregelen die hier worden opgesomd, hebben uiteindelijk één doel: een samenleving waarin iedereen vooruitgaat en waarin verdraagzaamheid en wederzijds respect primeren.

8 'Kennis van de streektaal leidt tot wederzijds respect'.

CHAPTER 8

1 'Wellicht zal een Centrum voor Etnische Gelijkheid zich moeten beperken tot het aan de kaak stellen van duidelijke veruitwendigingen van racisme, d.w.z. feitelijke discriminatie, of de politieke uitbuiting ervan'. (Blommaert and Verschueren 1992a: 159)

2 'Wij willen absoluut vermijden dat er een polarisatie ontstaat tussen ons en de ordehandhavingsdiensten van dit land. Het feit dat wij deze klacht indienen betekent geenszins dat wij willen insinueren dat alle politiemensen van dit land racisten zijn'. (DM 25 February 1994, p. 1)

3 GvA: Concreet. Ik wil mijn huis niet verhuren aan een Turkse familie met zes kinderen. Ben ik een racist?

JL: Niet per se. Als die Turk u aanklaagt wegens racisme, gaat hij niet per se door ons gevolgd worden. Alles hangt af van de manier waarop hij zich presenteert. Ik kan me voorstellen dat Belgen die zich op dezelfde manier presenteren, ook geweigerd worden door een bezorgde huiseigenaar. Als het om een bonafide migrant gaat die geweigerd wordt omwille van zijn huidkleur, gaan we wel optreden. Maar het zal niet eenvoudig zijn om de bewijslast aan te voeren. Daarom zullen we in eerste instantie bemiddelen tussen de huiseigenaar en de kandidaat-huurder. We gaan niet dadelijk het grote kanon in stelling brengen, omdat je racisme niet meteen repressief moet aanpakken.

GvA: Ik ben bakker, en zoek een winkeljuffrouw. Er biedt zich een keurige dame aan, maar zij draagt een (islamitische) hoofddoek. Ik weiger haar in dienst te nemen, omdat ik vrees dat ik anders klanten verlies. Ben ik een racist?

JL: Nee. Dat is een professioneel oordeel. Die man kan perfect verantwoorden waarom hij zo handelt. Voor het onthaal en de bediening van klanten mogen bepaalde eisen worden gesteld. Sorry dat ik het moet zeggen, maar dit speelt bv. ook voor punkers, en dat is dan geen kwestie van huidkleur.

GvA: Een andere, keurig uitziende dame die perfect Nederlands spreekt, wordt geweigerd omdat ze zwart is en ik bang ben klanten te verliezen. Ben ik een racist?

JL: Dit zou racistisch zijn, ja. Ik weet dat dit zeer delicaat is, en dit moet dan ook bepraat worden, maar hier raak je aan racisme. Al begrijp ik wel dat die winkelier wellicht handelt onder druk van zijn klanten'. (GvA, 8 February 1994, p. 2)

4 'Ik stel wel dat ik niet hou van mensen die per se een racismeklacht willen uitlokken en in de media willen komen als het eerste grote slachtoffer in België. Daar moet ik niet van weten, dat zeg ik rechtuit. De anti-racismewet kan zelfs het racisme voeden, als ze te pas en te onpas wordt gebruikt. Dat gaan we niet doen. We zijn trouwens geneigd om ons op de eerste plaats bezig te houden met gevallen van racisme in overheidsdiensten, eerder dan in de privésector'. (GvA, 8 February 1994, p. 2)

5 JL: Ik vind dat ongezond. Ge moogt daar uw ideeën over hebben maar ge moogt dat als overheid zomaar niet zeggen.

BRTN: Bijvoorbeeld, zeggen er zijn teveel Sikhs, da's gevaarlijk?

JL: Ja. Ik zou dat niet doen. Of zeggen d'r is een woningprobleem en het heeft exclusief of bijna exclusief te maken met de Sikhs – dat zou ik niet doen. Want in plaats van de Sikhs mag je zeker zijn dat er evenveel Belgen onder vallen. En ten tweede, in plaats van Sikhs, dat er evengoed Polen of, of andere mensen zouden kunnen zijn. En ik vind als OVERHEID moet je toch ENORM begaan zijn, zeker in crisismomenten, met gelijkwaardigheid tussen mensen en met niet de ene mens ergens meer met schuld gaan belasten dan anderen of dat te insinueren. En ik vind dat men daar wat onvoorzichtig in geweest is, ik blijf daarbij. Is dat daarom zwaar racisme geweest of als zwaar racisme bedoeld geweest, ik denk dat niet, maar sommige dwaze dingen gebeuren er. Mensen die niet per se de zwaarste racisten zijn maar die gewoon de gevolgen van hun daden niet inschatten, en DAT is hier een beetje gebeurd'.

6 'Je kunt op een bepaald moment onmogelijk dulden dat je als rechtsstaat ostentatief verliest. Je kunt dat niet dulden. Je moet alle middelen proberen. Als dat niet lukt bent ge – zijt ge aan de rechtsstaat verplicht om te zeggen "Sorry, maar we pakken u op en we nemen u weg!" – Strafkampen heeft natuurlijk een belaste naam, hé. Het is een belaste naam, maar je moet, je moet, je moet die jongens ook ergens wegrukken uit hun eigen negatieve spiraal waarin ze beland zijn, één, en je moet ook, je kan toch onmogelijk een situatie creëren waarin een paar honderden mensen eigenlijk moeten

een soort terreur ondergaan van een groep jongeren die eigenlijk het normbesef verloren heeft, compleet'.

7 In Dutch *onderwijs-voorrangsbeleid voor migranten*.

8 'Belgische ouders hebben niets te vrezen: aan hen worden geen extra inspanningen gevraagd. We rekenen wel op hun gastvrijheid en verdraagzaamheid'. (from a pamphlet distributed in schools in the Ghent area)

9 'Het onderwijs is vrij; elke preventieve maatregel is verboden [. . .]' and 'De Gemeenschap waarborgt de keuzevrijheid van de ouders'.

10 '[. . .] de grootmoeder langs moederszijde is niet in België geboren en is niet in het bezit van de Belgische of Nederlandse nationaliteit door geboorte [. . .]' and '[. . .] de moeder heeft ten hoogste tot het einde van het schooljaar waarin zij de leeftijd van 18 jaar bereikte onderwijs genoten [. . .]'.

11 As elsewhere (see Doupona, Verschueren and Žagar 1997), clear ethnic discrimination does not stop those who want to legitimate it from referring to international agreements. Thus the text of the non-discrimination declaration does not shy away from defining its concepts with reference to the Convention of New York (1966) concerning the fight against racial discrimination, where the latter is defined as 'every kind of distinction, exclusion, restriction or preference on the basis of race, skin colour, descent, national or ethnic origin' (back translation from Dutch), a definition that would seem to fit the proposed 'non-discrimination' measures quite neatly.

12 'Niemand kan mij vandaag nog bij benadering zeggen hoeveel illegalen er in ons land rondlopen. Maar het zijn er tienduizenden en blijkbaar zijn het brave mensen of we hadden al twintig keer een Brixton gehad! Al deze illegalen hebben geen enkele toegang tot de normale maatschappelijke voorzieningen en kunnen dus onmogelijk op een normale wijze functioneren in onze samenleving. Dat houdt men als rechtsstaat niet vol. Deze situatie kan elk moment exploderen en dat is precies mijn grootste bekommernis'. (from an interview in *Fuga*, October/November 1991, p. 20)

13 'Er komt nergens dwang bij kijken . . . Onze veiligheidsagenten zijn ambtenaren. Ze zijn niet gewapend en mogen geen geweld gebruiken'. (DS, 19–20 March 1994, p. 12)

14 'In een democratie is er een grens aan de opvangcapaciteit van de gemeenschap. Ik beweer niet dat die in België al is overschreden, maar er is wel degelijk een grens!' (*Fuga*, October/November 1991, p. 21)

EPILOGUE

1 See Christine Inglis (1996) for an elaborate example of this type of multiculturalism, developed within the paradigm of UNESCO's MOST programme (see Chapter 1).

2 '[. . .] een samenleving waar bekwame mensen uit de minderheden, die aan de uitgangspunten van een geslaagde integratie voldoen, volop een functie kunnen aanvaarden en een status kunnen verwerven op voet van gelijkheid met wie dan ook uit de meerderheid.' (Leman 1992: 710)

3 'Het is en blijft een van de grote problemen dat leden uit de migrantenbevolking die de Belgische samenleving genoeg kennen, nog steeds niet aan de besluitvorming deelnemen.' (interview in *Tijdschrift Universiteit Antwerpen*, 1992, 6(20): 20)

BIBLIOGRAPHY

Alen, André, Jaak Billiet, Dirk Heremans, Koenraad Matthijs, Patrick Peeters, Jan Velaers and Paul Van Rompuy (1990) *Rapport van de Club van Leuven: Vlaanderen op een kruispunt; sociologische, economische en staatsrechtelijke perspectieven*, Leuven: Lannoo.

Allemann-Ghionda, Cristina (1997) 'Ethnicity and national educational systems in Western Europe', in Hans-Rudolf Wicker (ed.), *Rethinking Nationalism and Ethnicity*, Oxford: Berg, pp. 303–18.

Anderson, Benedict (1983) *Imagined Communities: Reflections on the Origin and Spread of Nationalism*, London: Verso.

Arts, Herwig et al. (1991) *De onzijdige samenleving:over vrijheid en verdraagzaamheid in Vlaanderen*, Leuven: Davidsfonds.

Bakhtin, M.M. (1986) *Speech Genres and Other Late Essays*, Austin: The University of Texas Press.

Balagangadhara, S. and Filip Erkens (1990) 'Het migrantenvraagstuk: Een antropologische kijk', *PMS-Leven* 90, 1: 44–62.

Balibar, Etienne (1988) 'Y a-t-il un "néo-racisme"?' in Etienne Balibar and Immanuel Wallerstein (eds) (1988), pp. 27–41.

—— (1991) '"Es gibt keinen Staat in Europa": Racism and politics in Europe today', *New Left Review* 186: 5–19.

Balibar, Etienne and Immanuel Wallerstein (1988) *Race, nation, classe: les identités ambiguës*. Paris: Editions la Découverte.

Barth, Fredrik (ed.) (1982) *Ethnic Groups and Boundaries: The Social Organization of Culture Differences*, Oslo: Universitetsforlaget.

Bauman, Zygmunt (1991) *Modernity and Ambivalence*, Cambridge: Polity Press.

Beheydt, Ludo (1995) 'The linguistic situation in the new Belgium', in Sue Wright (ed.) (1995), pp. 48–64.

Bijttebier, Johan et al. (1992) *24 November 1991: De betekenis van een verkiezingsuitslag*, Leuven: Kritak.

Billiet, Jaak (1992) *De woorden van onwetenden*. Ms.

Billig, Michael (1995) *Banal Nationalism*, London: Sage.

Bloch, Maurice (1989) *Ritual, History and Power: Selected Papers in Anthropology*, London: Athlone Press.

Blommaert, Jan (1989) *Kiswahili politieke stijl*, unpublished Ph.D. dissertation, University of Ghent.

—— (1996) 'Language planning as a discourse on language and society: The linguistic ideology of a scholarly tradition', *Language Problems and Language Planning* 20, 3.

—— (1997) 'The slow shift in orthodoxy: (re)formulations of the concept of "integration" in Belgium', *Pragmatics* 7, 4: 499–518

Blommaert, Jan and Marco Martiniello (1996) 'Ethnic mobilization, multiculturalism and the political process in two Belgian cities: Antwerp and Liège', *Innovation* 9, 1: 51–73.

Blommaert, Jan and Jef Verschueren (1991) 'The pragmatics of minority politics in Belgium', *Language in Society* 20, 4: 503–31.

—— (1992a) *Het Belgische migrantendebat: de pragmatiek van de abnormalisering*, Antwerp: International Pragmatics Association.

—— (1992b) 'The role of language in European nationalist ideologies', *Pragmatics* 2, 3: 355–75. Reprinted in Christina Schäffner and Anita Wenden (eds) (1995), pp. 137–60.

—— (1993) 'The rhetoric of tolerance, or: What police officers are taught about migrants', *Journal of Intercultural Studies* 14, 1: 49–63.

—— (1994a) *Antiracisme*, Antwerp: Hadewijch.

—— (1994b) 'The Belgian migrant debate', *New Community* 20, 2: 227–51.

—— (1996) 'European concepts of nation building', in Ed Wilmsen and Patrick McAllister (eds) (1996), pp. 104–23.

Blommaert, Jan and Jef Verschueren (eds) (1991) *The Pragmatics of Intercultural and International Communication*, Amsterdam/Philadelphia: John Benjamins.

Blum, Alan F. (1971) 'The corpus of knowledge as a normative order: Intellectual critiques of the social order of knowledge and commonsense features of bodies of knowledge', in Michael F.D. Young (ed.) (1971), pp. 117–32.

Boon, James (1982) *Other Tribes, Other Scribes: Symbolic Anthropology in the Comparative Study of Cultures, Histories, Religions and Texts*, Cambridge: Cambridge University Press.

Bourdieu, Pierre (1982) *Ce que parler veut dire*, Paris: Fayard.

Briggs, Charles (1997) 'From the ideal, the ordinary, and the orderly to conflict and violence in pragmatic research', *Pragmatics* 7, 4: 451–9

Brown, Penelope and Stephen Levinson (1987) *Politeness: Some Universals in Language Usage*, Cambridge: Cambridge University Press.

Brunot, Ferdinand (ed.) (1927–43) *Histoire de la language française* (13 vols.) Paris.

Bulcaen, Chris and Jan Blommaert (1997) *Eindrapport VFIK project 307: Begeleiding van migrantenvrouwen en -meisjes in centra voor residentieel welzijnswerk*, Antwerp: IPrA Research Centre.

Cameron, Deborah (1994) '"Words, words, words": The power of language', in Sarah Dunant (ed.) (1994), pp. 15–34.

Carbaugh, Donal (1989) *Talking American: Cultural Discourses on Donahue*, Norwood, NJ: Ablex.

Certeau, M. de, D. Julia and J. Revel (1975) *Une politique de la langue: La Révolution Française et les patois*, Paris.

CGKR (see: Centrum voor Gelijkheid van Kansen en Racismebestrijding)

Centrum voor Gelijkheid van Kansen en Racismebestrijding (1995) *Op-stap naar gelijkwaardigheid*, Brussels: CGKR.

Cohn-Bendit, Daniel and Thomas Schmid (1992) *Heimat Babylon: Das Wagnis der multikulturellen Demokratie*, Hamburg: Hoffmann & Campe.

Collins, James (1996) 'Socialization to text: Structure and contradiction in schooled literacy', in Michael Silverstein and Greg Urban (eds) (1996), pp. 203–28.

Davidson, Alistair (1997) 'Multiculturalism and citizenship: Silencing the migrant voice', *Journal of Intercultural Studies* 18, 2: 77–92.

Dembour, Marie-Bénédicte (1996) 'Headscarf affair, please: The significant story of an identity photograph in Belgium', *Contemporary Issues in Law* 1, 4: 9–24.

Demeyere, Frank (ed.) (1993) *Over pluralisme en democratie: Verzuiling en integratie in een multiculturele samenleving*, Brussel: VUB Press.

Deprez, Kas (1994) 'Towards an independent and ethnically pure Flanders', in Martin Pütz (ed.) (1994), *Language Contact, Language Conflict*, Amsterdam: John Benjamins, 239–24.

Deslé, Els (1993) 'Geschiedenis van de immigratie: Enkele kritische bedenkingen bij de groei van een nieuw onderzoeksterrein', in Els Deslé *et al.* (eds) (1993), pp. 33–60.

Deslé, Els, Ron Lesthaeghe and Els Witte (eds) (1993) *Denken over migranten in Europa*. Brussel: VUB Press.

Detrez, Raymond (1992) *De Balkan: Van burenruzie tot burgeroorlog*, Antwerpen: Hadewijch.

Detrez, Raymond and Jan Blommaert (eds) (1994) *Nationalisme: Kritische opstellen*, Berchem: EPO.

Dewinter, Filip (1992) *Immigratie: de oplossingen. 70 Voorstellen ter oplossing van het vreemdelingenprobleem*, Brussels: Nationalistisch Vormingsinstituut.

—— (1996) *Immigratie: De tijdbom tikt*, Brussels: Nationalistisch Vormingsinstituut.

D'Hondt, Paula (1991) *Mens voor mens: een openhartig gesprek over het migrantenbeleid*, opgetekend door Manu Adriaens, Leuven: Kritak.

D'hondt, Sigurd, Jan Blommaert and Jef Verschueren (1995) 'Constructing ethnicity in discourse: A view from below', in Marco Martiniello (ed.) (1995), pp. 105–19.

Dijk, Rob van (1991) 'Cultuur als excuus voor een falende hulpverlening', Lecture at the symposium *De culturele factor in medische hulpverlening aan migranten*, 29 November 1991, Universitaire Instelling Antwerpen.

Dijk, T.A. van (1983) *Minderheden in de media: een analyse van de berichtgeving over etnische minderheden in de dagbladpers*, Amsterdam: SUA.

—— (1992) 'Discourse and the denial of racism', *Discourse and Society* 3, 1: 87–118.

—— (1995) 'Discourse analysis as ideology analysis', in Christina Schäffner and Anita Wenden (eds) (1995), pp. 17–33.

Douglas, Mary (1970) *Natural Symbols*, New York: Random House.

Doupona Horvat, Marjeta, Jef Verschueren and Igor Ž. Žagar (1997) 'The pragmatics of legitimation: The rhetoric of refugee policies in Slovenia', ms.

D'Souza, Dinesh (1995) *The End of Racism*, New York: The Free Press.

Dumont, Gérard-François (1995) *Les migrations internationales: les nouvelles logiques migratoires*, Paris: Sedes.

Dunant, Sarah (ed.) (1994) *The War of the Words: The Political Correctness Debate*, London: Virago Press.

Eco, Umberto (1990) *The Limits of Interpretation*, Bloomington: Indiana University Press.

—— (1992) *Interpretation and Overinterpretation*, Cambridge: Cambridge University Press.

Edwards, John (1995) *When Race Counts: The Morality of Racial Preference in Britain and America*, London: Routledge.

Eekert, Geert Van and Walter Van Herck (1993) 'Het migrantendebat', *Streven* 50, 5: 411–19.

Enzensberger, Hans Magnus (1992) *Die große Wanderung*, Frankfurt am Main: Suhrkamp.

Essed, Philomena (1991) *Understanding Everyday Racism*, Newbury Park: Sage.

—— (1994) *Diversiteit*, Amsterdam: Ambo.

Fabian, Johannes (1983) *Time and the Other: How Anthropology Makes its Object*, New York: Columbia University Press.

—— (1986) *Language and Colonial Power: The Appropriation of Swahili in the Former Belgian Congo, 1880–1938*, Cambridge: Cambridge University Press.

Fairclough, Norman (1989) *Language and Power*, London: Longman.

Foucault, Michel (1969) *L'Archéologie du savoir*, Paris: Gallimard.

Friedrich, Paul (1989) 'Language, ideology, and political economy', *American Anthropologist* 91, 2: 295–312.

Fukuyama, Francis (1992) *Het einde van de geschiedenis en de laatste mens*, Amsterdam: Contact.

Gabriel, John (1994) *Racism, Culture, Markets*, London: Routledge.

Galbraith, John Kenneth (1992) *The Culture of Contentment*, London: Sinclair-Stevenson.

Gijsen, Marnix (1928) *Ontdek Amerika*, Brussel: N.V. Standaard-Boekhandel.

Gilroy, Paul (1987) *'There Ain't No Black in the Union Jack': The Cultural Politics of Race and Nation*, London: Routledge.

Glenn, Edmund S. (1981) *Man and Mankind: Conflict and Communication between Cultures*, Norwood, NJ: Ablex.

Glenny, Misha (1992) *The Fall of Yugoslavia: The Third Balkan War*, London: Penguin.

Goldberg, David Theo (ed.) (1994) *Multiculturalism: A Critical Reader*, Oxford: Basil Blackwell.

Goldhagen, Daniel Jonah (1996) *Hitler's Willing Executioners: Ordinary Germans and the Holocaust*, New York: Knopf.

Goodwin, Charles (1994) 'Professional vision', *American Anthropologist* 96, 3: 606–33.

Goossens, Paul (1993) *Leuven '68, of het geloof in de hemel*, Zellik: Roularta Books.

Grillo, R.D. (1989) *Dominant Languages: Language and Hierarchy in Britain and France*, Cambridge: Cambridge University Press.

Grimes, Barbara F. (ed.) (1988) *Ethnologue: Languages of the World* (11th edition), Dallas, Texas: Summer Institute of Linguistics.

Gumperz, John J. (1982) *Discourse Strategies*, Cambridge: Cambridge University Press.

Gumperz, John J., T.C. Jupp and Celia Roberts (1979) *Crosstalk*, Southall: The National Centre for Industrial Language Training.

Gumperz, John J. and Celia Roberts (1991) 'Understanding in intercultural encounters', in J. Blommaert and J. Verschueren (eds), *The Pragmatics of Intercultural and International Communication*, Amsterdam: John Benjamins, pp. 51–90.

Heller, Monica (1995) 'Language choice, social institutions, and symbolic domination', *Language in Society* 24: 373–405.

Herman, Edward S. and Noam Chomsky (1994) *Manufacturing Consent: The Political Economy of the Mass Media*, New York: Pantheon.

Herriman, Michael and Barbara Burnaby (eds) (1996) *Language Policies in English-Dominant Countries. Six Case-Studies*, Clevedon: Multilingual Matters.

Herrnstein, Richard J. and Charles Murray (1994) *The Bell Curve: Intelligence and Class Structure in American Life*, New York: The Free Press.

Hinnenkamp, Volker (1995) 'Intercultural communication', in Jef Verschueren *et al.* (eds) (1995).

Hirschman, Albert O. (1991) *The Rhetoric of Reaction: Perversity, Futility, Jeopardy*, Cambridge, Mass.: Harvard University Press.

Hobin, Veerle and Frank Moulaert (eds) (1986) *Witboek integratiebeleid inzake migranten in Vlaanderen-België*, Brussel: ASLK.

Hobsbawm, Eric J. (1990) *Nations and Nationalism since 1780: Programme, Myth, Reality*, Cambridge: Cambridge University Press.

Hodge, Robert and Gunther Kress (1993) *Language as Ideology*, London: Routledge.

Hollinger, David A. (1995) *Postethnic America: Beyond Multiculturalism*, New York: Basic Books.

Hooghe, Liesbet (1991) *A Leap in the Dark: Nationalist Conflict and Federal Reform in Belgium*, Ithaca, New York: Cornell University, Western Societies Program.

Hymes, Dell (1996) *Ethnography, Linguistics, Narrative Inequality: Toward an Understanding of Voice*, London: Taylor & Francis.

Inglis, Christine (1996) *Multiculturalism: New Policy Responses to Diversity* (MOST Policy Papers 4), Paris: UNESCO.

Jäger, Siegfried (1991) *Alltäglicher Rassismus*, Duisburg: DISS.

—— (1996) *Brand Sätze: Rassismus im Alltag*, Duisburg: DISS.

KCM (see: Koninklijk Commissariaat voor het Migrantenbeleid)

Kissinger, Henry (1982) *Years of Upheaval*, Boston: Little, Brown.

Knapp, Karlfried, Werner Enninger and Annelie Knapp-Potthoff (eds) (1987) *Analysing Intercultural Communication*, Berlin: Mouton de Gruyter.

Koninklijk Commissariaat voor het Migrantenbeleid (1989) *Integratie(beleid): Een werk van lange adem* (3 volumes), Brussels: KCM/INBEL.

—— (1990) *Voor een harmonieuze samenleving* (3 volumes), Brussels: KCM/INBEL.

—— (1991) *Syllabus 'Omgaan met migranten'*, Brussels: KCM.

—— (1992a) *Culturele verscheidenheid als wederzijdse verrijking: Een verenigingsleven van en met migranten, door de overheid gesteund*, Brussels: KCM.

—— (1992b) *Oog voor jeugd met visie op morgen: Voor een jeugdbeleid dat integraal rekening houdt met de jongeren van anders-etnische herkomst*, Brussels: KCM.

—— (1992c) *Samen op weg in een multi-etnische samenleving*, Brussels: KCM.

—— (1993) *Tekenen voor gelijkwaardigheid*, Brussels: KCM.

Kraut, Alan M. (1994) *Silent Travelers: Germs, Genes, and the 'Immigrant Menace'*, New York: Basic Books.

Kristeva, Julia (1988) *Étrangers à nous mêmes*, Paris: Librairie Arthème Fayard. [English transl. *Strangers to Ourselves*, London: Harvester Wheatsheaf, 1991.]

Laqueur, Walter (1970) *Europe since Hitler*, Harmondsworth: Penguin.

Leman, Johan (1992) 'Vlaanderen en Nederland: De inpassing van allochtone minderheden', *Ons Erfdeel* 1992 (5): 705–10.

Lewontin, Richard (1982) *Human Diversity*, New York: Scientific American Library.

Lindemans, L., R. Renard, J. Vandevelde and R. Vandezande (1981) *De taalwetgeving in België*, Leuven: Davidsfonds.

Martens, Albert (1993) 'De integratieproblematiek binnen een multiculturele samenleving: Het verzuilingsmodel als hypothese', in Frank Demeyere (ed.) (1993), pp. 39–50.

Martín Rojo, Luisa et al. (eds) (1994) Hablar y dejar hablar (Sobre racismo y xenofobia), Madrid: Ediciones de la Universidad Autónoma.

Martiniello, Marco (1992) Leadership et pouvoir dans les communautés d'origine immigrée, Paris: CIEMI/L'Harmattan.

—— (1994) 'De communautaire kwestie en het migrantenvraagstuk in België', in Raymond Detrez and Jan Blommaert (eds) (1994), pp. 172–82.

Martiniello, Marco (ed.) (1995) Migration, Citizenship and Ethno-National Identities in the European Union, Aldershot: Avebury.

Martiniello, Marco and Paul Kazim (1991) 'Italy: Two perspectives', Race and Class 32, 2: 79–89.

Martiniello, Marco and Marc Poncelet (eds) (1993) Migrations et minorités dans l'espace européen, Bruxelles: De Boeck.

Mason, Peter (1987) 'Seduction from afar: Europe's inner Indians', Anthropos 82: 581–601.

—— (1990) The Deconstruction of America, Ph.D. dissertation, University of Utrecht.

Matouschek, Bernd, Ruth Wodak and Franz Januschek (1995) Notwendige Massnahmen gegen Fremde? Genese und Formen von rassistischen Diskursen der Differenz, Vienna: Passagen.

McAllister, Patrick (1997) 'Cultural diversity and public policy in Australia and South Africa – the implications of "multiculturalism" ', African Sociological Review 1, 2: 60–78.

McLellan, David (1986) Ideology, Minneapolis: University of Minnesota Press.

Meeuwis, Michael (1990) 'De identifikatie van migranten in de kleine-sensatie pers', Unpublished ms.

—— (1993) 'Nationalist ideology in news reporting on the Yugoslav crisis: A pragmatic analysis', Journal of Pragmatics 20, 3: 217–37.

—— (1997) Constructing Sociolinguistic Consensus: A Linguistic Ethnography of the Zairian Community in Antwerp, Belgium, Ph.D. Dissertation, University of Antwerp.

Mehan, Hugh (1996) 'The construction of an LD student: A case study in the politics of representation', in Michael Silverstein and Greg Urban (eds) (1996), pp. 253–76.

—— (1997) 'The discourse of the illegal immigration debate: A case study in the politics of representation', Discourse and Society 8, 2: 249–70.

Mey, Jacob (1985) Whose Language? A Study in Linguistic Pragmatics, Amsterdam/ Philadelphia: John Benjamins.

Miles, Robert (1993) Racism after 'Race Relations', London: Routledge.

Modood, Tariq (1992) Not Easy Being British: Colour, Culture and Citizenship, Oakhill, England: Trentham Books.

Morelli, Anne (ed.) (1992) Histoire des étrangers et de 'l'immigration en Belgique de la préhistoire à nos jours, Brussels: Vie Ouvrière.

Nederveen Pieterse, Jan (1990) Wit over zwart: beelden van Afrika en zwarten in de westerse populaire cultuur, Amsterdam: Koninklijk Instituut voor de Tropen.

Nietzsche, Friedrich (1957) The Use and Abuse of History, New York: Macmillan.

Obermeier, K.K. (1986) 'Human rights: An international linguistic hyperbole', in Nancy Schweda-Nicholson (ed.) (1986), pp. 105–14.

Östman, Jan-Ola (1986) Pragmatics as Implicitness, Ph.D. dissertation, University of California, Berkeley.

Pauw, Freddy De (1992) Volken zonder vaderland: Centraal- en Oost-Europa, Leuven: Davidsfonds.

Pinxten, Rik (1994) Culturen sterven langzaam: over interculturele communicatie, Antwerpen: Hadewijch.

Rampton, Ben (1995) *Crossing: Language and Ethnicity among Adolescents*, London: Longman.

Ratcliffe, Peter (ed.) (1994) *'Race', Ethnicity and Nation: International Perspectives on Social Conflict*, London: UCL Press.

Rath, Jan (1991) *Minorisering: De sociale constructie van etnische minderheden*, Amsterdam: SUA.

Réa, Andrea (1993) 'La construction de la politique d'intégration des populations d'origine étrangère en Belgique', in Marco Martiniello and Marc Poncelet (eds) (1993), pp. 143–66.

Rex, John (ed.) (1996) *Multiculturalism and Political Integration in European Cities*. Special issue of *Innovation*, 9, 1 (March 1996).

Ricento, Thomas (1996) 'Language policy in the United States', in Michael Herriman and Barbara Burnaby (eds) (1996), pp. 122–58.

Roberts, Celia and Pete Sayers (1987) 'Keeping the gate', in Karlfried Knapp *et al.* (eds) (1987), pp. 111–35.

Rodinson, Maxime (1993) *L'Islam: Politique et croyance*, Paris: Fayard.

Ronen, Dov (1979) *The Quest for Self-Determination*, New Haven: Yale University Press.

Said, Edward W. (1978) *Orientalism*, Harmondsworth: Penguin.

—— (1981) *Covering Islam: How the Media and the Experts Determine how We See the Rest of the World*, London: Routledge & Kegan Paul.

—— (1993) *Culture and Imperialism*, London: Chatto & Windus.

Schäffner, Christina and Anita Wenden (eds) (1995) *Language and Peace*, Aldershot: Dartmouth.

Schampheleire, Hugo De and Yannis Thanassekos (eds) (1991) *Extreem Rechts in West-Europa*, Brussels: VUB Press.

Schlesinger, Arthur M., Jr. (1991) *The Disuniting of America: Reflections on a Multicultural Society*, New York: W.W. Norton & Company.

Schweda-Nicholson, Nancy (ed.) (1986) *Languages in the International Perspective*, Norwood, NJ: Ablex.

Silverstein, Michael (1996) 'Monoglot "standard" in America: Standardization and metaphors of linguistic hegemony', in Donald Brenneis and Ronald Macaulay (eds) (1996), *The Matrix of Language: Contemporary Linguistic Anthropology*, Boulder: Westview Press, pp. 284–306.

Silverstein, Michael and Greg Urban (eds) (1996) *Natural Histories of Discourse*, Chicago: The University of Chicago Press.

Solomos, John and Les Back (1996) *Racism and Society*, London: Macmillan.

Sorenson, John (1991) 'Mass media an discourse on famine in the Horn of Africa', *Discourse and Society* 2, 2: 223–42.

Sowell, Thomas (1994) *Race and Culture: A World View*, New York: Basic Books.

Spencer, Sarah (ed.) (1994) *Strangers and Citizens: A Positive Approach to Migrants and Refugees*, London: Rivers Oram Press.

Thompson, E.P. (1993) *Customs in Common*, Harmondsworth: Penguin.

Thompson, Linda, Michael Fleming and Michael Byram (1996) 'Languages and language policy in Britain', in Michael Herriman and Barbara Burnaby (eds) (1996), pp. 99–121.

Todorov, Tzvetan (1989) *Nous et les autres: La réflexion française sur la diversité humaine*, Paris: Éditions du Seuil. [English transl. *On Human Diversity*, Cambridge, Mass.: Harvard University Press, 1992.]

Tulviste, Peter and James Wertsch (1990) 'Russia's value crisis', *Working Papers and Proceedings of the Center for Psychosocial Studies, Chicago*, 37.

Verhofstadt, Guy (1991) *Burgermanifest*, Gent: Verhofstadt personal distribution.

—— (1992) *De weg naar politieke vernieuwing*, Antwerp: Hadewijch.

Verschueren, Jef (1984) 'Linguistics and crosscultural communication', *Language in Society* 13, 4: 489–509.

—— (1994) 'Non-discriminatie: Het slachtoffer buitenspel', *De Standaard* 16 November 1994.

—— (1995a) 'The pragmatic return to meaning: Notes on the dynamics of communication, degrees of salience, and communicative transparency', *Journal of Linguistic Anthropology* 5(2): 127–56.

—— (1995b) 'Contrastive ideology research: Aspects of a pragmatic methodology', *Toegepaste Taalwetenschap in Artikelen* 52: 55–70.

—— (n.d.) 'The pragmatics of European nationalist ideologies', paper presented at the conference on *Language and International Communication in an Agenda for Peace*, United Nations, New York, 28 January 1994.

Verschueren, Jef, Jan-Ola Östman and Jan Blommaert (eds) (1995) *Handbook of Pragmatics: Manual*, Amsterdam/Philadelphia: John Benjamins.

Vološinov, V.N. (1976) *Freudianism: A Marxist Critique*, New York: Academic Press.

Vygotsky, L.S. (1978) *Mind in Society: The Development of Higher Psychological Processes*, Cambridge, MA: Harvard University Press.

Wallerstein, Immanuel (1988) 'La construction des peuples: racisme, nationalisme, ethnicité', in Etienne Balibar and Immanuel Wallerstein (eds) (1988), pp. 95–116.

Werbner, Pnina and Tariq Modood (eds) (1997) *Debating Cultural Hybridity: Multi-Cultural Identities and the Politics of Anti-Racism*, London: Zed Books.

West, Cornel (1993) *Race Matters*, Boston: Beacon Press.

Wetherell, Margaret and Jonathan Potter (1992) *Mapping the Language of Racism: Discourse and the Legitimation of Exploitation*, London: Harvester Wheatsheaf.

Wicker, Hans-Rudolf (ed.) (1997) *Rethinking Nationalism and Ethnicity: The Struggle for Meaning and Order in Europe*, Oxford: Berg.

Wilmsen, Ed N. and Patrick McAllister (eds) (1996) *The Politics of Difference: Ethnic Premises in a World of Power*, Chicago: The University of Chicago Press.

Wils, Lode (1992) *Van Clovis tot Happart: De lange weg van de naties in de lage landen*, Leuven: Garant.

Wodak, Ruth, Peter Nowak, Johanna Pelikan, Helmut Gruber, Rudolf de Cillia and Richard Mitten (1990) *'Wir sind alle unschuldige Täter': Diskurshistorische Studien zum Nachkriegsantisemitismus*, Frankfurt am Main: Suhrkamp.

Woolard, Kathryn (1985) 'language variation and cultural hegemony: Toward an integration of sociolinguistic and social theory', *American Ethnologist* 12, 4: 738–48.

Wright, Sue (ed.) (1995) *Languages in Contact and Conflict: Contrasting Experiences in The Netherlands and Belgium*, Clevedon: Multilingual Matters.

Young, Crawford (ed.) (1993) *The Rising Tide of Cultural Pluralism: The Nation State at Bay?* Madison, Wisconsin: The University of Wisconsin Press.

Young, Michael F.D. (ed.) (1971) *Knowledge and Control: New Directions for the Sociology of Education*, London: Collier-Macmillan.

INDEX